INTO THE VALUE ZONE

Gaining and Sustaining Competitive Advantage

Ron Wood

University Press of America,® Inc.
Lanham · Boulder · New York · Toronto · Plymouth, UK

Copyright © 2008 by
University Press of America®, Inc.
4501 Forbes Boulevard
Suite 200
Lanham, Maryland 20706
UPA Acquisitions Department (301) 459-3366

Estover Road
Plymouth PL6 7PY
United Kingdom

Library of Congress Control Number: 2008920218
ISBN-13: 978-0-7618-4019-0 (clothbound : alk. paper)
ISBN-10: 0-7618-4019-2 (clothbound : alk. paper)
ISBN-13: 978-0-7618-4020-6 (paperback : alk. paper)
ISBN-10: 0-7618-4020-6 (paperback : alk. paper)

Table of Contents

List of Tables

List of Figures

Acknowledgments

I want to thank my Executive Assistant, Miss Deborah Wells, and my editor, Miss Samantha Kirk, for all of their hard work and assistance in putting this final manuscript together. Their dedication to my project is deeply appreciated. I also want to thank Dr. Eric Abrahamson, Dr. W.S. Brown, Mr. John Elliot, Mr. Jim Parish, Mr. Dan Cantwell, Mr. Ron Williams, and Mr. Wayne McCray for being early readers of my work and for providing constructive criticism about my research.

Chapter One
A New Approach for Business Analysis

Value and Corporate Strategy

More than ever before, organizations exist in very dynamic and turbulent environments and face constant change. Challenges and demands come from every direction. Business leaders must deal with fierce competition; new technologies; new governmental regulations; new social concerns and emerging standards of ethical conduct; responsibilities to safeguard the environment; new challenges presented by globalization, political instability, terrorism, economic factors, and natural disasters; and their own well-being and mortality. This list highlights many of the major challenges facing businesses today, and we are sure that you could probably add more to this list. Understanding them correctly and fashioning an appropriate organizational response (if necessary) is part and parcel of the corporate strategic planning process. If you don't see them correctly (and you diagnose a symptom with the wrong illness), or you fashion an inappropriate response to the marketplace, it can spell the decline and demise of your organization. Sustaining value is strategic and critical to organizational survival.

In a now-classic work, Kenneth Andrews defines and articulates the concept of corporate strategy. Andrews states that corporate strategy is the sum and pattern of decisions an organization takes and that these patterns ultimately define the company's direction and success (what he calls the "central character" of the organization). In organizations that succeed, these patterns of decisions regarding corporate direction are based upon what he terms the distinctive competencies of the organization. We would argue that these patterns of decisions resulting in the distinctive competencies of an organization are value-creating mechanisms and are the foundational building blocks of the Value Zone.

We believe that identifying those things about an organization drives sustainable competitive advantage and that inculcating them into the organization's culture is at the heart of achieving the Sweet Spot of the Value Zone. Gary Hamel and C.K. Prahalad talk of organizations having strategic intent. They define strategic intent as a management process that captures the essence of winning and galvanizes personal commitment to the performance target on the part of everyone in the organization. Great sports teams that have dominated their fields of play have had this strategic intent. In American football, Vince Lombardi's Green Bay Packers, or Knute Rockne's Notre Dame teams; in basketball, Red Auerbach's Boston Celtics squads; Casey Stengel's New York Yankee baseball teams; the accomplishments of soccer's Manchester United, the Arsenal Gunners, or the multiple World Cup Champion Brazilian National Team—all of these star sports teams conjure up the essence of winning as strategic intent. We want to see your organization adopt value as its strategic intent. Ride it to competitive advantage. Imbue your organization with value practice consciousness. Develop a corporate ideology of value practices. Create a "missionary" organization built around value as the central tenet. Soak your corporate culture in it. It will pay dividends.

What is the Value Zone?

As we said earlier, many companies talk about creating value or being a value-added company. It is clear from our research that all businesses are buying and selling in the marketplace in an attempt to grow and be profitable (See Figure 1.1). To truly distinguish themselves, however, much more is needed. Sustained positioning in the Value Zone is the key metric for success. A critical question answered by a firm's customers is whether they view its products and/or services as possessing low value, average value, or high value over sustained periods of time (likely at least five years).

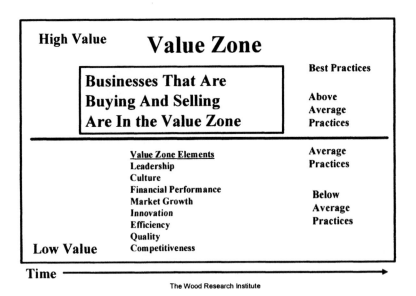

Figure 1.1

How do these companies sustain high organizational performance year in and year out? How do companies succeed against intense competition in their industries on a consistent basis? Our belief, which is supported by our extensive research, is that more than ever before, it is important for businesses and business leaders to know what the strategic "best practices" are that will help them sustain high organizational performance and succeed against intense competition. These "best practices" strategies lead to more efficient management of their organization's assets and, most importantly, *create meaningful and sustainable value. It is the creation of meaningful and sustainable value that can position a business in the High Value area of the Value Zone.*

In our analysis, we have found that business leaders are demanding uncomplicated business analysis models that can quickly highlight market trends, the impact of new technologies, economic changes, globalization, and government regulatory requirements. Too often in our corporate experience have we seen elegant and exhaustive analytical studies sit collecting dust on the corner of an executive's credenza simply because they required too much time and effort to review. We hope to provide a solution to this problem with a new and uncomplicated business analysis model. We believe that this uncomplicated model will help managers to see the competitive landscape through a new and clear lens that will help them to achieve new insights into the internal and external dynamics of success for their organizations. Our goal is to raise your organization's profile in the Value Zone through knowledge of the "best practices" that have brought other businesses success.

We seek to provide the global business community with a simple, yet powerful business tool that can help managers to build successful brands with sustainable results. We believe the Value Zone is a compelling approach that will help businesses provide products and services that will be highly valued in the marketplace. As executives craft new strategic initiatives for their organizations, they will find that using the Value Zone as a conceptual business model will assist them in forecasting, tracking, and measuring business outcomes. Through the use of the Value Zone over time, businesses will be able to identify faulty strategic practices and quickly develop and execute new initiatives.

The Value Zone is a business model that measures the performance of a business using eight key Value Zone elements. This business model also helps identify strategic initiatives that become the "best practices" that enable a business to achieve and sustain business prosperity. Our research has shown that companies that are consistently in the Value Zone have the following key elements, each containing embedded strategic "best practices":

- excellent leaders;
- an enduring culture;
- a well-managed financial portfolio with consistent and sustained growth in revenues and profits;
- a history of sustained market growth;
- a constant drive to innovate;
- consistent improvement of the efficiency and effectiveness in their business and manufacturing processes;
- outstanding quality in products and services;
- and substantial competitiveness.

Does your organization create value in the pursuit of its strategy? The level of value can vary; however, the position of a company in the Value Zone depends on whether its clients view its products and/or services as high value or low value in the Value Zone. Some companies create high value, but most create low value. How do the companies that create high value do it, and perhaps more importantly, how do they sustain it? Using the Value Zone, we will identify just how they do it and how they sustain it. In our research, we have found that the keys are the eight identified Value Zone elements, which are worth repeating here. Based on our comprehensive research involving 74,293 publicly owned companies in existence since 1981, this is where value can be created, measured, and more importantly, sustained. Once again, the eight Value Zone elements are:

1. Leadership
2. Culture
3. Financial Performance
    Grow Revenue
    Maintain Profitability
    Manage Liquidity Well
    Achieve Market Growth
    Enact Globalization
    Expand Existing Markets
    Develop New Markets
4. Market Growth

5. Innovation
    Develop New Products, Services or Business Processes
    Exploit New Technologies for Competitive Advantage
6. Efficiency
    Improve Enterprise Resource Processes
    Enhance Manufacturing/Business Processes
7. Quality
    Six Sigma Targets for Products/Services
    Malcolm Baldridge Award
8. Competitiveness
    Create High Barriers for New Entrants
    Out-Innovate, Out-Sell and Out-Market Top Competitors
    Increase Market Share

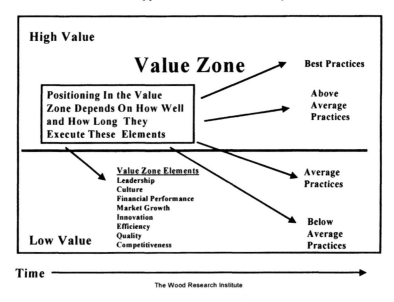

Figure 1.2

Embedded in each of these Value Zone elements are strategic initiatives that lead to outstanding business results. We have labeled these initiatives "Value Zone Practices." These practices can range from below-average practices to best practices (See Figure 1.2). A business's position in the Value Zone depends on how well and how long it executes the strategic initiatives embedded in each of these elements. Companies that are flying high in the Value Zone usually have two or three "best practices" embedded in several, if not all, of these elements each year. These key strategic initiatives could involve any of the following areas of business:

- Company Programs
- Products
- Pricing
- Projects
- Service Offerings
- Marketing Campaigns
- Lean Initiatives
- Business Process Reengineering
- Technology
- Supply Chain Optimization

In our research, we have found that companies with sustained excellence have several things in common. For one thing, they all seem to consistently sustain high value levels in the Value Zone for five years or longer (See Figure 1.3). In Chapter Three we will introduce the companies that have distinguished their excellence and which are included in the Value Zone Hall of Fame as a result. Each of these 38 companies was able sustain remarkable business results for 25 years or more. You will learn more about these companies later in this chapter.

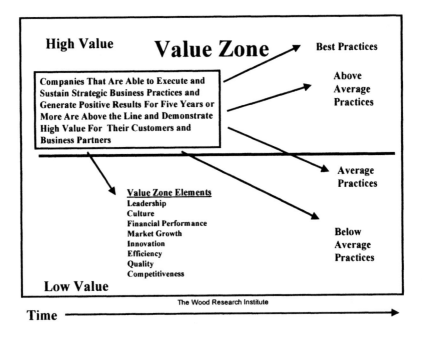

Figure 1.3

Strategic, Organic, and Learning Entities

Companies in the Value Zone develop winning strategies, adapt well to change, and constantly learn. These companies consistently learn to adapt to changing business, economic, and political environments. Peter Senge defines a learning organization as "an organization that is continually expanding its capacity to create its future." Creating an organization's future through learning is at the heart of strategic planning. A business must understand the challenges in the environment in which it exists. By understanding these challenges properly, the organization can fashion the appropriate responses. Repeated failure in this exercise can doom an organization to extinction. Senge tells us that one of the hallmarks of a thriving organization is the presence of both adaptive and generative learning in the company's culture. Adaptive learning is organizational learning that assists the company in coping with the commonplace and predictable. Generative learning, on the other hand, requires companies to think and learn creatively, finding new ways to look at the environment in which they function.

This book is about companies that thrive in the Value Zone. These firms consistently possess great leaders and achieve solid financial results. They also maintain an enduring culture, constantly seek new markets, are innovative, always seek to improve their efficiency, offer the highest quality in products or services, and are extremely competitive. The Value Zone method will help organizational leaders to view and think about their organization's futures in *both* adaptive and generative ways. We challenge you to use the Value Zone to energize your business's leaders to become more creative and imaginative thinkers. To give you, the reader, context for how the Value Zone can be used, we will briefly provide some examples of companies that each apply different Value Zone elements. Moreover, you will learn what strategic "best practices" (highlighted in Table 1.1 below) they use to achieve excellence in each of the Value Zone elements. In later chapters in the book, we will show you how the following table can be used to document the "best practices" strategic initiatives that are imbedded into each of the key Value Zone elements. In this book we will also describe for you how some outstanding companies demonstrate the execution of strategic "best practices" within each element. Table 1.1 illustrates how this analysis is done.

Table 1.1

Value Zone Elements with Strategic "Best Practices"	Results
Leadership	
Culture	
Financial Performance	
Market Growth	
Innovation	
Efficiency	
Quality	
Competitiveness	

In an effort to find companies that were able to sustain solid business performance for a period of five years or more, we evaluated 73,728 publicly owned companies worldwide beginning in 2005, and then we began working our way backwards in time to 2001 to see if these same companies were able to sustain their performance for even longer periods of time. We were able to find many companies that achieved this level from 2005 to 2001, but as we tested their performances for ten years, 15 years, 20 years, and finally, 25 years, the numbers dropped dramatically. What we felt was an amazing discovery in our research is that only 38 companies from a variety of industries were able to sustain solid business performance for the period beginning in 1981 and continuing until 2005. (In the Appendix of this book are tables that portray each company's revenue growth and profits over a 25-year period from 1981 through 2005.) To distinguish these companies from the rest of the companies that were examined, we have created the 1981 through 2005 Value Zone Hall of Fame. When we looked at the results for the 73,728 companies, we were surprised with some of the names of the companies that were included and equally surprised by the some of the more prominent Fortune 500 companies that were not on this short list. In Figure 1.4 below are the names of the 38 companies included in this list:

> **Value Zone Hall of Fame** <

Abertis SA	Home Depot Inc
ABM Industries Inc	Johnson & Johnson
Aeon Company Limited	Johnson Controls Inc
Alliance Unichem PLC	Land Securities PLC
Arthur J Gallagher & Company	Longs Drug Stores
Automatic Data Processing	Lowe's Companies Inc
Becton Dickinson & Company	McDonalds Corp.
Biomet Inc	Morrison (WM) Supermarkets PLC
Cbrl Group Inc	Nbty Inc
Cintas Corp.	Nordstrom Inc
Comcast Corp.	Omnicom Group Inc
Diagnostic Products Corp.	Pall Corp.
Family Dollar Stores Inc	Pick N Pay Stores Limited
Federal Realty Investment Trust	Stryker Corp.
Fraport AG	Sysco Corp.
G & K Services Inc	Teleflex Inc
Greene King PLC	Tesco PLC
Grupo Bimbo SA De CV	Wal Mart Stores Inc
Grupo Continental SA	Walgreen Company

Figure 1.4

With companies like GE, IBM, and ExxonMobil Corporation so prominent in the worldwide business spotlight, we were amazed at some of the companies on this list, such as Family Dollar Stores, Inc., Pall Corporation, Grupo Bimbo SA De CV, Tesco PLC, and AEON Company Limited, to name a few. Other companies on this list did not surprise us, including Automatic Data Processing, Johnson & Johnson, and Wal-Mart.

So the question we kept asking ourselves was: how were these companies able to sustain positive business results for so long? Which of the Value Zone core elements made the difference in creating sustained performance for these firms? As you read the rest of the book, we will provide some insights by examining many of these firms very carefully.

At the outset of this book, we decided that an examination of Family Dollar Store would be interesting. The fact that that a chain of discount stores offering inexpensive merchandise for family and home needs could consistently sustain value for customers in 43 states located mainly in the northeastern, southeastern, southwestern, and northwestern regions of the United States in an era with Wal-Mart thunderously establishing its retail brand merits attention. Let's learn a little more about this company and see how its leaders did it.

The first Family Dollar store opened in Charlotte, North Carolina in 1959. Since that time, the company has grown to more than 5,000 units with $4.75 billion in annual sales. Family Dollar stocks its stores with a wide variety of products ranging from food and housewares to apparel and linens, and most items are priced at less than $10. Family Dollar's founder was Leon Levine, who retired in 2003 and handed over the company reigns to his son Howard Levine.

The Family Dollar store concept was very popular with consumers who were shopping for value along with affordable prices. By the early 1970s, the company had gone public and had opened its 100th store in Brevard, North Carolina. Although it was not the first in the self-service, discount variety retail industry, Family Dollar became a leading player in this market. Key to its business model was reaching lower-income consumers who were often the first to be hit during bad economic times. This was due to either inflation or a recession which forced lower income consumers to cut back on spending. Family Dollar's challenge was to continue to provide value to its critical markets during hard times. The critical Value Zone elements for Family Dollar turned out to be market growth and diversification, enhanced efficiency, and competitive pricing. For example, during the mid-1970s, its stores were clustered in the southern states, and those states were hit by a major depression in the textile industry. Many of its customers in that region were textile workers, while others worked in the tobacco and furniture industries; all of them suffered the effects of the depression. Family Dollar profits dropped by one half during that time.

So what did the company do about it? For one thing, it became more efficient by making improvements in marketing and merchandising, diversifying geographically, tightening inventory controls, and adding an electronic data processing system. To be competitive, Family Dollar Store dropped its policy of pricing all merchandise at $3 or less. Despite the volatile economy in the late 1970s, it exceeded $100 million in sales in fiscal year 1978 and hit a record $151 million in sales in 1979.

In 1980, Family Dollar was operating about 400 outlets in eight states, all in the South. Most of its sales gains over the next several years occurred because it acquired additional stores, including 40 Top Dollar stores from Sav-A-Stop. It also opened 36 new units of its own, putting it ahead of its own expansion schedule.

Family Dollar's big draw in the 1980s was its bargain pricing, which included toys, automotive equipment, and school supplies. Key to its business model was the strategic fact that most of the company's merchandise was bought from vendors or suppliers who had overbought these items. Thus, Family Dollar was able to pass the savings on those under-priced goods to its customers. Another "best practices" strategy was gathering up manufacturer's overruns.

Efficiency, another Value Zone element, helped Family Dollar to sustain its performance during the 1980s. This was achieved through another strategic "best practice": leveraging an efficient distribution system. This system was handled completely in Charlotte, North Carolina, from whence the company could provide bulk deliveries to its stores. In 1980, the size of this distribution center was doubled, enabling Family Dollar to take advantage of discounts on single, bulk deliveries and launch more stores without the added headache of stock shortages.

Two other Value Zone elements that Family Dollar paid attention to were market expansion and prudent financial performance. Despite the fact that it was branching out geographically in the 1980s with approximately 80 new outlets in Georgia, it was still primarily a Carolinian chain. Family Dollar now set its sights on further opportunities in Alabama, Tennessee, the Virginias, Florida, Kentucky, and Mississippi. A key area of strength in financial performance for Family Dollar in the 1980s was that in spite of a recent Top Dollar stores acquisition, it had no long-term debt. This meant that the cash flow allowed Family Dollar to expand with little risk. Because of this, Family Dollar opened 33 new stores between September 1979 and September 1980 and had been boasting a 30% annual rate since 1975. Another strategic "best practice" that Family Dollar employed was housing its storefronts in leased buildings, thereby saving it capital investment. During the early part of 1982, the Family Dollar opened its 500th store in Brunswick, Georgia. We will provide more details about this remarkable company later in this book.

In future chapters of this book, we will provide you with examples of how to understand the Value Zone tables using the appropriate "best practices" and the positive business results. We will also go into more detail about each of these areas as the book develops. The key point we wish to make is that an organization's positioning in the Value Zone depends on how well and how long the organization achieves success in each of the Value Zone parameters. By studying what helps a business achieve and sustain high levels in the Value Zone, the leaders of organizations will learn to develop and adapt Value Zone "best practices" in their own strategic planning exercises.

We have learned in this chapter that the Value Zone business model is a tool that measures eight very important business elements that impact the sustained performance of a company and determine the embedded customer value "best practices" that are used to achieve outstanding, or in some cases even re-markable, business results. We again want to emphasize that our research dem-onstrates that prosperous companies have excellent leadership, an identifiable culture, consistent and proper management of liquidity, and consistent and sus-tained growth in revenues and profits. These organizations also constantly seek to improve the efficiency of their business processes; provide innovative prod-ucts, services, and business processes; maintain an attitude of consistent and fierce competition; sustain high-quality products and services; and maintain a track record of sustained market growth.

While we will go into greater detail about the definition and use of the Value Zone methodology in later chapters, an example of an organization that has achieved some merit in the Value Zone might be in order. Our first example is a company you probably know: Southwest Airlines. In Chapter Two, we use the Value Zone business model to examine an industry in crisis in the U.S.—the airline industry.

Chapter Two
Sustaining Your Performance in the Value Zone

You are probably wondering how to evaluate your company's positioning in the Value Zone. To help answer this question, we will analyze an industry in crisis—the airline industry. Why? For one thing, many people travel using the airlines and are therefore in a position to judge the value they receive during their travel experience. Furthermore, the airline industry has experienced economic downturns during recent years, and several major airlines have sought bankruptcy protection. Despite this disastrous period for the industry, some carriers are able to fly high in the Value Zone. As you read this chapter about the airline industry, we will guide you through an analysis of companies that are either flying high or low in the Value Zone. In each case, we will discuss our analysis of the eight Value Zone elements as they relate to the airline industry. You will see how some airlines are able to reach "critical mass" and the "'sweet spot" of the Value Zone and others are not. During this evaluating process, we will see "the good, the bad and the ugly" when it comes to businesses in this industry and their relative positioning in the Value Zone. We will start by reviewing the current state of the U.S. airline industry.

The 21st Century Airline Industry In Crisis

At the beginning of the 21st century, the airline industry was already anemic. This was caused by a lethargic economy and a significant drop in business and leisure travel. Then the September 11th, 2001 New York City World Trade Center tragedy brought on even more devastating business problems throughout the airline industry. This event, along with the rising cost of fuel, was catastrophic for the airline industry. Major carriers like American Airlines, Delta Air Lines, US Airways, and United Airlines suffered huge losses between 2001 and 2005, and for many of these airlines, the woes continue. For example, Northwest Airlines and US Airways reported substantial losses in January 2002, several months after the World Trade Center attack, and these airlines continue to operate in the red. Airframe manufacturer Boeing's orders dropped 45% in 2001.

The magnitude of the problems in the airline industry is obvious given the fact that a substantial number of companies in the U.S. airline industry have filed for or are currently in bankruptcy. Major players such as US Airways, Delta, Northwest, and United Airlines have all suffered record losses. Bankruptcies, terrorism, and high oil prices have rocked the airline industry. Household names such as Canadian, Swissair, and Trans World Airlines are gone. The losses are astounding, especially considering that during the past five years, the industry has been hemorrhaging at the rate of more than $1 million an hour, racking up losses in excess of $43 billion. Then there are the multitude of customers complaining about high ticket costs, poor service, and long lines. Is this industry faced with doom? Absolutely not! Simply put, the airline industry continues to provide value despite its troubles. The global economy cannot function without the airline industry. More than two billion people fly each year, a number that increases by almost 6% each year. Approximately $3.2 trillion worth of cargo is transported by the airline industry each year. Globalization as we know it would not exist without the airline industry. The critical questions for individual companies in this industry are: what value level are they providing? and where are they positioned in the Value Zone?

The questions we have just raised for companies in this industry are important when considering the opportunities and future projections for the airline industry. For example, using previous history as a guide, the world's airline industry will double its size every 15 years. This means that by 2020, passenger numbers will grow from two billion to four billion. Cargo will grow from 39.5 million tons to 79 million tons. In addition to the aforementioned airline industry statistics, another important one is that air traffic typically grows at two times the rate of the Gross Domestic Product. This means that in a thriving economy, the demand for air travel will soar. Consider these recent reports. Air India has ordered 68 Boeing planes, one of the largest aircraft orders ever, and no-frills airlines such as Kingfisher and Spicejet have taken off in India, where passenger demand is expected to increase by nearly 12% annually in the next four years. The rate will be greater in China, with close to 30 million Chinese traveling abroad in 2004; the World Tourism Organization predicts that that figure will exceed 100 million in 15 years. China's inbound traffic will also increase as China becomes the number-one destination for foreigners, with 137 million visitors projected in 2020. Given all of the factors just described, an airline company's positioning in the Value Zone is critical.

What we have previously discussed means that if you are in business in the airline industry in any capacity, you must ask tough questions about the state of your company. The bottom line is that you must look at your company critically and ask: what value is our company bringing to the table? Most importantly, you must ask whether or not your company is sustaining this value. A key incentive for this critical look is opportunity. The airline industry is poised for an unprecedented growth spurt involving a new generation of planes as well as huge growth in new markets. One other very important consideration for companies in the airline industry is traffic growth worldwide. For example, total airline traffic in the U.S. is up by 5.4%. In Europe, the rise is 6%; in Asia, the forecast is an annual growth of 6.8% through to 2009; and China and some eastern European countries will achieve an annual growth rate of approximately 10%. The opportunities will be unlimited for the businesses in this industry that soar high in the Value Zone.

So how do the airlines stack up in the Value Zone? Consider the flow of "red ink" in many of the carriers. For example, Delta Air Lines and Northwest tumbled into Chapter 11 bankruptcy protection in September of 2005, joining United Airlines and U.S. Airways. Because each of these companies is in bad shape financially, each is positioned in the low value area of the Value Zone. In fact, after three years in Chapter 11 bankruptcy, United Airlines reported a loss of $1.8 billion during the fourth quarter of 2005—its 21st consecutive quarterly loss. Now that's very low value for its stakeholders. Delta Airlines also reported whopping losses in 2005, as did Northwest Airlines. Companies that have had below-average to average ratings in the Value Zone include American Airlines and Continental Airlines. These carriers have avoided bankruptcy—American Airlines cut its losses through the second quarter of 2005, while Continental reported a profit of $61 million compared with a loss of $18 million in the third quarter of the previous year. In both cases, American Airlines and Continental have had consecutive increases in revenues. However, these two companies are both still struggling to post a positive profit. Depressing as all of this is for the airline industry, there is a "silver lining" in this dark cloud: several airline companies are still providing high value in the Value Zone. Let's see who they are and why they are soaring high in the Value Zone.

Discounters Flying High In The Value Zone

Low-cost airlines like JetBlue, Southwest Airlines, Malaysia's Air Asia, and Brazil's GOL have had solid business results despite the financial difficulties so rampant in the airline industry. Southwest Airlines has had decades of revenue growth and profit growth and has grown to be one of the largest carriers in the U.S.

The major carriers continue to be pricey, while the fares of companies like JetBlue are about one-third of the cost of the major airline carriers. A good example of cost reduction is JetBlue's strategy to use its 100-seat Embraers planes to compete in the major airlines' regional markets. The company is planning regional routes from JFK to Charlotte, Norfolk, and other East Coast cities. The majors typically charge one-way fares of $200.00 for these regional routes; JetBlue's, by comparison, are $70.00.

The bottom line here is that most major airlines are flying very low in the Value Zone. They are on a path towards extinction. The only "saving grace" for these major carriers is their lucrative international routes. Meanwhile, the discounter carriers are continuing to fly high in the Value Zone. Southwest, JetBlue, AirTran, America West, and Frontier airlines are attacking the major carriers' most profitable and protected routes. "The low-cost carriers are now dictating pricing in our business," states C. David Cush, the chief of sales at American Airlines. Bear Stearns, an investment banking and securities trading and brokerage firm, commented: "Every time the majors match the fares of the discounters, they lose money. That situation is clearly unsustainable." Let's take a closer look at the battlegrounds.

In the late 1990s, the Department of Transportation and local governments pressured airports to give more gates to newcomers. This significantly helped Frontier, Spirit, and AirTran to establish a presence at Washington National Airport and JetBlue to establish one at New York's JFK Airport. What about the major airlines' fortress hubs (airports where a single airline controls most of the passenger capacity)? They have started to crumble. For example, both Southwest and Frontier have invaded Philadelphia, a major hub for US Airways.

These discounter airlines have chipped away at US Airways' fares in dozens of destinations from Tampa to Las Vegas.

As we shift to the market share war front in the coast-to-coast markets, we see that the discounters have made major inroads. For example, JetBlue challenges American and United with increasingly frequent flights from JFK to the West Coast, and since its arrival in 2000, American and United Airlines have dropped around 30%. Just recently, former major airline America West has transformed itself into a discounter and has begun to roll out extensive West Coast service from both New York's JFK and Boston's Logan Airport. Its service now includes the Boston-to-San Francisco route dominated by United Airlines and American Airlines. One of America West's forays has forced United Airlines to match America West's three-day advance-purchase fare of $205 one way, replacing its old fare of $1,166 and resulting in a major coup for America West. Another battle line involves a number of routes between large cities. For example, Frontier Airlines recently broke through United's monopoly on nonstop service from Nashville to Denver by offering two flights a day between those cities. Frontier will charge $199 for a three-day advance purchase one-way ticket, whereas United charges $464. This has forced United Airlines to drastically reduce its fares in order to compete with Frontier's fares.

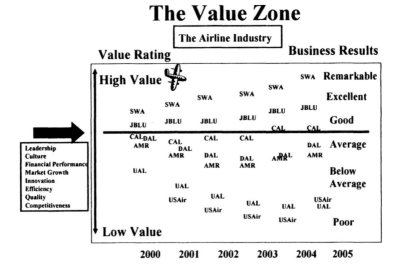

Source: The Wood Research Institute

Figure 2.1

Another major factor that enables airlines like Southwest, JetBlue and Frontier to fly high in the Value Zone is their ability to provide exceptional service. From their perspective, low pricing isn't their only advantage. Bad service is not a tradeoff for low prices. Instead, customers benefit from timely arrivals and take-offs, friendly flight attendants, leather seats, and in the case of both JetBlue and Frontier, live TV and sometimes movies. In fact, AirTran, America West, and Spirit offer business-class cabins just as plush as those of the major airlines. Figure 2.1 (above) displays a Value Zone five-year summary analysis of some of the major American airlines discussed in this chapter.

Southwest Airlines is clearly the leader of discount carriers and is an exceptional example of an airline carrier that is flying high in the Value Zone. Let's see why.

Southwest Airlines—Flying High In The Value Zone

Southwest Airlines (SWA) is a discount air-carrier that primarily provides short-haul, high-frequency, point-to-point, and low-fare services in 31 states in the U.S. The company operates only in the U.S. and has been ranked the top U.S. domestic airline by the Bureau of Transportation Statistics (BTS) of the U.S. Department of Transportation (DOT). The company has approximately 31,000 employees and is known as a carrier with excellent service. Having flown with Southwest myself many times, I can certainly attest to the quality of its service. Its employees really enjoy their jobs and provide exceptional service. It is not uncommon to see a pilot pushing a wheelchair passenger to and from an airplane or flight attendants speedily cleaning a plane to improve gate turn-around time. This type of incredible service has been a major factor contributing to SWA's remarkable history of revenue growth. With the exception of two years, Southwest has achieved revenue growth for over 32 years. Another amazing fact is that Southwest has always managed to be profitable since its start as an airline. In fact, Southwest was the only airline to report a profit in 2001.

Recent company reports indicate that SWA recorded revenues of $6.53 million during the fiscal year ending in December 2004, an increase of 10% over 2003. The increase was mainly related to an increase in revenue passenger miles (RPMs) flown and an improved load factor for the airline. The operating profit of the company during fiscal 2004 was $554 million, an increase of 14.7% over fiscal 2003. The net profit was $313 million during fiscal year 2004, a decrease of 29.2% from 2003.

Listed below are the Value Zone strategic initiatives developed by SWA's leadership team that are the key contributing factors to Southwest Airlines' success:

- Market Leadership
  - The airline has been ranked the top U.S. domestic airline (in terms of number of passengers) by the BTS. With approximately 12.9% of the share of total passengers in 2004, the company is far ahead of its next competitor, Delta Air Lines (a

difference of 1.7 million passengers). The airline currently
serves 59 cities in 31 states. Operating over 2,900 flights a day
gives Southwest a major market presence and strong competitive positioning.

- The Discount Business Model
  - o   A key competitive strength is Southwest's low operating cost.
    Southwest has the lowest cost on a per-mile basis in the airline
    industry. Value Zone "best practices" that contribute to low
    operating cost include a single aircraft type and an efficient,
    high-utilization, point-to-point route structure. The company is
    established in the low-cost airline market, and there is a sig-
    nificant customer awareness of the brand. This is why SWA is
    able to provide its customers with consistently lower prices
    than the other major carriers.

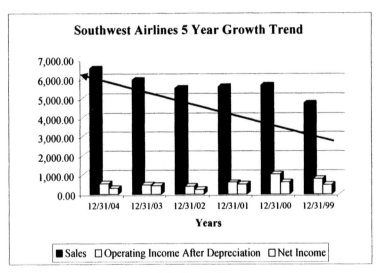

The Wood Research Institute

Figure 2.2

- Strong and Sustained Financial Performance
  The company recorded revenues of $6.53 million during the
  fiscal year ending in December 2004, an increase of 10% over
  2003. The operating profit of the company during fiscal year

2004 was $554 million, an increase of 14.7% over fiscal year 2003. Southwest therefore has a strong history of revenue growth (see Figure 2.2 above).

Value Zone Analysis Approach
A company's position in the Value Zone is influenced by eight Value Zone performance elements:

1) Leadership
2) A sustained and consistent culture
3) Well-managed and sustained financial performance
4) Market expansion
5) Innovativeness
6) Efficient business processes
7) Quality of products and/or services
8) Competitiveness

There also must be clearly embedded and identifiable strategic initiatives, which we call Value Zone "best practices," somewhere in most of the Value Zone elements. To fly high in the Value Zone, a company must sustain high ratings in each of the Value Zone's performance elements for a period of at least five years. Let's review Southwest Airline's great leadership first.

Leadership
The following joint statement in the 2004 annual report was issued by Herbert D. Kelleher, chairman of Southwest; Gary C. Kelly, chief executive officer of Southwest; and Colleen C. Barrett, president of Southwest.

> In 2004, Southwest Airlines recorded its 32nd consecutive year of profitability, which, we believe, is a record unmatched in the history of the commercial airline industry. Our 2004 profit of $313 million (or $.38 per diluted share) exceeded our 2003 profit (excluding a special federal government allowance to the airline industry) of $298 million (or $.36 per diluted share) by 5.0 percent.

Without question, those are remarkable results and they deserve, in our view, a standing ovation, especially during a time when the airline industry as a whole was struggling. These kinds of sustained and outstanding results are clearly manifestations of exceptional leadership.

Great leadership is pervasive at Southwest Airlines. Co-founder Herb Kelleher, who has been with Southwest since its beginning, put it quite succinctly by stating, "Everyone is looking for a formula in business like $E=MC^2$. But it's not a formula. It's got to be emotional, spontaneous, and from the heart." It is sustained leadership in the form of maintaining the original low-cost and low-pricing business model for over three decades that has led to Southwest's remarkable record. New CEO Gary Kelly sums it up this way: "I think what we see as the future of airline competition is that all carriers will be much lower cost and offer much lower fares, because that's what customers want. If an airline can't offer those things, then they're going to go out of business." In the area of customer service, SWA's leadership dictates again that the company invests in its people. Kelly explains it this way: "Our emphasis has been investing in our people. It is our people who make our product best, and they continue to be our focus. So the use of technology will simply be a further tool to make our people even more productive and provide even better customer service." He gives an example: "If you can call our reservation center today, our 800 number, you'll get a person. You won't get one of those voice response units. We could use that technology to reduce our costs. But we think that is lousy customer service." Southwest Airlines' leaders provide excellent examples of how to build a culture that sustains enduring value. Kelly puts it in a very straightforward way when he says, "I think the only thing that will derail Southwest Airlines from a great future is us. And as long as we can work together and treat each other with respect, we'll overcome the challenges that we face."

The Southwest Airlines Culture

To understand the Southwest Airlines culture, consider what was observed in a report involving job candidates interviewing for a job with Southwest Airlines. For example, one business analyst report described a group of Southwest Airline job candidates who were sitting together in a conference room at the airline's training center participating in an initial group interview. The interviewer asked the candidates to introduce themselves and provide a brief bio about themselves. They were then asked to address a hypothetical customer-relations problem. Each candidate responded accordingly. However, one candidate had his or her head down and eyes directed to the floor during this process. It appeared that this candidate was focused on preparing the best, most thoughtful response while waiting for his or her turn to speak. Unfortunately, this candidate's answer was a moot point because he or she left a negative impression on Southwest executives. What went wrong? The Southwest executive's perception of this candidate was one of selfishness. Why? Instead of politely listening to what the other candidates were saying, this candidate was focused on forming his or her response. A Southwest executive noted that the candidates are

> being evaluated as you're watching others say what they're saying, to see if you're giving them the appropriate amount of attention, or cheering them on...Our employees are enthusiastic team players, and they have the right to work alongside people who have the same standards as they do.

The bottom line is expressed by another Southwest executive: "We hire for attitude and train for skill."

Southwest executives believe that "attitude is king." Southwest's managers let their employees know that they are Southwest's number-one customers and that the paying customer is not always right. Southwest's senior leadership team believes that thinking that the paying customer is right all the time undermines trust between management and employees. The bottom line for Southwest's management is that if they "treat their employees well, the employees in turn will treat the customer well and that results in positive business results, namely profits."

Colleen Barrett embodies the Southwest Airlines culture. She has been with the airline since its inception. She grasps the essence of Southwest culture when she states, "If our employees don't feel good about their work environment and don't feel they have the tools to do their job, what kind of exchange are they going to have with our passengers?"

At Southwest, titles do not mean much. As Barrett points out, "One thing we won't tolerate at Southwest is someone saying, 'that's not my job.'" Southwest has a culture that drives its employees and managers to excel in customer service. It's about who they are. Barrett states succinctly,

> It has to be a way of life. And our way of life has evolved over the years. We are a different airline today than we were five years ago. But we have fun... and we're not a different airline when it comes to the way we treat people and customers. We are exactly the same airline. There are no inconsistencies with what we say to a new hire today vs. five years ago or 10 years ago or 20 years ago. I've always talked about the golden rule. I've always talked about spirit and enthusiasm and warmth and caring.

Southwest Airlines values its employees and calls them its customers. The Southwest Airlines' business model and culture are designed to offer an enjoyable and comforting work environment. Southwest Airlines "emphasizes an easy-going, relaxed corporate style that provides employees with extensive operational independence." Southwest also believes in rewarding its employees. The organization has created a profit-sharing program as well as a broad-based stock option plan for its employees. This allows employees to share in the financial successes of their company and helps to create an ownership culture. The program supports Southwest's belief "that people take better care of things they own." The ownership culture found at Southwest Airlines reflects the importance the company places on employee initiative and responsibility. This ownership culture provides Southwest's paying customers with high value. A successful company must have employees that believe and have confidence in their product. Southwest Airlines is an organization that truly works at making both the employee *and* the customer happy. The SWA culture can be experienced every day when customers fly Southwest Airlines. You see its culture in action as ticket agents, flight attendants, and pilots scurry to clean a plane that has just landed in preparation for the passengers waiting to get on; when a pilot is seen dutifully transporting a passenger in a wheelchair onto the plane; when a flight attendant helps a mother with her crying infant; when flight attendants or pilots tell a funny story or joke around with the passengers; or when flight attendants or ticket agents sing a cute jingle. The bottom line is that they are having fun, their passengers are having fun, flights are consistently on time, and the airline is making money. Now that's value.

Its current CEO, Gary Kelly, describes Southwest's success in this way: "The beauty of Southwest Airlines and one of the secrets of our success for over 35 years has been a pretty intense focus strategically...we don't want to be all things to all people. We want to be known for low fares, lots of flights, and high-quality, friendly customer service." When describing this insistence on superior customer service, Kelly points out that "you find...in so many industries today, an indifference, a lack of care and compassion for people and customers. That's just not the case at Southwest Airlines. Our employees take great care of each other and in turn take great care of customers." Regarding SWA's future outlook, he states,

> I think our future is very, very bright...we have a very strong balance sheet. We've got plenty of cash. We have an industry-leading fuel hedge position in place, which is like insurance protection against high energy costs...the hedges kept Southwest's jet fuel costs relatively low even as prices on the open market soared...we would expect 2006 to be our 34th year of consecutive profits, which is an unmatched record.

Sustained Financial Performance

Despite economic downturns in the airline industry, Southwest Airlines recorded its 30th straight year of profits in 2002. In sharp contrast to the huge losses some U.S. major airlines were reporting, Southwest Airlines emerged from the fourth quarter ending on December 31 with a net income of $42.4 million, only down 33.2% from a net income of $63.5 million in the 2001 quarter. Former CEO Jim Parker stated that although the results were "disappointing relative to historical standards," the airline's performance as compared against the industry as a whole had been "excellent." He also commented, "We will continue our diligent cost control efforts and remain committed to maintaining our competitive cost advantage and longstanding quality customer service."

Southwest is the only airline to have posted 30 consecutive years of profits. The profit growth for Southwest over the past five years has been 7%. Southwest has been affected by rising operating costs and decreases in travel, but it has still been able to operate in a manner that has generated it a profit. It is truly amazing to see the lines of passengers waiting to board a flight that has just landed. I can hear the Southwest Airlines employees and investors whispering under their breath during these times, "Ka-ching! Ka-ching! Ka-ching!"

From 1980 through 2004, SWA's revenues grew at an astounding compounded growth rate (CGR) of nearly 80%. Its net income's CGR was a remarkable 103.7%. At the year end of 2004, Southwest Airlines had posted a profit for its 32nd consecutive year and 55th consecutive quarter, an astonishing achievement in light of the anemic condition of the airline industry. Southwest's profits of $313 million in 2004 exceeded its profits for 2003.

The amazing thing about this strong profit performance is that SWA achieved these profit levels despite record-high energy prices and aggressive industry growth, two contributing factors to the continuing anemic economic environment of the airline industry. In fact, the airline industry as a whole suffered a substantial net loss for the fourth consecutive year, resulting in several major carriers being forced into bankruptcy protection. Other carriers have had to continue massive efforts to restructure their business, reduce the wages of their employees, and slash costs. These are all major factors that have helped Southwest Airlines to achieve high value ratings in the Value Zone.

One way that Southwest has significantly improved its financial performance is through an agreement with another airline, ATA Airlines, to a codeshare arrangement at Midway Airport in Chicago, Illinois. This arrangement was approved by the Department of Transportation in January 2005. With this codeshare agreement, each carrier will exchange passengers on select routes at Midway. Southwest believes this agreement could result in additional revenues of $25 to $50 million on an annual basis.

Efficiency/Effectiveness

Southwest has been able to sustain its low-cost competitive advantage by improving its cost structure. Doing this has helped it to greatly improve productivity. During November of 2003, Southwest announced that it was consolidating its Reservations Centers from nine to six. This strategic initiative was launched in February of 2004. Of the 1,900 employees affected, about 1,000 did not elect to move to one of the company's remaining reservations locations. This reduction in centers helped to alleviate an overstaffing problem exacerbated by slower passenger growth, changes in customer buying habits and boarding processes, and the federalization of airport security. As a result of these strategic initiatives and other productivity program efforts, Southwest's headcount per aircraft decreased from 85 on December 31, 2003, to 74 on December 31, 2004.

Southwest's use of the point-to-point route system as opposed to the hub-and-spoke system used by most of the major carriers allows more direct nonstop routings for customers. This does several things in terms of efficiency. For one thing, it minimizes connections, delays, and the total trip time. This results in more value for customers because approximately 78% of Southwest's customers fly nonstop. Another strategic initiative used by Southwest is providing services at many conveniently located secondary or downtown airports, including Dallas Love Field, Houston Hobby, Chicago Midway, Baltimore-Washington International, Burbank, Manchester, Oakland, San Jose, Providence, Ft. Lauderdale/Hollywood, and Long Island Islip. These airports are typically less congested than other airlines' hub-and-spoke airports. The use of these airports enhances Southwest's ability to sustain high employee productivity and provide its customers with significant value through reliable, on-time performance. Another important efficiency enhancement is its operating strategy, which permits Southwest to achieve and sustain high asset utilization.

Efficient aircraft scheduling minimizes the amount of time that Southwest's aircraft are at the gate to a mere 25 minutes on average, resulting in a reduction in the number of aircraft and gate facilities required. One other key efficiency strategic initiative is that Southwest operates only one aircraft type, the Boeing 737, which simplifies scheduling, maintenance, flight operations, and training activities.

Because we are talking about efficiency, let's take a hard look at ticketless travel. Southwest was the first major airline to introduce a ticketless travel option. That's right, Southwest was the first airline to do this. Why? Eliminating the need to print and then process a paper ticket saves time and money for the customer. Southwest took another step by introducing ticketless travel through the company's home page on the Internet, www.southwest.com. As of the end of 2004, Southwest reported that more than 90% of its customers chose the ticketless travel option, and approximately 59% of Southwest's passenger revenues came through its Internet site, which has become a vital part of Southwest's distribution strategy. One cost-saving result of this initiative has been that Southwest has not had to pay commissions to travel agents for sales since December 15, 2003. Now that's efficiency and sustained value!

What do you do as an airline if you fly over 80 million customers a year to and from 62 destinations? You are bound to get lots of mail, including email. At Southwest Airlines, there are four teams totaling 175 people working with the company's databases to manage all the incoming mail and the responses to all its customers.

Innovativeness

One of the ways that Southwest has shown exceptional innovativeness is by adding "blended winglets" to approximately 92% of its fleet of 737-700 aircraft. This initiative was completed on December 31, 2004. The addition of these wing enhancements, which reportedly included all of the company's aircraft by the end of 2005, provides the following benefits:

- It extends the range of these aircraft;
- It saves fuel;
- It lowers potential engine maintenance costs;
- and it reduces takeoff noise.

Any new 737-700 aircraft will now arrive from Boeing with winglets already installed. The company expects annual fuel consumption savings of approximately 3% for each aircraft outfitted with the winglets. The company also phased out commissions on travel agency sales in 2004, a move consistent with virtually all other U.S. airlines. This change in policy saved the company approximately $50 million in 2004. During 2004, the company added 47 new 737-700 aircraft to its fleet and retired 18 older 737-200 aircraft, resulting in a net available seat mile (ASM) capacity increase of 7.1% percent. This brought the size of the company's all-737 fleet to 417 aircraft at the end of 2004.

Southwest launched the first-ever "direct link" to customers' computer desktops in February 2005 through a product called "DING!" This application can be downloaded from www.southwest.com. The "DING!" application is used by Southwest to announce to its customers any new savings in airfares.

Quality of Products and Services

Southwest operated a total of 417 Boeing 737 aircraft as of December 31, 2004. By the end of 2004, it reported ownership of 322 of these aircraft and leased 95. The average age of Southwest's aircraft is nine years. Southwest made a key move towards its success by adding the Boeing 737-700 aircraft, the newest generation of the Boeing 737 aircraft type. The first 737-700 aircraft was delivered to Southwest in December 1997 and entered revenue service in January 1998. As of December 31, 2004, Southwest reported having 193 Boeing 737-700 aircraft in service as part of its Boeing 737 fleet. In order to maintain a high quality standard for the age of its aircraft, Southwest retired its five remaining Boeing 737-200 aircraft during January 2005. See Table 2.1 below:

Table 2.1

737 Type	Average Seats	Age (Yrs)	Number of Aircraft	Number Owned	Number Leased
200	122	22.0	5	5	--
300	137	13.7	194	110	84
500	122	13.7	25	16	9
700	137	3.4	193	191	2
Totals		52.8	417	322	95

Source: Southwest Airlines 2004 10K

Southwest mechanics perform most of the line maintenance on the company's aircraft and provide ground support services at most of the airports the company serves. In addition to achieving high quality standards in its maintenance of aircraft, Southwest also uses certain aircraft maintenance firms for major component inspections and repairs for its airframes and engines, which comprise the majority of the annual aircraft maintenance costs.

Market Expansion

In April 2005, Southwest announced plans to add new nonstop flights in 2005 to Baltimore/Washington, Fort Lauderdale/Hollywood, Las Vegas, Long Island/Islip, Oakland, Orlando, Philadelphia, Raleigh-Durham, San Diego, Tampa Bay, and West Palm Beach. The increasing demand for Southwest's low fares and customer-friendly flights in Philadelphia has been a major success, making this city one of Southwest's most profitable new city forays. In January 2005, Southwest also added Pittsburgh as its 60th city, with service scheduled to begin in May 2005.

Southwest leverages its low-cost competitive advantage, protective fuel hedging position, and excellent service to react quickly to market opportunities. Toward the end of 2004, Southwest was selected as the winning bidder at a bankruptcy court-approved auction for certain ATA Airlines, Inc. (ATA) assets, thus ensuring that Southwest could continue to add low-fare service in Chicago. As part of the transaction, Southwest agreed to pay $40 million for certain ATA assets, including leasehold rights to six ATA Chicago Midway Airport gates. In 2005, it re-opened Denver.

Competitiveness

To remain a formidable competitor, Southwest introduced a ticketless travel option, thus eliminating the need to print and then process paper tickets. After offering ticketless travel, it raised the bar again when it was the first airline to offer ticketless travel via Southwest's home page on the Internet, www.southwest.com. By the time the year ended on December 31, 2004, more than 90% of Southwest's customers chose to use ticketless travel, and approximately 59% of Southwest's passenger revenues came through its Internet site, which has become a key element of Southwest's distribution strategy. As pointed out previously, Southwest has not paid commissions to travel agents for sales since December 15, 2003.

Another equally competitive and innovative factor is the Frequent Flyer Awards program. Southwest's frequent flyer program, Rapid Rewards, is based on trips flown rather than mileage. Rapid Rewards customers earn a credit for each one-way trip flown or two credits for each round trip flown. Rapid Rewards customers also receive credits by using the services of non-airline partners such as car rental agencies, hotels, telecommunications companies, and credit card partners, including the Southwest Airlines Chase (formerly Bank One) Visa card. Another competitive feature of the Rapid Rewards program is the Companion Pass, which is granted to customers who have flown 50 round trips (or 100 one-way trips) on Southwest or who have earned 100 credits within a consecutive twelve-month period.

Unlike many of its competitors, Southwest does not limit the number of Award Tickets and Companion Passes. It also sells credits to business partners including credit card companies, hotels, telecommunications companies, and car rental agencies. These credits may be redeemed for Award Tickets with the same program characteristics as those earned by flying. The amount of free travel award usage as a percentage of total Southwest revenue passengers carried was 7.1% in 2004, 7.5% in 2003, and 6.8% in 2002. The number of fully earned Award Tickets and partially earned awards outstanding by the year's end of 2003 and 2004 was approximately 7.0 million. The numbers of outstanding Companion Passes for Southwest at the year end of 2004 and 2003 were approximately 60,000 and 53,000 respectively. Southwest estimates that an average of three to four trips will be redeemed per outstanding Companion Pass.

By 2004, Southwest Airlines had 31,011 active employees consisting of 11,442 flight attendants; 1,972 maintenance workers; 13,414 ground, customer, and fleet service personnel; and 4,183 management, accounting, marketing, and clerical personnel. Perhaps the most significant competitive advantages Southwest has this area are the ten collective bargaining agreements covering approximately 81.2% of Southwest's employees. Impressively enough, nine of these agreements will not have to be renegotiated until at least 2008 (see Table 2.2 on the next page). Now that's an enormous competitive advantage. These agreements show that Southwest's employees and the labor organizations representing them value their relationship with Southwest Airlines. In a volatile industry with an unstable labor and management relationship track record, Southwest Airlines has done a yeoman's job in this area.

Table 2.2

Employee Group	Represented by	Agreement Amendable
Customer Service and Reservations Agents	International Association of Machinists and Aerospace Workers	November 2008 (or 2006 at the Union's option and under AFL CIO certain conditions)
Flight Attendants	Transportation Workers of America, AFL-CIO (TWU	June 2008
Ramp, Operations, and TWU Provisioning and Freight Agents		June 2008 (or 2006 at the Union's option under certain conditions)
Pilots	Southwest Airlines Pilots' Association	September 2006
Flight Dispatchers	Southwest Airlines Employee Association	December 2009
Aircraft Appearance Technicians	Aircraft Mechanics Fraternal Association ("AMFA")	February 2009
Stock Clerks	International Brotherhood of Teamsters ("Teamsters")	August 2008
Mechanics	AMFA	August 2008

Southwest Airlines is clearly the leader in sustained growth, profitability, well-managed assets, and excellent market capitalization. The important key for Southwest Airlines is its sustained performance in all of the Value Zone performance categories (See Figure 2.3 below).

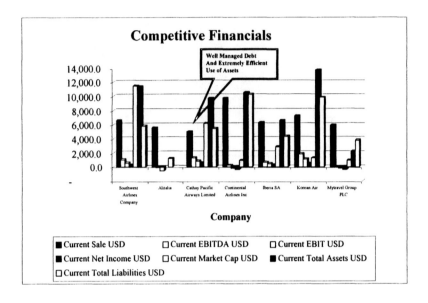

The Wood Research Institute

Figure 2.3

To continue to sustain its competitiveness, Southwest Airlines should monitor the following internal and external factors:

- The cost increases due to: the adverse impact of new airline and airport security directives related to the September 11th terrorist attacks, a
  decline in consumer demand for travel, new policies related to the
  Transportation Security Administration's scope for managing U.S. airport security, the availability and cost of war-risk and other aviation insurance, and the possibility of additional incidents that could influence
  consumers' view of the safety and/or efficiency of air travel and hence,
  their behavior.
- Competitive factors including fare sales, capacity decisions by Southwest Airlines and its competitors, changes in competitors' flight schedules, mergers and acquisitions, code sharing programs, and airline
  bankruptcies.
- Global economic conditions that could adversely affect the demand for
  leisure and business travel, consumer ticket purchasing habits, and decisions made by major freight customers on how they allocate freight
  deliveries among different types of carriers.
- Southwest's ability to control its costs as they relate to the results of labor contract negotiations; employee hiring and retention rates; costs for

health care; the largely unpredictable prices of jet fuel, crude oil, and heating oil; the continued effectiveness of Southwest's fuel hedges; capacity decisions made by Southwest and its competitors; unscheduled required aircraft airframe or engine repairs and regulatory requirements; changes in commission policy; the availability of capital markets; reliance on single suppliers for both Southwest's aircraft and its aircraft engines; disruptions to operations due to adverse weather conditions and air traffic control-related constraints; and internal failures of technology or large-scale external interruptions in technology infrastructure including power, telecommunications, or the Internet.

Southwest Airlines Value Zone Analysis Summary

In the preceding Value Zone analysis of Southwest Airlines, we have examined why this company is achieving and sustaining remarkable business results and a high value rating from its customers. Southwest Airlines' growing dominance in the airline industry clearly positions it well within the Value Zone. Southwest Airlines' outstanding record of sustained business results over a 26-year period is remarkable and demonstrates that it consistently provides its customers with high value. Although Southwest Airlines has stayed above the line with high ratings in the Value Zone during the period of 2001 through 2002, it has had some periods of slippage in its performance. Clearly, the tragic events that took place during September 11th, 2001, as well as the rise in fuel costs during that year, resulted in a decline in air travel that impacted Southwest and the rest of the airline industry dramatically. However, Southwest managed to eke out a small profit during 2001 despite a decline during the two years in revenue growth.

Our research has shown that all eight of the Value Zone elements—leadership, culture, financial performance, market growth, innovation, efficiency, quality, and competitiveness—are linked to clearly identifiable Value Zone "best practices." Southwest Airlines has scored high marks in the Value Zone. We have also seen that Southwest's Value Zone "best practices" strategic initiatives helped it weather the turbulent business environment of the early part of the 21st century (See Table 2.3 below). "Best practices" such as ticketless travel, hedging fuel costs, the code sharing arrangement with ATA, flying one type of aircraft, offering 78% of its customer base non-stop service with record gate turnaround time, the "DING!" linkage on its customers' computers alerting them to special low fares, and its Rapid Rewards program have kept Southwest Airlines flying high in the "Sweet Spot" of the Value Zone.

Table 2.3

Value Zone Elements Strategic "Best Practices"	Results
Leadership Colleen C. Barrett	One of Southwest's primary

Board: Executive Board
Job Title: President and Corporate Secretary
Since: 2001 Age: 60
Ms. Barrett has been president and director of the company since 2001. Prior to that time, she was executive vice president (customers) from 1990 to 2001 and vice president (administration) from 1986 to 1990.

Gary C. Kelly
Board: Executive Board
Job Title: Vice Chairman and Chief Executive Officer
Since: 2004 Age: 49
Mr. Kelly has been vice chairman of the board of directors and chief executive officer of the company since July 2004. Prior to that time, he was executive vice president and chief financial officer from 2001 to 2004 and vice president (finance) and chief financial officer from 1989 to 2001. Mr. Kelly joined the company in 1986 as its controller.

Herbert D. Kelleher
Board: Non-Executive Board
Job Title: Chairman
Since: 1978 Age: 73
Mr. Kelleher has been chairman of the board since 1978. He became interim president and chief executive officer of the company in 1981 and assumed those offices on a permanent basis in 1982, relinquishing those titles in 2001.

competitive strengths is its low operating costs. Southwest has the lowest costs, adjusted for stage length, on a per-mile basis of all the major airlines. Among the factors that contribute to its low cost structure are a single aircraft type; an efficient, high-utilization, point-to-point route structure; and hardworking, innovative, and highly productive employees.

Culture	Low operating costs
Hardworking, innovative, and highly productive employees	Sustained revenue growth
	Steady increase of loyal customers
Extraordinary customer service is institutionalized into Southwest's culture.	
Market Growth	In March 2005, SWA began providing nonstop service to 18 cities from Philadelphia, where its reception has been both heartwarming and enormously enthusiastic.
In December 2004, SWA successfully completed a significant transaction with ATA Airlines in the latter's Chapter 11 bankruptcy proceedings. SWA acquired the rights to six additional gates at Chicago's Midway Airport, which will soon be fully utilized by added Southwest flights and a much-needed six-bay Midway Airport maintenance hangar. In May 2004, SWA entered the Philadelphia market, and SWA routes and fares out of Pittsburgh were announced recently and the disclosure of its service plan engendered an enthusiastic reception and welcome.	Recently, SWA began service to Pittsburgh, which its executives view as a very promising opportunity because US Airways has so drastically reduced its service to the Pittsburgh area, in effect disassembling its Pittsburgh hub.
Innovation	Low operating and maintenance costs
• single aircraft type "blended winglets" lower fuel costs by 3% • Rapid Rewards program	Southwest's RAPID CHECK-IN Kiosks and automated boarding passes keep its boarding procedure quick and simple for its customers. Southwest's Rapid Rewards program won top honors as frequent flyer Program of the Year in *Inside Flyer* magazine's annual Freddie Awards, including awards for Best Customer Service, Best Award Redemption, and Best Bonus Promotion among all frequent flyer programs.

Efficiency efficient, high-utilization, point-to-point route structure	The Southwest staff of over 30,000 has fully supported numerous technological and security changes, helping to improve the overall customer airport experience and its operational efficiency. Southwest is the leading airline in on-time departure and arrival times.
Quality Southwest's mission statement states that it is dedicated to "the highest quality of Customer Service delivered with a sense of warmth, friendliness, individual pride, and Company Spirit."	Southwest was recognized for its 12th straight award as the airline with the best customer complaint record in the U.S. In March 2003, Southwest was again named by *Fortune* as one of the most admired companies in America and the most admired airline in America. Southwest ranked first among airlines for Customer Service satisfaction, according to a survey by the American Customer Satisfaction Index, as reported in the *Wall Street Journal.*
Competitiveness Ticketless travel Frequent Flyer Awards program Rapid Rewards program	Approximately 59% of Southwest's passenger revenues come through its Internet site, which has become a key element of Southwest's distribution strategy. Southwest has not paid commissions to travel agents for sales since December 15, 2003. The amount of free travel award usage as a percentage of total Southwest revenue passengers carried was 7.1% in 2004, 7.5% in 2003, and 6.8%

| | in 2002. The number of fully earned Award Tickets and partially earned awards outstanding by the year end of 2003 and 2004 was approximately seven million. The numbers of Companion Passes for Southwest outstanding at the year end of 2004 and 2003 were approximately 60,000 and 53,000 respectively. Southwest estimates that an average of three to four trips will be redeemed per outstanding Companion Pass. |
| | |

What we have learned by studying the airline industry in crisis, and in particular, by studying Southwest Airlines, is that companies can fly high in the Value Zone despite operating within a tumultuous industry. Companies can experience success if they focus as Southwest did on the eight critical elements of the Value Zone. Using the Value Zone table just displayed, we can see the "best practices" strategic elements and their results. It is clear that any business can do this type of an assessment. We will introduce a tool along with this book that you can use to do a self-assessment and test your own company to determine its areas of strengths and weaknesses as they relate to the application of strategic "best practices" embedded in each of the Value Zone elements. This tool is easy to use. The tough part is conducting an honest evaluation and "gutchecking" that you and your company's leadership have the right strategic "best practices" in place. In many cases, you will find that there are some areas in which you are doing well and some areas in which your company needs work. The next step is to address these problem areas. But before you do this, please learn more about the Value Zone by reading Chapter Three. In this chapter, we re-introduce the first group of companies that qualify for the distinction of being included into the Value Zone Hall of Fame. Each of these companies has been able to sustain remarkable business results for 25 years or more. In fact, some companies are distinguished even more by being included in the Value Zone Hall of Fame Ring of Honor for sustaining remarkable business performance for 50 years or more. To learn more about these companies and how they have achieved this distinction, please read Chapter Three and the rest of this book.

Chapter Three
The Value Zone Hall of Fame

Companies that thrive in the Value Zone have strong leaders and an enduring culture. They also consistently achieve solid financial results, constantly seek new markets, are innovative, always seek to improve their efficiency, offer the highest quality in products or services, and are extremely competitive. In our research to determine companies that were able to sustain solid business performance for a period of five years or more, we evaluated the performance of 73,728 publicly owned companies worldwide from 2005 to 2001. Then we worked our way backwards in time to see if these same companies were able to sustain their performance for even longer periods of time. We were able to find many companies that achieved this level from 2005 to 2001, but as we tested their performances for ten, 15, 20, and 25 years, the numbers dropped dramatically. Amazingly enough, only 38 companies from a variety of industries were able to sustain solid business performance from 1981 through 2005 (see the Appendix for charts portraying each company's revenue growth and profits from 1981 through 2005). To distinguish these companies from the rest of the companies that we examined, we have created the Value Zone Hall of Fame. Because our research was based on a benchmark time span (1981-2005), it is very possible that we will have to add other companies into the Value Zone Hall of Fame for past consistent performances that meet our criteria. You will find many other companies with this distinction at our website, www.TheValueZone.net. We will discuss our website more in the last chapter of this book.

We will now provide you with a list of the companies that are included in the 1981-2005 Value Zone Hall of Fame as well as an overview of each of these companies. Then we will take you on an incredible journey that will remind you of all the external and internal environmental forces and factors that have affected businesses from 1981 through 2005. We will explain how these 38 companies dealt with them more effectively than the other 73,728 companies that we examined in our research. As you read about these past events, we believe that you too will marvel at what these 38 companies were able to achieve despite all of the external and internal forces that could have impacted or impeded their progress as businesses. The next eight chapters will highlight some of the strategic "best practices" initiatives embedded in each of the Value Zone core elements and used by these and other companies that have exhibited exceptional performance for more than five years. One of our goals in conducting this research is to determine if there are any common strategic "best practices" that transcend time and industry and can be applied to other companies.

The 1981-2005 Value Zone Hall of Fame
    The following companies are included in the Value Zone Hall of Fame for
the years 1981 through 2005 (Figure 3.1):

Value Zone Hall of Fame	
Abertis SA	Home Depot Inc
ABM Industries Inc	Johnson & Johnson
Aeon Company Limited	Johnson Controls Inc
Alliance Unichem PLC	Land Securities PLC
Arthur J Gallagher & Company	Longs Drug Stores
Automatic Data Processing	Lowe's Companies Inc
Becton Dickinson & Company	McDonalds Corp.
Biomet Inc	Morrison (WM) Supermarkets PLC
Cbrl Group Inc	Nbty Inc
Cintas Corp.	Nordstrom Inc
Comcast Corp.	Omnicom Group Inc
Diagnostic Products Corp.	Pall Corp.
Family Dollar Stores Inc	Pick N Pay Stores Limited
Federal Realty Investment Trust	Stryker Corp.
Fraport AG	Sysco Corp.
G & K Services Inc	Teleflex Inc
Greene King PLC	Tesco PLC
Grupo Bimbo SA De CV	Wal Mart Stores Inc
Grupo Continental SA	Walgreen Company

Figure 3.1

Historical External Forces from 1981 to 2005
    As we peer back into the 1980s, the 1990s, and the beginnings of the 21st
century, we find ourselves witnessing momentous years that will impact companies all over the world. Imagine that you are leading one of these 38 companies.
As these leaders traversed the corridors of time, how did they navigate their
companies safely through turbulence and adversity? Let's briefly look at those
years and imagine how the key events that occurred from 1981 to 2005 could
have affected the decisions and strategies of our 38 Hall of Fame companies.
Think about the challenges you would face if you were at the helm of one of
these firms.

1981
    In 1981, the Social Security wage base increased from $25,900 to $29,700.
Iran released 52 U.S. hostages who had been held captive for 444 days. Deregu-

lation of the oil and gas industries was announced in the U.S. IBM unveiled the first Personal Computer. Japan agreed to limit car exports to the U.S. from April 1, 1981, to March of 1983. The Organization of Petroleum Exporting Countries (OPEC) failed to agree on a uniform price schedule, and OPEC officials froze prices. The dollar reached its highest level in international trading since December 1971. U.S. Social Security checks increased by 11.2% due to Cost of Living Adjustment (COLA). Two Libyan jets were shot down by U.S. Navy fighters about 60 miles from the Libyan coast after the Libyan fighters opened fire on the U.S. jets. Libya claimed that it had control of all of the Gulf of Sidra, where the Navy was holding military exercises, while the U.S. maintained that the Gulf was an international body of water. The U.S. dollar hit a new high exchange rate against European currencies, while the Canadian dollar closed at $0.809 U.S., the lowest exchange rate since 1931. The Professional Air Traffic Controller's Organization (PATCO) began a nationwide strike, and President Reagan announced that the strikers must return to work by August 5th or face dismissal. Many stayed home and were fired. Food shortages in Warsaw had the Polish populace protesting. President Reagan signed the Economic Recovery Act of 1981, thereby writing both the tax- and budget-cut bills into law. The Federal Aviation Administration began accepting applications for new air traffic controllers to replace the strikers who were fired on August 5, 1981. U.S. federal employees received a 4.8% general pay increase and regular step increases, while military pay increased by 14.3%. Egyptian President Sadat was assassinated. The Federal Labor Relations Authority decertified the Professional Air Traffic Controller's Organization (PATCO), ending any possibility of a negotiated settlement with the remaining striking air traffic controllers. The OPEC price was set at $34.00/barrel—the Saudi benchmark—and we will probably never see it that low again. The Polish government instituted martial law to quell political unrest. In retaliation, President Reagan announced economic sanctions against Poland's government to protest the imposition of martial law. The long-dormant Mount St. Helens volcano erupted. President Reagan announced sanctions against Russia for its role in the Polish crisis.

1982

In 1982, the Social Security wage base rose again from $29,700 to $32,400. AT&T agreed to divest itself of 22 Bell Telephone operating systems, ending an eight-year antitrust suit by the U.S. Justice Department, which had charged AT&T with being a monopoly. This was truly a momentous decision that opened the way for many new competitors in the telecommunications industry to be born. The U.S. Justice Department dropped its 13-year antitrust suit against IBM. The Reagan administration announced economic sanctions against Libya in response to Libya's involvement with international terrorist organizations; the sanctions included an embargo on Libyan oil shipments to the U.S. and a ban on exports of high-technology products to Libya. OPEC cut production from 18.2 million barrels to 17.5 million. Argentine forces seized the Falkland Islands, and in retaliation, the United Kingdom imposed economic sanctions on Argentina. In the wake of the seizure of the Falkland Islands, limited sanctions by other Western countries followed. The U.S. consumer price index declined 0.3% in March—the first decline in 17 years and the largest drop in nearly a quarter of a century. Israeli troops invaded southern Lebanon to attack PLO guerillas. The U.S. Department of Commerce determined that imported foreign steel should receive government subsidies. The French franc was devalued by 6% and the Italian lira by 3%. Argentine forces in the Falkland Islands surrendered to British forces, ending the Falklands War. In the U.S., the 10% personal income tax cut became effective. Social Security checks increased by 7.4%. The Tax Equity and Fiscal Responsibility Act (TEFRA) raised taxes by cutting loopholes, eliminating about a third of 1981 corporate tax cuts. Cyanide placed in Tylenol capsules caused the deaths of seven persons in the Chicago area; by October 6th, a nationwide alert was sounded, and the makers of Tylenol recalled 264,000 bottles of the drug. The killer was never found. Social Security was borrowed from in November 1982 for the first time. Voluntary restrictions on steel exports from the European community to the U.S. went into effect. Japan renewed its ceiling of 1.68 million auto exports to the United States. The U.S. national unemployment rate hit 9.0% in March, tying the post-WWII high in May 1975. The U.S. unemployment rate reached 9.4% for a post-WWII record.

1983

This year began with a major work stoppage due to an Independent Truckers strike. The strike paralyzed the shipment of goods and ended several weeks later. The United American Bank of Knoxville, Tennessee was declared insolvent. Toyota and GM agreed to build a small car together in late 1984. The FTC approved the venture on December 22, 1983. OPEC set a benchmark price of $29 per barrel and a production quota of 17.5 million barrels—an amazing feat because here we are in 2006, and the rate is now $75 per barrel. The U.S. Embassy in Beirut, Lebanon was almost totally destroyed by a car-bomb explosion that killed 63 people, including 17 Americans. An earthquake measuring 6.5 on the Richter scale struck Coalinga, California. The Soviet Union shot down Korean Airlines Flight 007 from New York to Seoul for violating Soviet airspace near the Soviet island of Sakhalin just north of Japan. All 269 people aboard were killed. The U.S. Marine headquarters in Beirut, Lebanon were destroyed when a massive car bomb exploded outside the building, killing 241 Navy and Marine personnel. The U.S. invaded Grenada after a bloody coup of the island's leadership. The hostilities in Grenada ended on November 2, 1983.

1984

This year was marked by tragedy when Indira Ghandi was murdered by two of her bodyguards while walking home from her office. Her assassins were Sikh extremists retaliating for the raid she ordered on their shrine in Amritsar that had resulted in the deaths of over 1,000 Sikh separatists. Hindu rioting after the assassination killed more than 2,000 Sikhs. In 1984, the United Kingdom and

China agreed on terms for the return of Hong Kong to China when the 99-year lease of portions of Hong Kong expired in 1997. Under the agreement, Hong Kong was to maintain its capitalist system after its return to Chinese control. A major disaster occurred in India when poison gas escaped a Union Carbide plant in Bhopal, India. The gas, which was methyl isocyanate (used in the manufacture of insecticides), killed 2,000 people, and an additional 200,000 suffered long-term harm. Over 300 people died when India's army attacked the Golden Temple, one of the Sikh's holiest shrines. The army claimed that the temple was an arms depot. Moderates won the election in El Salvador. Free elections held in El Salvador brought Jose Napoleon Duarte to power as President; he became the first civilian leader in El Salvador in 49 years. As Acquired Immune Deficiency Syndrome (AIDS) "broke out" several years prior to 1984, French scientists reported isolating the virus that causes AIDS. In the United States, 7,000 cases of AIDS were reported, and 3,300 of its victims were dead by the end of the year. Mikhail Sergeyevich Gorbachev became the new leader of the Soviet Union on March 11, 1985 after the death of Secretary General Cherenenko. Gorbachev represented a younger generation of Soviet leaders and began a series of reforms aimed at invigorating the communist system in the Soviet Union while at the same time improving relations with the West. The changes he began soon developed a momentum of their own.

1985

The *Rainbow Warrior*, which was owned by Greenpeace, was sunk in the Auckland harbor as it prepared to protest French nuclear tests. The French government admitted to blowing up the ship, and the French defense minister was forced to resign. Palestinian terrorists seized the cruise ship *Achille Lauro* and threw the body of American tourist Leon Klinghoffer off of the ship. The terrorists agreed to surrender to Egyptian authorities. These authorities promised them safe passage when they were flown out of Egypt. The U.S. intercepted the plane and forced it to land in Italy, where the terrorists were put on trial. A TWA Boeing 727 was hijacked by two Shiite terrorists, and 153 people were held hostage. Women, children and the elderly were eventually released, and one American hostage was killed. His body was thrown out of the plane, and the remaining passengers were held in various parts of Beirut. After Israel released 31 of its Shiite prisoners, the hostages being held in Beirut were released. Because the United States owed more money to foreigners than was owed to the U.S., the U.S. became a debtor nation for the first time since 1914. President Reagan unveiled a new tax program that would simplify tax laws and lower America's tax rates. The new laws lowered the maximum personal income tax rate of 35.5% and decreased the number of rates from 11 to three. These new tax laws also lowered corporate rates. Columbian terrorists executed 100 people, including 11 judges. Colombian terrorists of the M-19 group stormed the Palace of Justice in Bogotá and held two dozen justices and over 100 others hostage.

1986

United Steelworkers leaders agreed to allow rank-and-file members to vote on labor contracts for the first time in the union's history. The space shuttle *Challenger* exploded, killing all seven crewmembers. Corazon Aquino took over the Philippines as its new president. Meanwhile, conservative Jacques Chirac was appointed as Prime Minister of France. U.S. warplanes attacked two Libyan ships and a shoreline missile site after Libyan missiles were fired at U.S. planes in the Gulf of Sidra. Federal Chair Paul Volcker warned that public and private debt buildup was a threat to the economy. A Soviet nuclear plant at Chernobyl was destroyed by fire. The U.S. proposed a 35% tariff on Canadian cedar shakes and shingles for roofing, which led to a trade dispute between the U.S. and Canada. The U.S. Supreme Court ruled that the Gramm Rudman Hollings mechanism for across-the-board automatic spending cuts was unconstitutional. In 1986, President Reagan signed into law his economic program calling for spending curbs and higher taxes to reduce the then-projected federal budget deficit by $496 billion over a five-year period. United Steelworkers went on strike for the first time since 1959; 44,000 workers were involved. General Motors Corporation introduced a new incentive program to lure consumers with an unprecedented auto loan rate of 2.9%. Union employees from Kaiser Foundation Hospital, Kaiser Permanente Medical Group, Inc., and Kaiser Foundation Health Plan went on strike on October 27th; they ended the strike on December 13th.

1987

Fannie Mae raised the mortgage ceiling from $133,250 to $153,100. OPEC's 7% production cut went into effect, and U.S. oil prices hit $18 per barrel. When you consider today's oil prices, that is simply amazing. The U.S. dollar fell to a post-WWII low. A U.S. warship, the *USS Stark*, was struck by an air-launched Iraqi missile in the Persian Gulf. Kuwaiti tankers were placed under the U.S. flag for transit through the Persian Gulf. Alan Greenspan was sworn in as chairman of the Federal Reserve Board. A severe earthquake with its epicenter near Whittier hit southern California.

1988

Former Soviet Union leader Gorbachev addressed the U.N. to announce a unilateral troop reduction of 500,000 Soviet conventional forces in Eastern Europe. The Soviets also agreed to remove 120,000 troops from Afghanistan. An Iranian passenger jet was shot down by the U.S. in a case of mistaken identity. The *USS Vincennes* shot down the Iranian passenger plane, an Airbus carrying nearly 300 passengers. Sadly, all were killed. The longest undersea tunnel in Japan was opened between Aomori on the island of Honshu and Hakidate on the island of Hokkaido. The tunnel, called "Seikan," is 33.44 miles long and is as deep as 787 feet below water at one point. Free elections were held for the Soviet Congress of Deputies for the first time in its history. The formation of the new Soviet Congress of Deputies brought many leading dissidents to elected positions in the Congress, including Andrei Sakharov. Boris Yeltsin was also elected. Yeltsin had been ousted from the Central Committee a year earlier.

1990–1991

Iraq invaded Kuwait; as a result, the U.S. Congress approved the use of force in Iraq. The U.S. took military action against Iraq in Operation Desert Storm. Iraqi troops withdrew from Kuwait. President George H. W. Bush ordered a cease-fire in the war against Iraq, and Desert Storm ended.

1992

Retailer R. H. Macy filed for Chapter 11 bankruptcy protection. Trans-World Airlines filed for bankruptcy protection. In Los Angeles, there was widespread flooding, an earthquake in Palm Springs, and racial riots.

1993

President Clinton announced an economic plan that cut defense spending by $188 billion from 1994 to 1998. There was a major bomb blast at New York's World Trade Center that resulted in considerable damage. The U.S. Department of Defense announced a plan to close 31 major military bases, seven of which were in California. The Great Flood of '93, which stretched from Minnesota to Missouri, caused estimated damages of $12 billion and covered over 10 million acres. President Clinton declared more than 200 counties federal disaster areas, including all 99 counties in Iowa. President Clinton signed into law an economic program that called for spending curbs and higher taxes to reduce a projected federal budget deficit by $496 billion over a five-year period. Thirteen wildfires raged through Southern California, and some were attributed to arson. Five counties were declared disaster areas. The North American Free Trade Agreement (NAFTA) was passed. Japan and the U.S. agreed on a plan to open Japan's markets to rice import.

1994

An earthquake registering 6.8 on the Richter scale and centered in Northridge struck Southern California. Congress approved the General Agreement on Tariffs and Trade (GATT). Orange County, California filed for bankruptcy protection under Chapter 9 provisions.

1995

California was battered by its worst series of storms since 1986. Severe floods forced the evacuation of thousands of residents and caused an estimated $2 billion of damage, making it the costliest winter storm series in the history of the state. The U.S. trade deficit soared by 68% to $12.2 billion. A powerful earthquake measuring 7.2 on the Richter scale struck Kobe in central Japan, killing more than 5,000 people. The Clinton administration announced a program of loans and currency swaps to prop up the Mexican peso. The plan utilized existing authority and involved several international agencies. The peso had been devalued by more than 40% against the U.S. dollar since early December 1994.

Britain and Ireland unveiled their framework document for a political settlement in Northern Ireland. British merchant bank Barings PLC collapsed after trader Nick Leeson lost more than $1 billion on Japanese shares and bonds in Singapore. Boeing won a $1.17 billion order from Scandinavian Airlines for its 737-600 airliners. Turkish troops launched a three-pronged attack across the Iraqi border against Kurdish rebels. Eleven people died and more than 5,000 were injured in a nerve gas attack on the Tokyo subway by the Aum Shinri Kyo religious sect. Border controls between seven European Union countries disappeared as the Schengen agreement came into force. A huge car bomb devastated a federal building in Oklahoma City, Oklahoma, killing at least 167 people. President Clinton announced a cutoff of all trade between U.S. companies and Iran. NASA intended to cut 28,860 jobs and consolidate space-shuttle activities under a single contractor during the next five years. Boeing cut 5,000 more jobs during 1995, more than previously projected, bringing the total to 12,000 by the year's end. A major flare-up in the Bosnian war occurred when NATO launched air strikes and the Serbs retaliated by shelling U.N. safe areas, killing 68 people. An earthquake struck the oil-producing town of Neftegorsk on Russia's Sakhalin Island, killing about 2,000 people. Meanwhile, Bosnian Serbs took 372 U.N. peacekeepers hostage. Lord Owen resigned as the European Union key peace negotiator. Boeing won at least two-thirds of a $6 billion commercial jetliner order from Saudi Arabian carrier Saudia; the remainder of the order went to McDonnell-Douglas Corp. Chechen fighters launched a commando-style raid on the Russian town of Budennovsk, taking hundreds of hostages. More than 120 people were killed. Gunmen attempted to assassinate Egyptian President Hosni Mubarak in the Ethiopian capital of Addis Ababa. The U.S. space shuttle *Atlantis* successfully docked with the Russian space station *Mir*. Part of a department store in Seoul, South Korea collapsed, killing nearly 500 people. French commandos stormed the Greenpeace ship *Rainbow Warrior* after it entered an exclusion zone near the French nuclear test site at Mururoa Atoll. Bosnian Serb forces overran the U.N.-declared safe area of Srebrenica while Croatia launched an offensive to regain the Krajina enclave held by its Serb minority for four years. Israel and the Palestine Liberation Organization signed an agreement in Washington, D.C. extending Palestinian rule to most of the West Bank. Hurricane Opal hit Florida's panhandle. O. J. Simpson was acquitted. In a referendum on independence, Quebec voted by a narrow margin to remain part of a budget impasse that was causing a partial federal government shutdown and furlough of nonessential federal employees. Boeing won a $12.7 billion order from Singapore Airlines. Strikers at Caterpillar rejected a proposed six-year contract, but the United Auto Workers union called an end to the 17-month walkout anyway. President Clinton authorized a vanguard of U.S. troops to move into Bosnia. The advance troops set up headquarters in preparation for thousands more U.S. soldiers to follow.

1996

AT&T decided to eliminate at least 40,000 jobs over the next three years as part of its plan to split into three companies. The federal government was partially shut down because of a budget crisis. Wells Fargo & Co. merged with First Interstate Bancorp. President Clinton signed a landmark telecommunications bill into law. Boeing intended to fill 7,000 new jobs by early 1997 in its rebounding commercial-jet division. Between March and June, gasoline retail prices in California increased by 28%—much higher than the sizable nationwide increase of about 12%. United Auto Workers went on strike at General Motors Corporation's brake-parts plants in Dayton, Ohio. Bell Atlantic and Nynex agreed to merge. The California Public Employees Retirement System reached the $100 billion mark. Packard Bell and NEC Corp. merged their personal computer operations to create one of the largest PC makers in the world. Lockheed Martin won a $1 billion federal contract to build a prototype for a next-generation space shuttle. Hurricane Bertha hit the North Carolina coast. First Nationwide Bank acquired Cal Fed Bancorp Inc., creating the nation's fourth-largest savings and loan association. Standard & Poor's raised California's credit rating from an A to an A+. Rockwell International Corp. agreed to sell most of its aerospace and defense business to Boeing. Aerojet landed a $30 million contract that gave it a role in developing the nation's next-generation space shuttle. PacifiCare Health Systems Inc. bought competitor FHP International, making it the second-largest managed healthcare organization in California. A massive disruption in a major power system triggered a widespread electricity outage affecting millions of people in parts of at least nine western states. Hurricane Fran hit the Carolina coast. The U.S. minimum wage rose from $4.25 to $4.75 per hour. Countries representing most of the world's high-technology trade agreed to abolish tariffs on computers, software, and related goods.

1997

Rivers in the western United States overflowed as rain and melting snow brought a great deal of flooding in California, Nevada, and several northwestern states. The damage from the flooding was estimated at $155 million. Faced with unprecedented demand for new phone lines for Internet surfers and home offices, Pacific Bell hired more than 2,500 employees in California. Kaiser Corporation consolidated its northern and southern California operations into one division to streamline operations and cut costs. Mexico announced that it would repay a U.S. loan three years ahead of schedule. General Motors' Hughes Electronics was acquired by Raytheon Corporation. Banc One Corporation agreed to buy First USA Inc. As a result, Banc One became the nation's third-largest credit card company at that time. The U.S. Treasury issued the first $7 billion in ten-year inflation-indexed notes. The U.S. trade deficit hit an eight-year high. California's minimum wage increased from $4.75 to $5.00. A federal 10% tax on airline tickets was reimposed. U.S. Bancorp agreed to be acquired by First Bank System. The U.S. unemployment rate fell to its lowest rate in 24 years. Boeing won an order from Russia's Aeroflot, its first big push into one of the world's untapped markets. At the end of the first quarter, the U.S. Gross Domestic Product (GDP) grew at a rate of 5.6%, fueled by a large inventory buildup, warm weather, and the biggest increase in consumer spending in ten years. Coffee shortages pushed coffee prices to a 20-year high. China regained sovereignty over Hong Kong. Lockheed Martin agreed to buy Northrop Grumman. British Telecom's planned acquisition of MCI was approved by the U.S. Justice Department. The European Commission formally cleared the merger of Boeing and McDonnell Douglas. The Teamsters union went on strike against United Parcel Service and subsequently settled.

1998
El Niño-fueled storms caused widespread flooding and landslides in California. Thirty-five counties were declared federal disaster areas, and California's agriculture industry estimated a flood-related loss of $57.4 million as a result. The U.S. trade deficit widened to its worst level in six years in January. Boeing announced that it would reduce approximately 6,200 jobs in California by the year 2000. Xerox Corporation cut 10,000 jobs worldwide—11% of its workforce. NationsBank formally announced its merger with BankAmerica while Banc One confirmed its planned merger with First Chicago. Intel announced that it would eliminate up to 3,000 jobs over a period of six months. National Semiconductor announced its plans to cut its worldwide workforce by 10% (about 1,400 people). Compaq eliminated 15,000 jobs after it purchased Digital Equipment. Motorola announced its plan to lay off 10% of its workforce (about 15,000 workers). The United Auto Workers went on a strike at General Motors that lasted months. Wells Fargo & Co. and Norwest agreed to merge. California's unemployment rate fell in May to its lowest level in nearly eight years. Texas Instruments announced its plans to eliminate 3,500 jobs worldwide, about 8% of its payroll. OPEC cut crude oil production by 1.4 million barrels per day. Rockwell International Corporation announced that it planned to cut 9% of its workforce. Lockheed announced its plan to lay off 2,500 workers. Chinese and U.S. companies signed $1.1 billion in new business deals such as China's agreement of intent to purchase 27 Boeing jetliners. Japan officially declared a recession.

1999
A new reserve currency, the "euro," was introduced, creating a single market in Europe. It became the currency of reference for the 11 countries participating in the European Monetary Union. Brazil devalued its currency, sending U.S. stocks into a free-fall.
The 1998 trade deficit hit an all-time high of $175 billion, 58% more than the shortfall recorded in 1997. OPEC agreed to reduce crude oil production by 2.1 million barrels per day and maintain lower levels of output for the full year. The bombing of Kosovo began. The Dow Jones Industrial Average closed at over 10,000 (10,006) for the first time. The European Central Bank cut its key discount rate for the first time, from 3% to 2.5%. The Dow Jones Industrial Av-

erage closed at over 11,000 (11,014.69) for the first time. A peace agreement was signed for Kosovo. Japan's economy grew 7.9% in the first quarter. Hurricane Floyd battered the East Coast. A 7.6 magnitude earthquake hit Taiwan. The U.S. poverty rate fell to 12.7%, its lowest level in 20 years. Real median household income hit a growth rate of 3.5%, surpassing its pre-recessionary peak in 1989, and for the first time since 1975, all four U.S. regions experienced significant increases. MCI WorldCom announced its intent to buy Sprint. The Dow Jones Industrial Average replaced four companies with Microsoft, Intel, and two other issues. NASDAQ closed above 3,000 for the first time. Packard Bell announced that it was going to close its Sacramento manufacturing facility and lay off 80% of its workforce.

2000

Pfizer Inc. and Warner-Lambert Co. completed a merger deal. Crude oil prices dropped below $30 a barrel. Boeing engineers and technical workers returned to work after a 40-day strike, ending one of the biggest white-collar walkouts in U.S. history. Microsoft lost an antitrust suit. President Clinton signed into law a bill allowing older Americans to work without losing any of their Social Security benefits. Wells Fargo & Co. agreed to acquire First Security Corporation of Utah. One of the worst weeks on Wall Street ended with the Dow Jones Industrial Average down 5.5% and NASDAQ down nearly 10%. The employment cost index jumped 1.4% in the first quarter, the sharpest increase in 11 years. A contract dispute between Time Warner and Disney resulted in a blackout of the Disney network in 3.5 million homes. The "I Love You" computer virus disrupted computers worldwide. The U.S. unemployment rate fell below 4%. A controlled blaze set by the U.S. National Park Service blew out of control, forcing the evacuation of 25,000 people and destroying hundreds of homes in Los Alamos, New Mexico. United Airlines announced that it had agreed to buy US Airways. U.S. private employers cut 116,000 jobs in May. A court ordered the breakup of Microsoft. Microsoft won a delay on breakup penalties, and the case went to U.S. Supreme Court. An orbiting spacecraft reported grooved surfaces on Mars suggesting relatively recent water flow. Philip Morris bought Nabisco holdings. The Human Genome Project was completed. Wildfires destroyed 500,000 acres in California, Arizona, Colorado, Idaho, and Montana. A Concorde crash killed 113 people near Paris. World oil prices rose because of increasingly tight supplies. U.S. inventories were at their lowest level since 1976 and crude prices increased significantly, contributing to costlier gasoline and heating oil. Bridgestone/Firestone admitted to tire defects and began a massive recall. Artic visitors reported a mile-wide area of ice-free ocean in the North Pole ice cap. A 15-day strike against Verizon Communications occurred. Mitsubishi admitted to a defect cover-up and the concealment of customer complaints about defective cars; it recalled over 600,000 cars. OPEC agreed to increase crude oil output by 800,000 barrels a day. High fuel prices sparked protests in Europe. Clinton released 30 million barrels of oil reserves to offset rising fuel costs. European, American, and Japanese central banks acted to bolster the euro. Danish voters rejected joining the European Union's common currency (the euro) in their first popular test of the EU's economic and political integration. The China Trade Bill was signed, giving China permanent normal trade relations. Terrorists blew a hole in the side of the *USS Cole* while it was refueling in the Yemeni port of Aden. Israeli combat helicopters attacked Palestinian command centers in retaliation for the killing of three Israeli soldiers. The Dow Jones Industrial Average closed below 10,000 for the first time since March of 2000. Chevron announced that it had agreed to buy Texaco. Social Security and Supplemental Security income payments were set to increase by 3.5% in 2001, the biggest increase in almost a decade. The Clinton administration announced a record $237 billion surplus, the third in a row, for the fiscal year ending September 2000. OPEC planned to increase oil production by 500,000 barrels per day, making it the fourth increase of 2000.

2001

California's minimum wage rose from $5.75 to $6.25. The federal government lowered the Discount Rate by 0.25% and the Federal Funds Rate by 0.5%. California's power system was under a continuous Stage 3 electrical emergency in the middle of January. OPEC reduced its oil production by 1.5 million barrels a day—5.6% of its current output. California suffered two days of rolling blackouts. California regulators approved a retail electric rate increase. A Tosco refinery explosion pushed gas prices to near-record highs. The federal tax cut was signed into law. The Federal Energy Regulatory Commission adopted a price "mitigation" plan designed to reduce spikes in wholesale electricity prices in California and other western states. Terrorists attacked the World Trade Center and the Pentagon. Enron filed for bankruptcy protection. China became a member of the World Trade Organization (WTO).

2002

Taiwan became a WTO member. OPEC cut oil production by 6.5%. The euro became legal tender in 12 European countries. Unemployment insurance benefits were increased in California. California's Job Creation and Worker Assistance Act of 2002, which provided temporary extended unemployment compensation, was signed into law. The Security and Exchange Commission launched a formal investigation of Wall Street analysts' conflicts of interest.

President George W. Bush signed a ten-year, $190 billion farm bill promising to expand subsidies to growers. Foreign direct investment flows to developed countries declined by 56% in 2001. The United States saw the largest falloff in the flow as it sunk to its lowest level since 1997. Intel launched its Itanium 2 chip. President Bush called for stiffer penalties in an effort to eradicate corporate fraud. Pfizer announced that it would buy Pharmacia. Intel announced plans to eliminate 4,000 jobs. The dollar sank against the euro for the first time in more than two years. WorldCom filed for bankruptcy protection. The Dow Jones Industrial Average sank to its lowest level in nearly four years. Both the NASDAQ and the S&P 500 were at their lowest levels since the first half of 1997. President Bush signed the Public Company Accounting Reform and Investor Protection Act into law. Venture capital investments hit a four-year low. The previous year's data was also revised, indicating that the economy shrank in each of the first three quarters. The International Monetary Fund signed an emergency loan to Brazil. US Airways filed for bankruptcy. The U.S. trade deficit narrowed in June following two consecutive record monthly deficits. Cargo operations at 29 West Coast ports halted when terminal operators locked out unionized workers. The operations resumed when terminal operators ended the lockout of unionized workers. Standard & Poor lowered California's bond rating from an A+ to an A. United Airlines filed for bankruptcy protection.

2003

Moody's lowered California's bond rating from A1 to A2. A major snowstorm hit the mid-Atlantic and eastern states. Doctors in Hong Kong reported the first case of a flu-like virus, "Atypical Pneumonia," more commonly known as Severe Acute Respiratory Syndrome (SARS). Operation Iraqi Freedom began. Baghdad fell and U.S. troops toppled the statue of Saddam. President Bush declared the conclusion of major combat operations in Iraq. Standard & Poor's lowered California's bond rating from an A to a BBB. The United States Treasury began mailing $400-per-child tax rebate checks. Light vehicle sales in the U.S. reached 19.0 million in August, the second-best monthly annual rate ever. Wildfires broke out in Southern California. They eventually burned 743,000 acres and destroyed over 3,500 homes. President Bush ended steel tariffs. The Dow Jones Industrial Average closed above 10,000 for the first time since May 24, 2002. Saddam Hussein was captured by American troops. The GDP grew by 8.2% in the third quarter of 2003, its fastest rate since 1984. The U.S. confirmed its first case of "mad cow" disease.

2004

An unexpected cut in OPEC quota and cold weather contributed to higher oil prices. International oil prices hit a three-and-a-half year high. Michael Melvil piloted SpaceShipOne into space, becoming the first person to do so in a privately developed aircraft. Tropical Storm Bonnie hit the Florida panhandle. Hurricane Charley hit Florida's west coast with winds up to 145 mph. Hurricane Frances hit Florida, causing about $40 billion in damages. Hurricane Ivan hit Alabama and Florida and caused the evacuation of more than two million people. Floods and mudslides from Tropical Storm Jeanne killed 550 in Haiti. The federal government raised the federal funds target 0.25% to 1.75%. Hurricane Jeanne hit Florida (the third hurricane in 22 days and the fourth of the season), causing severe flooding and killing five people. A 9.0 magnitude earthquake off of the Indonesian island of Sumatra triggered a major tsunami that killed approximately 140,000 in the Indian Ocean area.

2005

The aircraft carrier *USS Abraham Lincoln* began distributing tsunami aid on Sumatra Island in Indonesia. Indonesia's president said that Indian Ocean nations would work on a tsunami warning system. President Bush invited former Presidents Clinton and the elder Bush to raise tsunami relief funds. The Department of Energy said that the average retail gas price was $1.78 a gallon nationwide. Palestinians elected Mahmoud Abbas as president and successor to the late Yasser Arafat. The *Deep Impact* spacecraft began its 268 million-mile journey to smash into the comet Tempel 1. Major League Baseball adopted a steroid-testing program that would require the suspension of first-time offenders for ten days and the random testing of players year-round. The world's largest commercial jet, an Airbus A380 able to carry 800 passengers, was unveiled. Cancer surpassed heart disease as the top killer of Americans age 85 and younger. President Bush was inaugurated for a second term. Iraqis voted in the country's first free election in a half-century. The Senate confirmed Alberto Gonzales as attorney general. North Korea boasted publicly for the first time that it had nuclear weapons. Former Lebanese Prime Minister Rafik Hariri was assassinated, and suspicions were focused on Syria. A gas explosion inside a Chinese mine killed 214 people, the worst reported mining disaster since the 1949 Communist Revolution. The National Hockey League cancelled its entire season after a prolonged lockout. The Kyoto Protocol environmental treaty took effect. Certified election results showed that a Shiite alliance won the majority of seats in Iraq's National Assembly. The New York chief medical examiner stopped trying to identify victims of the 2001 terrorist attack on the World Trade Center, leaving more than 1,000 victims unidentified. Martha Stewart left prison to begin five months of home confinement. Bush nominated John Bolton as U.S. ambassador to the United Nations and then bypassed Senate opposition with a recess appointment five months later. Former WorldCom chief Bernard Ebbers was convicted of engineering the largest corporate fraud in U.S. history. Later, he was sentenced to 25 years in prison. Baseball players told Congress that steroids were a problem in the sport, and stars Rafael Palmeiro and Sammy Sosa testified that they hadn't used them. Mark McGwire refused to answer. A woman claimed that she found a fingertip while eating Wendy's chili, costing the fast-food chain millions in lost sales before she admitted it was a hoax. An explosion at a BP oil refinery in Texas City, Texas, killed 14 people. President Bush authorized quarantines if needed to prevent the spread of particularly deadly flu outbreaks, a worry raised by bird flu cases in Asia. Bush signed legislation making it harder for people to wipe out debts by declaring bankruptcy. Tony Blair won his third term as British prime minister. A bankruptcy judge approved United Airlines' plan to terminate its employees' pension plans, clearing the way for the largest corporate-pension default in American history. The National Association for the Advancement of Colored People selected retired Verizon executive Bruce S. Gordon as its new president. Six months after the Indian Ocean tsunami, the death toll was 178,000 in 11 countries, with another 50,000 missing and presumed dead. Oil prices settled at a record high of over $60 a barrel. Wal-Mart heir John Walton died in a plane crash. The investigator of the *Columbia* disaster said that he approved of NASA resuming its shuttle launches even though some safety recommendations were not followed. Spain became the third country to legalize gay marriage. Justice Sandra Day O'Connor, the first woman on the Supreme Court, said that she would retire. The *Deep Impact* probe collided with the Tempel 1 comet, leaving a crater and kicking up dust that would be studied for clues to the workings of the solar system. A repeat attack on London's transit system failed. Four suspected would-be bombers were later detained. China stopped pegging its currency to the U.S. dollar. Six nations resumed nuclear disarmament talks that North Korea boycotted for 13 months, but little progress was made. *Discovery* blasted off on the first space shuttle flight in two-and-a-half years. A South Korean cloning pioneer announced the world's first cloned dog, an Afghan hound named Snuppy. Iran resumed work at a uranium conversion facility after suspending nuclear work for nine months to avoid U.N. sanctions. In the first damage award from thousands of pending lawsuits, Merck & Co. was ordered to pay millions for the death of a man who took the painkiller Vioxx. Hurricane Katrina hit Florida with 80 mph winds and headed into the Gulf of Mexico. The mayor of New Orleans ordered everyone in the city to evacuate after Katrina grew to become a monster storm. Category Four Hurricane Katrina struck Louisiana, and the first levee broke in New Orleans. Floodwaters covered 80% of New Orleans, and residents were rescued from rooftops. New Orleans Convention Center and the Superdome swelled with thousands of desperate people stranded by Katrina. Health and Human Services Secretary Michael Leavitt said that thousands of people died due to Katrina and its aftermath. The official toll was later found to be 1,300. President Bush nominated John Roberts as chief justice and said that he would choose an associate justice in a timely manner. The Department of Energy said that retail gas prices skyrocketed. Federal Emergency Management Agency (FEMA) Director Michael Brown resigned. Delta Air Lines and Northwest Airlines filed for bankruptcy. North Korea pledged to drop its nuclear weapons development and rejoin international arms treaties, but its leaders quickly backpedaled and disarmament talks stalled. John Roberts took his oath of office as chief justice of the United States. The Nobel Peace Prize was awarded to the International Atomic Energy Agency and its chief Mohamed ElBaradei. A major earthquake flattened villages on the Pakistan-India border, killing an estimated 86,000 people and leaving 3.5 million more homeless. Delphi Corp., the largest U.S. auto supplier, filed for bankruptcy. Engineers finished pumping floodwaters out of New Orleans six weeks after Katrina. China launched its second manned space flight, which had two astronauts orbiting Earth for five days. A strain of bird flu that had killed humans in Asia spread to Europe; a case was confirmed in Turkey. Apple Computer introduced an iPod that could play videos and television shows. Iraqis voted to approve a constitution. Hurricane Wilma struck Mexico's Yucatan peninsula, then sped across Florida three days later. Civil rights icon Rosa Parks died. Merck & Co. won in court a suit about painkiller Vioxx for the first time. Oil executives testified to Congress that their huge profits were justified, even as consumers struggled to cope with soaring gasoline and winter heating costs. Germany's Christian Democrats sealed a deal with Social Democrats to form a coalition government, allowing Angela Merkel to become the first female chancellor. A plant explosion in Jilin, China spilled toxic chemicals into the Songhua River, the water source for major cities downstream in China and Russia. Baseball players and owners agreed on a tougher steroid-testing policy that would increase suspension for first-time violators from ten games to 50 games and impose a lifetime ban for a third offense. Representative John Murtha of Pennsylvania called for immediate U.S. withdrawal from Iraq, saying that the troops have done their duty and that "It's time to bring them home." General Motors said that it would close 12 facilities and lay off 30,000 workers in North America. Doctors in France performed the world's first partial face transplant, attaching a donor's nose, lips and chin to a woman disfigured by a dog bite. A Southwest Airlines jet slid off a runway and onto a busy street during a snowstorm in Chicago, killing one boy in a car.

Summary

Our snapshot in time has revealed startling events occurring between 1981 and 2005. Our 38 companies were facing turbulent times during these years because of unpredictable economies, an unprecedented occurrence of natural disasters, political instability, a rapidly growing world population, regional warfare, threats of terrorism, a growth in the number of countries boasting nuclear capabilities, disruptive technologies, an alarming decline in ethical values, a growing energy crisis, and healthcare problems at levels never faced by mankind before. All of these events introduced disruptive change and challenged business leaders relentlessly. Companies like Johnson & Johnson, AEON, Abertis SA, and ADP are just a few examples of businesses that were able to achieve and sustain remarkable business results (see the names and read the overview of all 38 companies in the 1981-2005 Value Zone Hall of Fame in the Appendix). It is an amazing achievement, and we salute these companies as the first inductees into the Value Zone Hall of Fame. As we peer into the upcoming chapters, it will become clear how these 38 companies leveraged the eight elements of the Value Zone to sustain enduring value for their clients. Let's now examine how great leadership helped some of these companies sustain exceptional performance levels in the Value Zone.

Chapter Four
The Interconnectivity of the Elements of the Value Zone

We have learned from the first three chapters of this book that the Value Zone is all about sustaining outstanding business performance for five years or longer. Doing well in each of the elements of the Value Zone is essential for success. Critical to this success are the strategic initiatives embedded within each of those elements. As shown in Figure 4.1 below, the Value Zone core elements are interconnected.

Source: The Wood Research Institute

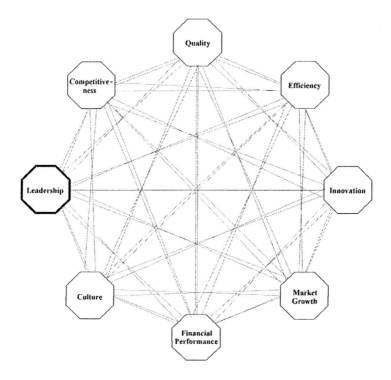

Figure 4.1

Our research indicates that each of these elements in some way interconnects with all of the other elements. The leadership element, however, guides all of the other elements. Great leaders:

- provide a clear vision with strategic objectives that are communicated well;
- develop enduring cultures which provide lasting value;
- achieve superior financial performance;
- are always seeking new ways to reach global markets;
- nurture an environment of ceaseless innovation;
- constantly seek to improve efficiency and effectiveness;
- demand Six Sigma quality in products and services; and
- always seek superior and substantial competitive advantage.

This means that leadership represents the heart of the Value Zone and is the engine that drives the other seven Value Zone elements.

Effective leaders help their companies to define their Value Zone; for this reason, it is very important to sustain excellent performance in each strategic initiative embedded within the Value Zone elements. Effective leaders understand and manage all the elements of the Value Zone; they also strive to guide their organizations toward remarkable business results. These leaders also leverage interconnectivity in the Value Zone to build enduring value for their clients. Great leaders are also good communicators who can communicate critical messages that drive and sustain organizational growth and vitality.

Great leaders recognize the importance of succession planning at all leadership levels. They realize that succession planning is crucial in building and sustaining an organization's culture. Business executives leverage business intelligence to help them make decisions based on the best information that is available. They also act in an entrepreneurial way by using an informed risk-taking approach that minimizes failures and maximizes successes. They understand why "doing things right" and "doing the right thing" are essential to sustaining value for clients.

A great leader creates and communicates a culture to her organization. She does this by understanding her enterprise's history and root culture. She helps to nurture a climate of deep-seated values and underlying assumptions that guide not only her own behavior but that of her subordinates as well. Leaders understand why it is imperative to learn to adapt a company's culture to change while maintaining core values. They also learn that it is vital to effectively and persuasively communicate an enterprise's culture throughout that enterprise. Most importantly, great leaders learn how to build and sustain culture that creates enduring value for their companies' clients.

Leaders of organizations must understand the numbers that count in evaluating financial performance as well as what they mean and what they do not mean. Managers must distinguish long-term thinking versus short-term thinking and understand the trade-offs of each. Business leaders must be able to grasp the impact and implications of globalization on effective leadership. They must also focus on learning about the impact of international trade and foreign exchange rates on their businesses. Furthermore, managers must keep up with the ways in which government regulatory bodies affect their organizations. Another very important area for managers to consider is knowledge and awareness of meaningful and competitive financial analysis techniques.

Organizational leaders must understand why reaching new and emerging markets should be an essential element in their enterprises. They need to comprehend why globalization is a key catalyst for reaching and creating new markets. Leaders who excel know why growth is important and how remaining stagnant can stunt a business's growth. They must learn why understanding different cultures is key to market growth.

Exceptional executives have learned that continuous innovation helps them to avoid extinction. They understand why imagination and creative thinking are essential to sustaining value for their clients. The key to innovation is the protection of intellectual property rights. Leaders who are innovators have learned to engage in creative innovation while taking calculated risks. They "get it" and understand the importance of "out-of-the-box thinking."

The 21st-century business environment provides compelling reasons for business executives to learn to eliminate waste and become more efficient in their business operations. They need to learn why "lean" concepts and principles should be deeply ingrained in their companies. Other key challenges include managing costs and liquidity—both of which are critical to a firm's success. Executives must be up to speed on productivity and know why learning to do more with less is so important. They need to comprehend why it is important to manage their assets to achieve capital efficiency. It is critical that they understand and grasp how to use knowledge management to improve their firms' profit picture.

Business leaders who excel in offering high quality products and services understand the importance of achieving Six Sigma standards. They work hard to create a quality culture in their businesses. They are very effective at leading quality teams that get sustained "best practices" results. They are keenly aware of the importance of quality standards and benchmarking organizations.

Vince Lombardi, a great leader in the NFL, coined this famous statement related to competition: "Winning isn't everything—it's the only thing." Business leaders who excel understand this and compete to win by sustaining value. To quote Lombardi again, "You don't do things right once in a while, you do them right all the time." Winning leaders also are great at scanning the environment, which is a critical building block towards providing solutions and products with sustaining value. Winning leaders also have a great grasp of the new competitive landscape caused by globalization and an understanding of how to compete in emerging markets.

It should be clear not only how these elements are interconnected but also how they interlock with each other. For a business to be in the high value quadrant in the Value Zone, its leaders must pay careful attention to each of these elements and the strategic initiatives embedded in each one. As shown in Figure 4.2 below, leaders must guide their organizations to "sustain value" for their clients over periods of five years or longer to achieve the "sweet spot" representing high value in the Value Zone. To accomplish this, they must develop and execute Value Zone "best practices" strategic initiatives in each of the elements.

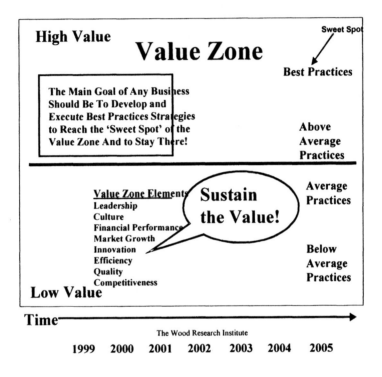

Figure 4.2

In the following chapters, you will learn about 38 remarkable companies that were able to achieve outstanding business results not just for 5 or 10 consecutive years but for a period of 25 years beginning in 1981 and continuing through 2005. We will highlight many of the Value Zone strategic "best practices" that these firms developed, executed, refined, overhauled, and sustained. At the end of this book, we will discuss businesses that have sustained excellent performance for 50 years or more and that we have therefore included in the Value Zone's Hall of Fame Ring of Honor.

Chapter Five
Leadership—The Heart of the Value Zone

Six companies with outstanding leadership are ADP, AEON, Biomet, Grupo Bimbo S.A. DE C.V., Home Depot, and Johnson & Johnson (see the Appendix for their long-term, sustained financial performance). There are many others; however, these were chosen to clearly show you, the reader, how great companies in the Value Zone demonstrate great leadership.

Biomet

Today Biomet is one of the largest and fastest-growing U.S. manufacturers of orthopedic medical devices and supplies. Biomet and its subsidiaries design, develop, manufacture, and market products used mainly by orthopedic specialists in surgical and non-surgical therapy; Biomet's products include reconstructive implants and artificial joints, electrical bone-growth stimulators, and operating room supplies. The firm is located in Warsaw, Indiana. Dane Miller and three other business colleagues, in the way of true leaders and entrepreneurs, did something about what they all saw as a stifling corporate culture within the orthopedic medical devices and supplies industry. In 1978, the founders of Biomet risked $130,000 from their personal assets, took a bank loan for $500,000 from the U.S. Small Business Administration, and secured a $100,000 line of credit from a local bank. When Biomet began, recent amendments to the Federal Food and Cosmetics Act had placed squelching legislation on the artificial implants industry, thus giving Miller and his colleagues their first test as leaders. According to Miller, "People laughed at us for starting up a new company after the new device legislation went into effect." However, despite some major challenges, Biomet was able to find a place in the marketplace as a developer and marketer of orthopedic products, contracting with independent manufacturing shops to make its implants. During its first year of operation, Biomet developed a breakthrough titanium "total hip replacement" implant, the first of which was implanted in Dane Miller's grandmother. Total hip replacement devices and the use of titanium both became the industry standard by the late 1980s. Although Biomet had only $17,000 in sales during its first year of operation and lost a total of $63,000, by 1980 the struggling enterprise was turning a meager profit, and as shown in the Biomet chart in the Appendix section of this book, they have a financial history of revenue growth and profits since 1980.

In 2005, Biomet's revenues were over $1.879 billion. Biomet is now one of the leading manufacturers of musculoskeletal products worldwide. The company holds the fourth-largest position in the orthopedic reconstructive device and spinal products markets in the U.S., and it holds the second-largest position in the shoulder devices, fixation products, bone cements and accessories, and dental reconstructive implant markets in the U.S. Furthermore, Biomet recorded its 26th year of record performance in fiscal 2004, and its revenues and earnings continue to grow steadily.

During 2005, Biomet announced that Dane A. Miller, Ph.D., the company's president, CEO, and co-founder, had informed the Board of Directors of his decision to retire. He decided to remain a director and serve as a consultant. In his place, Biomet's Board appointed Senior Vice President Daniel P. Hann, the company's general counsel and a member of the Board, to be president and chief executive officer on an interim basis. Regarding Dr. Miller's long leadership tenure, Dr. Scott Harrison, a Biomet lead director, stated,

> Biomet is a true American success story, and Dr. Miller's extraordinary vision, talent and leadership over the course of nearly three decades has been central to its progress and development. He and his co-founders built this Company into a worldwide leader in the design and manufacture of reconstructive products with revenues of nearly $2 billion... and strong values and organizational standards.

What Dr. Miller and his team have achieved is truly remarkable. One key to great leadership is the ability to launch strategic "best practices" that sustain enduring value. This is clearly what Biomet has done. Also important to the successful leadership of a firm is effective succession planning as a "best practices" strategic initiative. By announcing an interim replacement for Dr. Miller, Biomet's leadership clearly demonstrated that they understood this initiative. Chairman of the Board Niles L. Noblitt stated about Biomet's new CEO and president, Mr. Daniel P. Hann,

> The Board shares my confidence in the selection of Mr. Hann, a talented and results-oriented executive with more than 17 years at Biomet, to lead the Company during this period. He knows the Company intimately, shares our commitment to building shareholder value, and is well-positioned to move the Company forward.

Mr. Hann added,

> The Biomet team has built a great company through its passion for engineering excellence and innovation... Biomet will remain true to its heritage, and I believe we are well-positioned to capitalize on the momentum of our successful exhibition at the recent American Academy of Orthopedic Surgeons' Annual Meeting, at which the Company introduced over 100 new products.

Dr. Miller stated, "I believe in Biomet and its team members, and their ability to continue to deliver quality products and enhance shareholder value. As I begin a new stage in my life, I will always be grateful to have worked with the great people at Biomet and to have played a role in its growth and success."

The Home Depot

When Bob Nardelli, a former General Electric senior executive, was asked to step in as chairman and CEO of The Home Depot, he said, "The Home Depot has a proud past and a bright future built on several pillars: broad product assortment, low pricing, and excellent service. Our company has been able to

achieve consistent revenue growth with profits." Before Mr. Nardelli was selected as CEO of The Home Depot, the company's founders knew that they had
a great company that needed better leadership to cope with rapid growth. They
had run their company for years under autonomous leadership, with store general managers acting as individual entrepreneurs. New competition from companies like Lowe's was beginning to eat away at Home Depot's dominance in the
market. Mr. Nardelli commented about this, stating, "A major problem that had
the potential to limit the growth was operating by a decentralized and autonomous model where it was hard to scale. There was no leverage. We resolved this
by adding more rigorous measurement and accountability to our operations." In
addition to this problem, Mr. Nardelli described another threat that required visionary leadership to solve: "Another threat was that we were looking at business opportunities primarily through the lens of a $200 billion industry. When
we widened our span of interest—to the residential, commercial, and industrial
arenas—the marketplace of opportunities grew to more than $970 billion." As
shown below, the results have been remarkable.

In a comment on Home Depot's incredible growth during the past five
years, Mr. Nardelli stated,

> We focused on transforming a fragmented, ineffective, local, stagnant, do-it-
> yourself U.S. market by driving growth, consolidation and innovation. We
> made an aggressive number of store openings in new markets and in those ar-
> eas where we already had an presence—to the point where we impacted sales at
> our existing stores in order to maintain our lead of providing customers with
> more shopping locations.

Nardelli has since taken over the reins of Home Depot and accomplished some
solid business results. To help centralize Home Depot's management structure,
Bob Nardelli has focused on hiring people with extensive experience in the military who are accustomed to giving and following orders and functioning in a
more rigorous management environment. He has chosen to take this strategic
tack while also emphasizing to his staff the importance of excellence in customer service. To that end, Home Depot will do 23 million hours of training
during 2006. Nardelli has put an executive leadership program in place and has
had great internal and external learning results. Under his leadership, what has
served the company well is setting, not unrealistic goals, but challenging goals.
The important point here is that under Nardelli's leadership, Home Depot is
providing its clients with sustained and enduring value. We believe that it is
inevitable that the stock price will catch up with the strategy.

Finally, regarding his leadership and focus, Mr. Nardelli further states,

> More recently, over the past five years, we have accelerated our efforts to meet
> three strategic priorities:
> Enhancing our core retail network—with distinctive and innovative merchan-
> dise, store modernization and technology.
> Extending the business—through new store formats, online sales, and home in-

stallation services for do-it-for-me customers.

Expanding our market—to capture international opportunities and to attract a greater percentage of the professional customer's business.

AEON

AEON is a Japanese retail chain company that develops shopping centers and operates retail stores, general merchandise stores, and specialty stores. It also leases and manages commercial facilities in Japan. The company also operates in other Asian countries and in the U.S. Headquartered in Chiba, Japan, AEON employs about 195,000 people.

Two of AEON's key leaders include its chairman, Toshiji Tokiwa, and its president, Motoya Okada. These leaders stress the importance of remaining constantly focused on enhancing global management standards and local customer needs. They also stress the importance of maximizing group synergies. By emphasizing these factors, AEON has been able to achieve sustained and profitable growth. AEON's leaders constantly refresh their governance and group management "in pursuit of transparency and management responsiveness." AEON leadership is guided by three core principles: respect for humanity, contribution to local communities, and the pursuit of peace centered on customers. AEON's leadership team is committed to fulfilling principles by working to satisfy the requirements of all customers and ensuring sustained and long-term growth by responding swiftly to changes in the business environment and consumer needs.

AEON's long-term target is to become one of the world's top ten retailers. Its leadership team believes that reforms in group management and corporate governance are among the company's most important priorities. The company leaders hold a fundamental belief that leadership through group management reforms enhances the total value of AEON. By leveraging group synergy and corporate governance reforms, they believe that they can achieve a world-class management structure. AEON's inclusion in the Value Zone Hall of Fame certainly provides evidence that its leaders guide the company in sustaining enduring value for its clients.

Automatic Data Processing

Automatic Data Processing also has a leadership culture built on performance, merit, and rewards. From its outset, ADP has been built on these three leadership principles. With an investment of $6,000, the company's founder Henry Taub began a business based on a simple business model: a payroll preparation service for a variety of businesses. As ADP grew, Henry, who was later joined by his brother, began to build a staff of professional accountants to handle the increased workloads. Two very significant leadership decisions made early on were to build a sales force to sell ADP's services and to hire Frank Lautenberg as the company's first salesman in 1954. The latter move paid off enormously. In fact, Mr. Lautenberg eventually became the CEO of ADP.

Under Frank Lautenberg's leadership, the ADP sales team began to sell the concept of outsourcing—in this case, the outsourcing of payroll services.

Slowly, ADP's client list grew. This led to other major leadership decisions. As Henry Taub stated it, "I really think we bet the company when we made the move from a manual to an automated environment." That decision, which was made in the late 1950s, significantly accelerated ADP's growth. Another key leadership decision was to expand the business by acquiring other service bureaus that were doing payroll. This led to the development of ADP's brokerage services. Of course, ADP's leadership was visionary and recognized the value of technology, so during the 1960s, they anticipated that the advent of the computer would change their business dramatically. This gave ADP enormous competitive advantage due to two things: speed and capacity. Now the company could go after business on Wall Street, the financial capital of the world. For example, during 1962, it was processing 300 trades per night for a company named Oppenheimer; by 1999, ADP would be handling a million trades a day.

Frank Lautenberg's vision was to enhance ADP's image. One of the steps taken to achieve this vision was the construction of a brand-new facility in New Jersey along Route 3, one of the main arteries into New York City, in 1968. Henry Taub wholeheartedly supported Frank's vision. Lautenberg commented, "405 Route 3 was modern and forward-looking in every respect…For a long time, it was our flagship facility. It represented to everyone who would drive by or visit us what we were and, equally important, what we were striving to become."

Another ADP leader, Josh Weston, who got his early training in payroll services while serving in the U.S. Navy, created ADP's culture of associates and clients. Weston's concept of teams is what drove his passion to view everyone who worked in ADP as an associate. He pointed out that when he started at ADP during the early 1970s, "The common understanding in business is that the 'employer' is the boss and the employees are underneath….on the other hand an associate is part of a team. So on my first day on the job I started calling people associates and every time I saw a letter or some other piece of copy that said employee, I crossed it out and wrote in the word associate. Gradually the idea took hold." Frank Lautenberg, who was CEO at that time, concurred, stating, "The Associate concept was a wonderful addition to our culture. Associates share common goals and have common missions. That's what ADP is all about." The term "client" was a concept that also shaped the culture at ADP. As Josh Weston explained back in the 1970s, "Anybody can be a customer. If you buy a bag of tomatoes at the grocery store and never come back again you're still a customer….a one-time transaction. A client connotes an enduring professional relationship. All of our businesses have that type of relationship, and using the word 'client' reinforces that to us and the companies we serve." When you think about it, ADP's leadership results were based on the relationship that employees nurtured with their clients. ADP was able to sustain outstanding business results by providing enduring value for its clients.

Today, under Arthur F. Weinbach's leadership as chairman and CEO, ADP continues to successfully achieve outstanding business results. Arthur comments about ADP's progress, stating the following to its investors:

Nothing is more important to ADP's continued success than our 44,000 associates around the globe who continually strive to provide quality products and world-class service to our 590,000 clients. Our associates are exceptionally client-oriented, motivated, committed, and dedicated. They are the reason we win in the marketplace.

GRUPO BIMBO S.A. DE C.V.

Grupo Bimbo's core business is producing, distributing, and marketing baked goods, including sliced bread, buns, cookies, snack cakes, pre-packaged foods, tortillas, salty snacks, and confectionery products. This company has 71 plants and more than 980 distribution centers located in 14 countries throughout the Americas and Europe. Some of the company's brand names include Bimbo, Marinela, Barcel, Ricolino, Coronado, Oroweat, Mrs. Baird's, Plus Vita, Pullman, Monarca, and Trigoro.

Grupo Bimbo's Chairman Roberto Servitje made the following comment in his company's 2004 Annual Report:

> I am pleased to report to you that the Grupo Bimbo's performance in 2004 was highly satisfactory. These are the kinds of results we were expecting when we began the far-reaching internal reorganization, and the intensive process of modernizing the Company's systems around the world. We know there is still much to do, but we are pleased to see our expectations being met.

Under Roberto's leadership, the results of Grupo Bimbo's systems modernization initiatives and its efforts to reorganize its internal teams have been prosperous. The company's total revenues in 2004 totaled 51.55 billion pesos and increased in 2005 to 56.10 billion pesos. According to Grupo Bimbo, this growth was largely related to growth in the Bimbo and Barcel divisions along with modest growth in the Latin America Division (OLA). During 2004, Bimbo and Barcel accounted for all of Grupo Bimbo's profits. Their U.S. operation is very important to Grupo Bimbo, accounting for just over 26% of total sales. However, U.S. operations continue to report very modest results.

Grupo Bimbo's leaders made some very significant developments in the company's operations. Some key initiatives during the last two years include:

- the opening of the Barcels Mérida plant and the Fripans plant in Toluca;
- the expansion of Ricolinos plants in San Luis Potosí and the Valencia plant in Costa Rica;
- the shutdown of the Dallas plant;
- the assets acquired from George Weston Ltd.; and
- the closure of plants in La Paz, Baja California in Mexico, Alajuela in Costa Rica, La Mejor in Guatemala, and Tia Rosa in Ohio.

During 2004, Grupo Bimbo acquired Joyco de México, a leading producer of various candy products like Duvalín, Bocadín, and Lunetas. This transaction was completed in May 2004, with Joyco's sales total at about 500 million pesos. This is certainly not bad, considering that Grupo Bimbo purchased this company for 290 million pesos. Grupo Bimbo has benefited from some important synergies that will allow it to completely recover its investment in the short term and deliver positive results. Grupo Bimbo's leaders assert that the results of these changes have helped them to run the company's 71 plants more efficiently and have also helped them to improve Grupo's 30,000 distribution routes.

Grupo Bimbo's leadership team also reported that because of the company's strong operating results, it ended 2004 with substantial cash in its treasury. Grupo Bimbo was able to achieve this even after setting aside reserves for future acquisitions and pre-paying as much debt as possible. In 2004, the company was able to declare an extraordinary dividend, which was well-received by the financial community and the company's shareholders.

Roberto Servitje notes that one key area of central importance to Grupo Bimbo's leadership culture "is remaining true to our fundamental objective of being highly productive and people-oriented." An example of excellent leadership in this area is Grupo Bimbo's recent announcement that the annual review of all its labor unions contracts was amicably concluded with favorable conditions for all parties.

Servitje also discusses Grupo's corporate social responsibility initiatives and highlights one area where the company provided a lot of assistance; namely, the "Reforestamos México." Grupo Bimbo helped to establish this organization, which has completed a number of successful programs in "green management." This organization has ambitious plans for the short term that will undoubtedly contribute significantly to environmental protection and preservation in Mexico. Grupo Bimbo also demonstrated great leadership in its traditional practice of community involvement by supporting social programs with an emphasis on education and rural development.

Johnson & Johnson

It was during 1943 that Johnson & Johnson CEO Robert Johnson, known as the "General" because of his military service during WWII, created the Johnson & Johnson Corporate Credo. Johnson wrote this Credo, which outlines the company's four areas of social responsibility: first to its customers; second to its employees; third to the community and environment; and fourth to its stockholders. The intent of writing the Credo was to institutionalize a leadership culture of social responsibility at Johnson & Johnson that would guide future leaders of this company in their behaviors and decision-making processes. On the heels of the Credo came the company's change from a family-owned firm to a publicly owned company when J&J was listed on the New York Stock Exchange in 1944. The importance of this Credo as the centerpiece and heart of the Johnson & Johnson culture would be tested over and over throughout the years to come as the company grew at staggering speeds through a number of carefully selected acquisitions.

In addition to the Credo, the "General" firmly believed in decentralization. He was the driving force behind J&J's organizational structure, in which divisions and affiliates were given autonomy to direct their own operations. He insisted that the leaders of the decentralized organizations understood, agreed to, and adhered to the J&J Credo as they led their enterprises. This policy of decentralization coincided with a move into pharmaceuticals, hygiene products, and textiles. During the 1960s, 1970s, and 1980s, Johnson & Johnson grew by expanding its product lines through key and strategic acquisitions. This growth was greatly accelerated during the 1980s and 1990s. For example, from 1989 to 1999, the company made 45 such acquisitions of companies and product lines.

In succession planning, future leaders of J&J were groomed to adhere to the Credo like breathing air. During the tenure of former CEO and Chairman James Burke, J&J as a company faced a significant test of the Credo and the J&J culture. During September 1982, tragedy struck J&J when seven people died from ingesting Tylenol capsules that had been laced with cyanide. J&J immediately cancelled all advertising and recalled all Tylenol products from store shelves. Despite the great losses suffered by J&J, this was a "no-brainer" for Burke and the J&J leaders. The Credo and the culture compelled Burke and J&J leaders to "do the right thing." Now, a new problem arose after the Food and Drug Administration found that the tampering had been done at the retail level rather than during manufacturing. J&J's leadership was left with the problem of how to save its number-one product, its reputation, and its brand. In the week after the deaths, J&J's stock had fallen 18%, and its prime competitors' products, Datril and Anacin-3, were in such demand that supplies were back-ordered.

J&J's leadership team became innovative and was able to recoup its company's losses by executing a series of marketing strategies. The company ran a one-time advertisement explaining how to exchange Tylenol capsules for tablets or refunds and worked closely with the press by responding directly to reporters' questions as a means of keeping the public informed. The company also placed a coupon for $2.50 off of any Tylenol product in newspapers across the country to reimburse consumers for Tylenol capsules they may have discarded during the tampering incident and offered an incentive to purchase Tylenol in other forms.

Within weeks of the poisoning incidents, the FDA issued guidelines for tamper-resistant packaging for the entire food and drug industry. To bolster public confidence in its product through innovation, J&J used three layers of protection, two more than recommended by the FDA, when Tylenol was put back on store shelves. The results were staggering. Within months of the cyanide poisoning, J&J was gaining back its share of the pain-reliever market, and it soon regained more than 90% of its former customers. Customers recognized that J&J's consistent leadership was able to provide them with enduring value by producing safe products. By 1989, Tylenol sales were $500 million annually, and the line was expanded in 1990 into the burgeoning cold remedy market with several Tylenol Cold products; the following year saw the launch of Tylenol P.M., a sleep aid. James Burke's savvy yet honest handling of the Tylenol tampering incident earned him a spot in the National Business Hall of Fame, an honor awarded in 1990. This is just one of many stories from a number of companies that, through great leaders, have cultivated consistent cultures that sustain enduring value. The financial performance of Johnson & Johnson for the last ten years clearly demonstrates that the incident in 1982 and the decision based on adherence to the corporate J&J Credo not only was the right thing to do but also was viewed as being of significant value to J&J's customers worldwide. James Burke summed it up well, stating, "Despite the enormity of the Tylenol tragedy, we are impressed that our value system at Johnson & Johnson survived the challenge placed against it and serves society well."

Today, William C. Weldman is at the helm of Johnson & Johnson. He made the following comments in the company's 2005 Annual Report:

> A year ago I reported to you our excitement about the prospect of broadening our presence in cardiovascular devices through the acquisition of Guidant Corporation. We extended considerable effort throughout the year to conclude this transaction. Unfortunately, a combination of adverse developments in Guidant's business and competition for the asset forced the price to a point where we concluded it was no longer in the best interest of our shareholders to pursue this business opportunity. Nonetheless, we remain committed to strengthening our business in this important therapeutic category.

This is an excellent example of savvy Johnson & Johnson leaders providing and sustaining enduring value for their investors, which is a fundamental aspect of their Corporate Credo.

> Commenting further, Weldman praises Johnson & Johnson employees:
> The men and women of Johnson & Johnson are to be recognized for their strong performance this past year. They remain the engine that drives our business forward. They make it possible for Johnson & Johnson to continue to touch people's lives in a more meaningful way, as the stories in this year's annual report relate.

This is another powerful example of exemplary leadership guided by an enduring Corporate Credo that emphasizes the importance of employees and the importance of giving back to the communities that Johnson & Johnson touches as a business.

Consider the case of Huntley Neita, a diabetic patient who had triple-vessel diffuse disease. He was able to return to the life he enjoys with his wife, Doreen, a few weeks after receiving three CYPHER® Stents following a heart attack in 2002. Another powerful example is a Johnson & Johnson company, The LifeScan, Inc., which

> is creating a world without limits for people with diabetes. An important part of achieving this vision is educating patients on the importance of monitoring blood glucose and the compelling need to manage their disease. In markets around the world, diabetes 'Heroes,' such as singer Patti LaBelle in the U.S. and actor Naseeruddin Shah in India, communicate to other diabetes patients

the benefits of regular blood glucose self-monitoring with products such as the ONETOUCH® ULTRA® and the ONETOUCH® HORIZON™ Blood Glucose Monitoring Systems.

These are just a few examples of Johnson & Johnson's leadership in providing and sustaining enduring value for its clients. It is not surprising, therefore, to see that Johnson & Johnson has enjoyed over 73 years of profitable growth, and that it is one of the few companies globally to earn the distinction of being included in the Value Zone Hall of Fame's Ring of Honor. The Ring of Honor is a special recognition for those companies that have achieved profitable growth for a period of 50 years or more. In the next chapter, we will learn about the culture of great companies like Johnson & Johnson, Nordstrom, and ADP, to name just a few.

Chapter Six
Building and Sustaining an Enduring Culture

Companies that are able to sustain their performance in the Value Zone generally have enduring cultures that are also adaptable to change and have underlying beliefs, values, and norms that stand the test of time. Culture influences the behavior of people within an organization. Cultures are nurtured within organizations by individuals who interact with one another and communicate ways of managing change. Figure 6.1 below provides interesting insights about organizational cultures. It illustrates the three levels of culture. The branches and leaves of the tree represent the artifacts that are visible manifestations of the culture, the tree trunk symbolizes the values and enduring beliefs that provide the vital nourishment to the artifacts, and the roots of the tree symbolize the assumptions and deeply hidden beliefs in a culture.

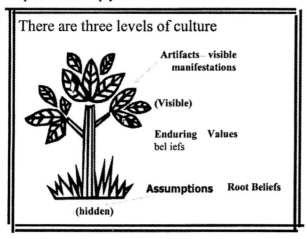

The Wood Research Institute

Figure 6.1

We will discuss several examples of companies that have very rich and clearly discernible cultures. These companies include ADP, Family Dollar Stores, Johnson & Johnson, Nordstrom, and Walgreen.

Automatic Data Processing

Automatic Data Processing (ADP)'s culture began to develop in 1949 and was built on the premise of service. The company's principle founder, Henry Taub, established this premise as a result of an incident early in the company's history. While Mr. Taub was visiting a company, panic developed because a critical person who did the company's payroll had unexpectedly gotten ill. Because of the employee's illness, the status of payroll was in jeopardy. The results were awful: unhappy employees, frustrated managers, and a disruption in productivity. That incident caused Mr. Taub to wonder how many other companies would be faced with similar problems in the payroll area. This led to the birth of an automatic payroll service offered by ADP.

Another important component of ADP's culture was its adoption of innovative technologies that were used to transform ADP from a manual environment to an automated one. The decision to do this was risky but key to ADP's culture. Mr. Taub commented about this, stating, "I really think we bet the company when we made the move from a manual environment to an automated environment."

Another core area in the ADP culture was quality service. For example, when ADP introduced brokerage services, Henry Taub commented, "Wall Street was a carousel, known for up-and-down volumes, which made it difficult for most suppliers of back-office accounting to sustain a high level of quality." The adoption of computers enabled ADP to provide quality services with capacity and speed.

Former ADP CEO Josh Weston added another critical part of the ADP culture. He introduced the term "associate" into the company. No matter what title or position a person held in the company, Josh Weston would refer to him or her as an associate. Mr. Weston explained it this way:

> The common understanding in business is that the 'employer' is the boss and the 'employees' are underneath...On the other hand, 'an associate' is part of a team. So on my first day of the job, I started calling people associates and every time I saw a letter or some other piece of copy that said employee I crossed it out and wrote in the word associate.

Commenting further on this, former ADP CEO Frank Lautenberg stated, "The associate concept was a wonderful addition to our culture. Associates share common goals and have common missions. That's what ADP is all about."

Another term deeply imbedded in the ADP culture is "client." Mr. Weston explained this term's meaning in the ADP culture this way:

> Anyone can be a customer. If you buy a bag of tomatoes at the grocery store and never come back again you're still a customer—a one-time transaction. A client connotes an enduring relationship. All of our businesses have that type of relationship, and using the word 'client' reinforces that to us and the companies we serve.

These two terms are at the heart of the ADP culture. CEO Arthur F. Weinback and Chief Operating Officer Gary C. Butler stated the following in ADP's 2005 Annual Report about the remarkable business results during 2005:

> Nothing is more important to ADP's continued success than our 44,000 associates around the globe who continually strive to provide quality products and

world class service to our 590,000 clients. Our associates are exceptionally client-oriented, motivated, committed, and dedicated. They are the reason we win in the marketplace. ...We are very proud of our results, the outstanding leadership of our executive team, and the contributions of our many associates. We are building momentum and are poised for a positive future.

Family Dollar Store

Leon Levine founded the Family Dollar Store. The store, located in Rockingham, North Carolina, was branded as a department store, although it could probably be more closely characterized as an old-fashioned general store. Leon opened the first Family Dollar store in Charlotte, North Carolina, with a target customer base of lower middle-income families who could not afford fancy name brands and were not interested in high fashion but who did require good clothing and durable shoes. The Family Dollar Store was quite popular among value shoppers, and soon new outlets were opened. By the early 1970s, the company had gone public and had opened its 100th store in Brevard, North Carolina. Although it was not the first in the self-service, discount variety field, Family Dollar secured a leading role in that space. At its outset, the Family Dollar culture centered around providing value to lower middle-income families who were not enamored with high-fashion brands.

Family Dollar's key draw continues to be its bargain-priced goods—such items as toys, automotive equipment, and school supplies—all displayed within 6,000 to 8,000 square feet of store. Its key strategy is purchasing merchandise from vendors or suppliers who have overbought in order to get lower-than-market pricing so that Family Dollar's savings on those under-priced goods can be passed on to its customers. This is an essential facet of the Family Dollar Store culture. Another strategic value is gleaning from manufacturer's overruns. For example, Procter & Gamble refused to give Family Dollar stores a deal on Pampers disposable diapers at one point in recent years. Family Dollar's Levine figured he would have to stock them anyway, so he stocked more Kleenex and Family Dollar brand disposable diapers, and soon the Pampers became irrelevant.

Since Family Dollar's nascence, its shoppers have been low-income families making less than $25,000 a year. This is an essential element of Family Dollar's culture, as is the fact that most stores are situated in rural areas, usually in towns of less than 15,000, and are quite often within walking distance or a very short drive from home. The average Family Dollar customer shops there at least once a week and spends roughly $8 each visit. The size of each store is approximately 10% the size of a Wal-Mart or Kmart, which means that Family Dollar's product lines have to be meticulously selected and are limited.

While the bigger stores can offer more products, the draw of Family Dollar stores is often location, a key cultural factor. "Location, location, location" is a critical part of the culture of Family Dollar, and that part includes strategically locating stores to be convenient to their target markets. To their credit, Family Dollar Store executives recognized the importance to their culture of offering low and competitive pricing and made adjustments after they realized that they were preoccupied with expansion and had lost sight of the competition's pricing. The adjustments were made based on the fact that Wal-Mart was pricing its goods as much as 10% below Family Dollar's, and the goods it was discounting were often things such as health and beauty products that Family Dollar was heavily advertising sales on. To further strengthen its cultural resolve to be a low-price provider, Family Dollar instituted a new pricing policy during 1987: it would not be undersold. The results were immediate and solid, with same-store sales up 10% in just a few months.

Another important facet of Family Dollar's culture is its outstanding management of debt. In fact, Family Dollar has been debt-free throughout its existence. This has helped it to squeeze into urban store spaces without fear of a large Wal-Mart moving in next door.

Another cultural factor is Family Dollar management's policy of aggressive markdowns. During the late 1980s, the company's management also created a new policy requiring that any item tagged at more than $15 receive approval by top management. In harmony with the chain's return to "everyday low prices," Family Dollar Store did bounce back. What helped it was its healthy cash flow and the minimal debt it rode during the recession years of the 1980s and 1990s.

In Family Dollar's 2005 Annual Report, Howard Levine, its CEO and Chairman, stated, "At the heart of Family Dollar's mission is the determination to provide exceptional value to the people who are the most important to us—our Shareholders, our Customers and our Associates." This consistency in providing exceptional value is an overarching culture for Family Dollar. Here are a few examples from the 2005 Annual Report:

- The Cooler Initiative: Family Dollar's stores provide value and convenience to their customers through an expanded food assortment that includes refrigerated coolers for those frequent "milk and eggs" fill-in trips that keep customers coming back day after day.
- The Urban Initiative: The Urban Initiative addresses the opportunities and challenges of operating in urban markets. Better customer service and store presentation standards, a more flexible organizational structure, and improved processes drive higher financial performance and create value for shareholders, customers, and associates.
- The Treasure Hunt Initiative: Family Dollar's customers appreciate the tremendous value the store delivers as it offers both exciting and unique Treasure Hunt items as well as everyday home and family necessities that customers count on.
- The New Store Initiative: By expanding into new areas and increasing their presence in existing markets, Family Dollar's stores provide value and neighborhood convenience to one of the fastest-growing, yet vastly under-served, consumer segments.
- Its Associates: Family Dollar's most valuable asset is its team of talented and dedicated associates. Its executives are committed to provid-

ing the skills and development tools to allow associates to build, not just a job, but also a career with Family Dollar Store.

Johnson & Johnson

Johnson & Johnson operates over 230 companies with locations in 57 different countries. These firms provide products and services internationally. Johnson & Johnson's culture centers on its Credo. The company's leaders expect their employees to live by the Credo and make it their guiding light. In fact, employees are expected to make all of their business-related decisions by living the Credo. The Credo in its entirety is shown in Figure 6.2 below:

Johnson and Johnson Corporate Credo

We believe our first responsibility is to the doctors, nurses and patients, to mothers and fathers and all others who use our products and services. In meeting their needs everything we do must be of high quality. We must constantly strive to reduce our costs in order to maintain reasonable prices. Customers' orders must be serviced promptly and accurately. Our suppliers and distributors must have an opportunity to make a fair profit.

We are responsible to our employees, the men and women who work with us throughout the world. Everyone must be considered as an individual. We must respect their dignity and recognize their merit. They must have a sense of security in their jobs. Compensation must be fair and adequate, and working conditions clean, orderly and safe. We must be mindful of ways to help our employees fulfill their family responsibilities. Employees must feel free to make suggestions and complaints. There must be equal opportunity for employment, development and advancement for those qualified. We must provide competent management, and their actions must be just and ethical.

We are responsible to the communities in which we live and work and to the world community as well. We must be good citizens – support good works and charities and bear our fair share of taxes. We must encourage civic improvements and better health and education. We must maintain in good order the property we are privileged to use, protecting the environment and natural resources.

Our final responsibility is to our stockholders. Business must make a sound profit. We must experiment with new ideas. Research must be carried on, innovative programs developed and mistakes paid for. New equipment must be purchased, new facilities provided and new products launched. Reserves must be created to provide for adverse times. When we operate according to these principles, the stockholders should realize a fair return.

Figure 6.2

As another part of its culture, Johnson & Johnson also expects its employees and management team to adhere to the guiding principles of the Credo using an internal document entitled "Johnson & Johnson Living the Credo." This document identifies the Credo's Six Pillars of Character. The Six Pillars are highlighted below:

- Trustworthiness—Involves four major qualities: integrity, honesty, promise-keeping, and loyalty.
- Respect—People are not things, and everyone has a right to be treated with dignity. The Golden Rule: Do unto others as you would have them do unto you.
- Responsibility—Our capacity to reason and our freedom to choose make us answerable for whether we honor or degrade the ethical principles that give life meaning and purpose.
- Fairness—Essentially implies a balanced standard of justice without reference to one's own biases or interests.
- Caring—Caring is the heart of ethics. An ethical person feels and demonstrates sincere concern for the well being of others.
- Good Citizenship—Relates to our obligation to be a constructively contributing part of a community.

Johnson & Johnson has had a succession of executive leadership cultures that have strictly adhered to its Credo. For example, in 1971, former CEO P.B. Hofmann stated the following:

As a company, we firmly believe that we must assume our share of social responsibility. This has been traditional with Johnson & Johnson, and through the years we have made commitments to health and medical education, environmental protection, preservation of our water resources, transportation and minority employment. Johnson & Johnson is fully committed to a policy of equal opportunity for all persons.

Mr. Hofmann stressed something very central to the Credo; namely, the importance of being good corporate citizens and participating in community service. He stressed the importance of equal opportunity, another essential element of the Credo. He discussed social responsibility at a time when many corporations were totally ignoring issues like the environment, the preservation of water resources, and minority employment.

Ten years later, Johnson & Johnson CEO James Burke discussed an incident that truly tested the heart and soul of Johnson & Johnson's Credo. His comments about the 1982 incident were as follows: "Despite the enormity of the Tylenol tragedy, we are impressed that our value system at Johnson & Johnson survived the challenge placed against it and serves society well." During September 1982, Mr. Burke and other senior executives at Johnson & Johnson were faced with a major crisis. In the city of Chicago, seven people died after ingesting Tylenol capsules. Sadly, those capsules were cyanide-laced. As Mr. Burke stated above, Johnson & Johnson acted "by doing the right thing." Johnson & Johnson recalled all Tylenol products and stopped Tylenol advertisements. To bring to a stop to plummeting stocks, J&J allowed consumers to exchange capsules for tablets or refunds, and it distributed coupons for $2.50 off any Tylenol product. Meanwhile, the U.S. Food and Drug Administration (FDA) determined that the tampering occurred at the retail level, not during manufacturing. That was a critical finding because it demonstrated that the poison capsules were localized and J&J did not have to worry about future deaths in other areas of the country. Within weeks of the poisoning incidents, the FDA issued guidelines for tamper-resistant packaging for the entire food and drug industry. To bolster public confidence in its product, J&J (under Mr. Burke's leadership) used three layers of protection, two more than recommended by the government. Tylenol was put back on store shelves within months of the cyanide poisoning, and J&J gained back its share of the pain-reliever market. It soon regained more than 90% of its former customers.

Johnson & Johnson absorbed a loss in recalls, advertising, and repackaging exceeding $240 million. Despite this great loss for J&J, the consumer public rewarded J&J by returning as customers. As Mr. Burke stated, the public could clearly see within the Johnson & Johnson value system that J&J valued its customers' safety over the major losses incurred due to the massive recalls.

A more recent decision made by Johnson & Johnson showing that this Credo culture of Johnson & Johnson has not changed with time was the Guidant decision. Johnson & Johnson made the decision to back out of the acquisition of Guidant for the following reasons, as explained by current J&J CEO William C. Weldon:

> A year ago I reported to you our excitement about the prospect of broadening our presence in cardiovascular devices through the acquisition of Guidant Corporation. We extended considerable effort throughout the year to conclude this transaction. Unfortunately, a combination of adverse developments in Guidant's business and competition for the asset forced the price to a point where we concluded it was no longer in the best interest of our shareholders to pursue this business opportunity. Nonetheless, we remain committed to strengthening our business in this important therapeutic category.

Again, it was the value system embedded within the Credo that drove this decision, as Mr. Weldon explained. In this case, it was to protect J&J's investors, the fourth and last Credo category. Perhaps Mike Dormer, group chairman of the Medical Device Division of Johnson & Johnson, best described it when he stated at the Banc of America Securities 2006 Health Care Conference on May 17, 2006:

> This slide I think is enormously important in terms of the understanding of Johnson & Johnson. We have essentially four strategic principles that we use to drive our business into the future. First is that we are broadly based in human

health care, and I think that gives us enormous strength. There is no one product or business unit that makes up more than 10% of our portfolio. That enables us to withstand any, if you would like, shock to the system where we could have any threats to individual businesses and I think goes a long way to explaining the consistency of results that we have been able to deliver over long periods of time. We want to, as well as look at short-term financial results, look at the strategic value of our growth opportunities in terms of delivering long-term value to the Company and obviously our shareholders. And the last things, which is [sic] extremely important and in the sense is the umbrella that over-launches everything in Johnson & Johnson, is our value system, which is well-defined in our credo, which interestingly puts patients, mothers, fathers first in terms of what our responsibilities are, and we utilize that as in a sense the fabric of the Company.

Nordstrom

Nordstrom's culture began in 1901 when John W. Nordstrom and Carl F. Wallin opened the Nordstrom and Wallin shoe store in Seattle, Washington. John Nordstrom stressed the value of customer service, a vast selection of merchandise, and high-quality products. Thus were born the underpinnings of the Nordstrom culture. Interestingly, Nordstrom's first-day sales total was $12.50. By 1968, Nordstrom was still a family-owned business with a total of five stores that offered apparel and shoes and grossed over $40 million in annual sales. In 1971, Nordstrom decided to go public, with family members retaining the majority of the stock. The company was then operating 11 stores in three states and earning $3.5 million on sales of $80 million. The fundamental culture passed on through the family from one generation to the next still remained the same: an emphasis on the value of customer service, a vast selection of merchandise, and high-quality products.

During 1975, Lloyd Nordstrom led a group of investors to found the Seattle Seahawks, a National Football League franchise, for $16 million. They also bought three stores in Anchorage, Fairbanks, and Kenai, all in Alaska, from the Northern Commercial Co.

By 1980, Nordstrom was the third-largest specialty retailer in the United States, only ranking behind Saks Fifth Avenue and Lord & Taylor. At that time, Nordstrom operated a total of 31 stores, and sales reached $407 million with earnings of $19.7 million. Its fundamental culture remained the same.

By 1985, Nordstrom had become the number-one specialty retailer in the United States. In 1988, another major milestone was reached. Nordstrom opened its first East Coast store in McLean, Virginia. The store's first-day sales reached $1 million, and its annual sales then were $100 million. The grand opening day sales of a Nordstrom San Francisco store were $1.7 million, and its luxurious amenities included 103 brands of champagne, 16 varieties of chilled vodka, and a health spa.

In 1989, Nordstrom won the National Retail Merchants Association's Gold Medal, and envious competitors began to imitate the company's strategies of maintaining a large inventory and providing lavish customer service, which are core to Nordstrom's culture.

Nordstrom consistently relied on an aggressive sales staff, but the corporate policy of encouraging clerks to go out of their way to make sales caused Nordstrom some problems. For example, the employees' union (which was later de-certified) complained about the pressure on employees to sell.

Nordstrom's culture insists on excellence in customer service; however, this led to some problems in 1989, when unionized employees in Washington state charged that they were not paid for extra services provided to customers or for attending mandatory meetings and doing paperwork. This began an interesting test of Nordstrom's ability to hold onto its core culture, now almost ninety years old.

During 1990, after a three-month investigation, the Washington State Department of Labor & Industries found that Nordstrom had systematically violated state laws by failing to pay employees for a variety of duties such as delivering merchandise, writing customer correspondence, and doing inventory work. The agency ordered Nordstrom to change its compensation and record-keeping procedures and to pay $15 million in back wages.

In that same year, Nordstrom began trading on the New York Stock Exchange under the symbol JWN. As part of its global expansion during 1999, Nordstrom announced its partnership with The Seibu Department Stores, Ltd. and The Daimaru, Inc., to introduce select Nordstrom products in Japan. By 2001, U.S. stores in operation totaled 131; international stores in operation totaled 24.

As it entered into the 21st century, Nordstrom increasingly came to be recognized as an efficient, upscale, full-service department store. Nordstrom's culture-driven aggressive customer service plainly brought results. The firm consistently sustained the highest sales per square foot of retail space ratios in the industry, nearly twice those of other department stores.

Nordstrom's success has been due to a consistent culture. For example, throughout the company's history, shoes have traditionally accounted for a good deal of the firm's sales. During 1989, for example, shoes were about 18% of total sales. This is far different from most of Nordstrom's competitors, for whom shoes constitute a smaller percentage of sales. In addition, Nordstrom has consistently maintained huge inventories and a huge selection, both of which are usually twice the size of other department stores'. However, the key to Nordstrom's success, which reflects the heart of its culture, is a service-oriented and aggressive sales strategy. The vast majority of Nordstrom clerks work on commission, and Nordstrom managers generally promote from within the ranks of salespeople, intensifying the clerks' desire to sell.

During the 1980s, Nordstrom's customer service became legendary, and tales of heroic efforts by salespeople were common. For example, salespeople were known to:

- pay shoppers' parking tickets;

- rush deliveries to offices;
- unquestioningly accept returns;
- lend cash to strapped customers; and
- send tailors to customers' homes.

To this day, Nordstrom's salespeople receive constant pep talks from management, and motivational exercises are a routine part of life at Nordstrom. Nordstrom has also created an extremely customer-friendly environment. Many stores have free coat check service, free foot massages, concierges, and piano players who serenade shoppers.

President of Stores Eric Nordstrom sums it up nicely in the 2005 Nordstrom Annual Report, stating, "In simple terms, fashion is what sells. With compelling merchandise and an unyielding commitment to customer service, we can be the retailer customers trust."

Walgreen

Walgreen's culture centers around three core elements:

- a tradition of trust;
- long-term profitable growth; and
- the ability to be the most convenient and technically advanced provider of prescription drugs, basic needs, and managed care services.

It all began in 1901, when Charles R. Walgreen opened his first drugstore on Chicago's South Side. Over the next 14 years, Walgreen's expanded to five drugstores. By 1925, Walgreen's had grown to 65 stores, and its total annual sales were $1.2 million. In 1929, just four years later, it had grown to 397 stores. With this kind of expansion, we can clearly see the core culture element of sustained growth and profitability becoming traditional for Walgreen.

In 1934, Walgreen was listed on the New York Stock Exchange. During that year, it reported operating over 600 stores in 33 states, primarily in midwestern communities with populations of less than 20,000. That growth is an excellent indicator that the second core cultural element, a tradition of trust, was consistently being met. Why? Well, consider that all of these consumers were purchasing and ingesting prescription drugs. Therefore, they must trust their Walgreen pharmacy stores to provide the right drugs safely. Another way to look at this is that during 1962, Walgreen sold its 100 millionth prescription. Also, because Walgreen locates its stores in small communities, it also provides convenience to customers.

In 1984, Walgreen celebrated the grand opening of its 1,000th drugstore, and in 1985, sales were recorded at $3 billion. What a remarkable record of sustained profitable growth, drugstore expansion, and the ability to provide convenient and safe prescription drugs to consumers throughout the U.S.! During the mid-1990s, Walgreen was recognized as the largest drugstore chain in the U.S.

Another core facet of the Walgreen culture was (and continues to be) the desire to be the most technologically advanced provider of prescription drugs. In 1995, Walgreen introduced its Intercom Plus system, an automated touch-tone telephone system that takes refill orders 24 hours a day and transfers them into the pharmacy computer. The system was installed in all of its stores within a few years.

Today, Walgreen is the largest drugstore chain in the United States in terms of sales, more than 60% of which derive from retail prescriptions. During 2003, Walgreen filled 400 million prescriptions, a figure which represents about 13% of all retail prescriptions in the country. That shows a lot of trust on the part of the consumer public, and that trust is a key cultural element. There are now more than 4,400 Walgreen drugstores in 44 states and Puerto Rico. Clearly, the critical cultural element of convenience is there. About 80% of these outlets are freestanding locations, more than three-quarters have drive-through pharmacies, and nearly all of them offer one-hour photofinishing. In addition to the flagship Walgreen, the company also runs Walgreen Health Initiatives, a prescription benefit manager serving small and medium-sized employers and managed care organizations. Walgreen's century-plus history has been marked in more recent years by explosive growth fueled almost entirely by the opening of new stores. This is in stark contrast with its fiercest rivals, CVS Corporation and Rite Aid Corporation. Another major cultural factor is that by 2004, more than half of Walgreen outlets were less than five years old.

According to its 2005 Annual Report, the following facts certainly provide compelling evidence that its cultural triad of core elements mentioned earlier were all being sustained:

- Walgreen opened 435 new stores, bringing its total store count to 4,953 stores in 45 states and Puerto Rico.
- It filled 490 million prescriptions—15% of the U.S. retail market. Pharmacy is 64% of its business.
- Walgreen drugstores served 4.4 million customers daily and averaged $8.3 million in annual sales per store. That's $747 per square foot, among the highest in the drugstore industry.
- As of 2005, Walgreen had 179,000 employees and approximately 750,000 shareholders.
- Walgreen added 15,700 jobs in fiscal 2005.
- Walgreen's digital photo service now offers customers the ability to up-load photos from home and pick up their prints at nearly any store chain-wide in one hour.
- Walgreen was ranked number one among food and drug stores on *Fortune* magazine's Most Admired Companies in America list. Walgreen also ranks 38th on the Fortune 500 list of the largest U.S.-based companies.

- *Barron's* magazine lists Walgreen as one of the top 10 "most respected" companies in the world.

All 38 companies that were included in this year's Value Zone Hall of Fame achieved exceptional financial performance consistently for 25 years from 1981 through 2005. In the next chapter, we will discuss several examples of these companies and why they were able to sustain profitable revenue growth for such a long period of time.

Chapter Seven
Sustaining Profitable Growth

The Value Zone Hall of Fame companies that sustained exceptional business performances between the years 1981 and 2005 and were introduced in Chapter Three all posted consistent financial performances throughout this period. Their distinguished performances of sustained and profitable revenue growth during the 25-year period of study are quite remarkable, especially considering all of the internal and external forces affecting their business strategies. Their remarkable financial performances are on display graphically in the Appendix of this book. In this chapter, we will discuss several of these companies and review some of the turbulent forces that they were able to navigate through while sustaining exceptional business results.

Nordstrom

By 1980, Nordstrom was the third-largest specialty retailer in the country, with only Saks Fifth Avenue and Lord & Taylor ranked ahead of it. That year, Nordstrom operated 31 stores in California, Washington, Oregon, Utah, Montana, and Alaska. Nordstrom launched an aggressive expansion strategy in the early 1980s with a new plan to open 25 new stores. Its projection for growth was that both earnings and total square footage would double by 1985.

It turns out this forecast was more modest than what actually happened. But it is always best to under-promise and over-achieve. In 1980, Nordstrom's revenues were $407 million, and between 1980 and 1983, sales rose to $787 million. In addition, earnings more than doubled, increasing from $19.7 million to $40.2 million. In 1982, Nordstrom launched Nordstrom Rack, a string of outlet stores, as its third division. Nordstrom's biggest growth area, however, was in the enormous California market. In 1984, there were seven Nordstrom stores in California. By 1989, Nordstrom had 22 full-size stores in California.

Another factor contributing to this growth was Nordstrom's development of a highly spirited sales force. Managers were generally promoted from within the ranks of salespeople, a practice which provided an incentive for salespeople to sell. For example, clerks were known to pay shoppers' parking tickets, rush deliveries to offices, accept returns with no questions asked, lend cash to customers who were short on cash, and send tailors to customers' homes. The sales force received constant pep talks from management, and motivational exercises were institutionalized. Nordstrom also created a very customer-friendly environment. Many stores had free coat check service, concierges, and musicians who serenaded shoppers. As the economy boomed in the 1980s, Nordstrom's financial performance soared. During 1985, sales first topped $1 billion, then jumped to $1.3 billion. In 1987, Nordstrom had profits of $92.7 million on revenues of almost $2 billion. By the end of 1988, Nordstrom had 21,000 employees toiling in its 58 stores. Together, they persuaded customers to buy $2.3 billion worth of merchandise, creating $123 million in profits.

In the late 1980s, Nordstrom continued to rely on an aggressive sales force. However, the corporate policy of encouraging the sales force to go out of its way to make sales caused Nordstrom some problems. The employees' union (which was later decertified) complained about the pressure on employees to sell. In late 1989, a group of unionized employees claimed that they were not being paid for performing extra services to customers. In February 1990, after a three-month investigation, the Washington State Department of Labor and Industries charged that the company had systematically violated state laws by failing to pay employees for a variety of duties such as delivering merchandise and doing inventory work. The agency ordered Nordstrom to change its compensation and record-keeping procedures and to pay back wages to some of Nordstrom's 30,000 employees. Not long after this, Nordstrom created a $15 million reserve to pay the back-wage claims. Nordstrom, however, remained a target of class-action lawsuits on these matters; the lawsuits were finally settled out of court in early 1993, when Nordstrom agreed to pay a set percentage of compensation to employees who worked at Nordstrom from 1987 to 1990. The settlement cost the company between $20 and $30 million.

Another unforeseen external factor impacting Nordstrom was the San Francisco earthquake of 1989, which resulted in the company's retail sales taking a significant hit in the San Francisco Bay area. The general nationwide slowdown in retailing hurt the company more, however. In September 1990, Nordstrom, then a 61-store company, announced it would cut costs between 3% and 12% and lay off some employees. Despite all of this, however, sales increased in 1989 from $2.33 billion to $2.67 billion, an increase of nearly 15%.

A recession caused slower growth during the early 1990s. Despite the recession, Nordstrom continued to expand and open new stores in the East Coast and the Midwest. In September 1990, Nordstrom launched a store in Paramus, New Jersey, its first in the metropolitan New York area. In April 1991, Nordstrom debuted its first Midwest store in Oak Brook, Illinois, a Chicago suburb. In typical Nordstrom style, the store featured 125,000 pairs of shoes, a concierge, an espresso bar, and a wood-paneled English-style pub. In 1991, the company also opened stores in Riverside, California; Edison, New Jersey; and Bethesda, Maryland. Sales and earnings rebounded a tad in 1990 as revenues rose 8% to $2.89 billion; profits rose a tiny 0.7% to $115.8 million. In 1990, women's apparel and accessories accounted for 59% of Nordstrom's total sales; men's apparel accounted for 16%; and shoes, still a company mainstay, constituted 19% of all sales.

This single-digit growth became the norm for Nordstrom throughout the early and mid-1990s as sales grew sluggish largely due to fluctuations in demand for women's apparel and the severe recession in southern California, where more than half of the company's total store square footage was located in the early years of the 1990s. The double-digit growth of the 1980s was gone; however, the sales increases achieved during the 1990s were largely attributable to new store openings.

Nordstrom continued its strategy of expanding while shying away from the troubled California market. Nordstrom increasingly sought out new territory for expansion, particularly in the Midwest, South, and Northeast. For example, in 1996 alone, the Philadelphia, Dallas, Denver, and Detroit metropolitan areas were added to the Nordstrom chain via new store openings. While it continued its steady expansion, Nordstrom also made a number of other strategic moves that were indicative of a company in transition. Nordstrom produced its first mail-order catalog in the early 1990s, opened the first Nordstrom Factory Direct store near Philadelphia in 1993, and launched a proprietary Visa card in 1994. Also in 1993, the company opened a men's boutique in New York called Façonnable in partnership with the French firm Façonnable S.A. Nordstrom had been the exclusive U.S. distributor of Façonnable's line of upscale men's and women's apparel and accessories since 1989.

Meanwhile, profits slipped from 5.3% in 1988 to 3.91% in 1993. To resolve this problem, Nordstrom cut costs, especially its selling, general, and administrative costs, which accounted for 26.4% of sales in 1992. This fairly high figure was related to Nordstrom's generous employee incentive program, which fueled the company's reputation for customer service. By 1995, however, these costs had actually increased to 27.2% of sales, while net earnings improved only slightly to 4.01%.

Nordstrom was innovative in many areas; however, the company had stayed away from large investments in information technology prior to the mid-1990s. In 1995, it invested in a new information system along with a new system for personnel, payroll, and benefits processing. Another major technology investment was Nordstrom's first inventory control system. Company executives rolled the system out during 1995 in southern California and planned a company-wide rollout for 1996. Despite these investments in new technology, Nordstrom continued its traditional decentralized buying, bucking an industry trend toward centralization.

Between 1997 and 1999, Nordstrom continued its expansion and opened another ten new stores, adding 3.7 million square feet to the chain total. Among these was a new flagship store in downtown Seattle. Other states receiving their first Nordstrom store during the late 1990s were Arizona, Connecticut, Georgia, Kansas, Ohio, and Rhode Island. By the year 2000, there were 77 full-line Nordstrom stores, 38 Nordstrom Racks, and 23 Façonnable boutiques. In the latter part of 1998, the company entered the e-commerce world by launching its first online store at nordstrom.com. Furthermore, Nordstrom stock began trading on the New York Stock Exchange in June 1999.

Nordstrom's struggles continued during this period because many customers began to think that its merchandise was too formal and not in line with the latest lifestyle changes. Centralized purchasing was instituted in order to provide a consistent chain-wide merchandise look and to increase leverage with vendors. Along the same lines, regionally created advertising was replaced with the firm's first national television campaign, which helped create a consistent Nordstrom image. Nordstrom's outdated computer systems began to be upgraded in order to more easily track merchandise and collect more data about customer trends.

Unfortunately, these merchandising changes did not work for long, and "Reinvent Yourself," Nordstrom's new national ad campaign emphasizing a more youthful fashion, failed. Although this ad was appealing to 20-somethings, it alienated Nordstrom's core baby-boomer shoppers. Sales remained lackluster and earnings were down; these factors led to an August 2000 management shakeup. Bruce Nordstrom came out of retirement to take over the chairman's position, while his son Blake assumed the day-to-day operations as president. These developments occurred during one of Nordstrom's least profitable years; net income for fiscal 2000 totaled a mere $101.9 million on sales of $5.53 billion. Same-store sales increased just 0.3% over the previous year's sales. Also in 2000, Nordstrom acquired Façonnable S.A. for about $170 million, gaining full control of the Façonnable brand and the 53 Façonnable boutiques located around the world, mainly in Europe.

Nordstrom's new management team, while attempting to help its firm rebound from the recent slide in profits, had the further problem of an economic downturn to deal with. After a brief upturn, same-store sales began falling in August 2001. This led to Nordstrom's decision to lay off thousands of employees late in the year as part of a cost-cutting initiative. During this time, Nordstrom also held its first-ever fall clearance sale to try to reduce excess inventories (unlike most competitors, who conducted regular sales, Nordstrom had traditionally held few promotions: two half-yearly sales for men and women and an anniversary sale in July). Same-store sales fell 2.9% for the year, while net sales increased just 1.2% despite the opening of four new Nordstrom department stores and eight Nordstrom Racks. During the early 2000s, new store openings for the Nordstrom flagship centered around the Sun Belt. These openings included the first locations in Florida and several additional ones in Texas.

By 2003, Nordstrom appeared to have regained some brand equity through cost containment, technology initiatives, and a returned focus on its niche—luxury goods at affordable prices. Industry experts considered technology to be the key component of Nordstrom's upswing. Nordstrom added a state-of-the-art merchandising system in 2002. This system could track sales minute-by-minute throughout Nordstrom's stores, enabling the firm to reduce markdowns and better target its offerings to customers. On the merchandise side, the retailer began introducing more trendy fashion offerings in a department called "via C" as part of an attempt to leverage its core customer base, which was younger and had a wider age range than its main competitors, Neiman Marcus Co. and Saks Incorporated. In 2003, Nordstrom enjoyed its most profitable year ever: $242.8 million in net income on record revenues of $6.49 billion. Same-store sales rose 4.3%, Nordstrom's best performance in a decade. Nordstrom hoped to maintain this forward momentum by continuing to roll out its technology initiatives, keeping a tight rein on expenses, and avoiding large investments in new real estate—only 11 new stores were slated to open from 2004 through 2008—in favor of enhancing existing stores and maximizing sales per square foot. However, Nordstrom continued to open new stores, increasing from $319 a square foot in 2002 to $327 in 2003, but those figures were still far behind the industry leader Neiman Marcus's figure of $466 a square foot.

As reported in Nordstrom's 2005 Annual Report, total sales increased 8.3% to $7.7 billion and same-store sales increased 6%; this was Nordstrom's fourth consecutive year of same-store sales gains. A key long-term strategy for Nordstrom's was to drive profitable growth by earning more business from current customers, serving more customers, and increasing Nordstrom's presence where the company's customers shop.

As the leadership team at Nordstrom guided its organization through some significant changes, its members were very pleased with their staff's ability to adapt to change. For example, company executives praised their people for their ability to adapt to new technology while building on the momentum of the last few years. In 2005, Nordstrom spokespeople reported that the company was honored to be included among *Fortune* magazine's "100 Best Companies to Work For in America" for the ninth time. Nordstrom's leaders were especially proud of that recognition because they have always strived to create a positive environment for their employees, one that allows them to deliver great service and achieve their own goals.

They also extended a deep and heartfelt appreciation to Bruce and John Nordstrom, both of whom retired from the Board of Directors after four decades of service. Along with Jack McMillan and the late Jim Nordstrom, these men were part of the third-generation leadership team that guided the company from a small northwestern retailer to a leading national specialty store. The company went public in 1971. It has grown from an $80 million company in 1971 to a nearly $8 billion company today. Now that's a remarkable achievement, and we can clearly see why Nordstrom is in the Value Zone Hall of Fame.

Johnson & Johnson

Johnson & Johnson has the distinction of being included in the Value Zone Hall of Fame Ring of Honor, an honor reserved for those companies that have sustained profitable growth for 50 years or more. This is quite remarkable because Johnson & Johnson is comprised of over 230 companies that are located in 57 countries and provide products and services in virtually every country in the world. Considering the fierce competition J&J has faced in its three lines of business—pharmaceuticals, medical devices and diagnostics, and consumer segments—it is quite an achievement to get most of the CEOs and executive teams running these businesses to consistently produce great financial results.

During the 1980s, there were a number of important developments that J&J leaders had to deal with. To begin with, they made a number of key acquisitions. The challenge for J&J leadership was to bring new managers and employees of the acquired companies into J&J culture while remaining steady in growth and profitability. For example, in the late 1980s, J&J acquired LifeScan, Inc., maker of at-home blood-monitoring products for diabetics. In that same year, the company expanded its world-leading position in baby care products with the acquisition of Penaten G.m.b.H., a market leader in Germany. After the acquisition of Frontier Contact Lenses (now Vistakon), J&J introduced the Acuvue brand of disposable contact lenses in the United States in 1988. The popularity of the Acuvue lenses helped launch Vistakon into the number-one position in contact lens companies worldwide. In 1989, J&J and drug giant Merck & Co., Inc. entered into a joint venture, Johnson & Johnson-Merck Consumer Pharmaceuticals Co., to develop OTC versions of Merck's prescription medications. These versions were meant initially for the U.S. market, and later expansion into Europe and Canada was planned. One of the first product lines developed by this venture was the Mylanta brand of gastrointestinal products.

Another important factor is Johnson & Johnson's succession planning. Jim Burke retired in 1989 and was succeeded by CEO and Chairman Ralph S. Larsen, who came from the consumer sector; Vice-Chairman Robert E. Campbell, who had headed the professional sector; and President Robert N. Wilson, who had headed the pharmaceutical sector. These three men were responsible for overseeing the network of 168 companies operating out of 53 countries.

Ralph Larsen immediately began reducing some of the inefficiencies that a history of decentralization had caused. Some examples of efficiency improvements occurred during 1989 when the J&J infant products division merged with the health and dental units to form a broader consumer products segment. This move reduced costs by eliminating approximately 300 jobs. This reorganization was extended to overseas units over the next couple of years through consolidation under three primary companies: Ethicon, Johnson & Johnson Medical, and Johnson & Johnson Professional. As a result, a number of professional operating departments in Europe were reduced from 28 to 18 products. In 1990, J&J formed Ortho Biotech Inc. to consolidate the company's research in the burgeoning biotechnology field.

As part of its effort to apply the principles of its Corporate Credo to issues of social responsibility, J&J was able to address rising criticisms of higher healthcare costs in the United States and around the world in the 1990s. J&J developed several progressive programs, including childcare, family leave, and "corporate wellness," that began to be recognized for lowering healthcare costs. Furthermore, weighted average compound prices of J&J's healthcare products, including prescription and OTC drugs and hospital and professional products, grew more slowly than the U.S. consumer price index from 1980 through 1992. These strategic initiatives or "best practices" provided support for J&J's claim that it was part of the solution to the healthcare crisis. In 1992, J&J launched its "Signature of Quality" program, which urged the corporation's operating companies to focus on three general goals: "Continuously improving customer satisfaction, cost efficiency and the speed of bringing new products to market."

J&J growth was consistent but moved at a relatively slow pace during the early 1990s largely because of a difficult economic climate. Revenues increased from $11.23 billion in 1990 to $14.14 billion in 1993, an increase of just 26%. However, a series of acquisitions during the mid-1990s was the catalyst for a period of more rapid growth as revenues hit $21.62 billion by 1996, a jump of

53% from the 1993 level. J&J's skin care line received a tremendous boost in 1993 through the purchase of RoC S.A. of France, a maker of hypoallergenic facial, hand, body, and other products under the RoC label. Even more significant was the acquisition the following year of Neutrogena Corporation for nearly $1 billion. Neutrogena was well known for its line of dermatologist-recommended skin and hair care products. Moreover, in 1995, J&J spent another billion dollars for the clinical diagnostics unit of Eastman Kodak Company, which was particularly strong in the areas of clinical chemistry (the analysis of simple compounds in the body) and immuno-diagnostics. In 1997, J&J combined its existing Ortho Diagnostics Systems unit with the operations acquired from Kodak to form Ortho-Clinical Diagnostics, Inc. LifeScan, acquired in the late 1980s, remained a separately-run diagnostics company.

Another key acquisition during the early 1990s was Ethicon Endo-Surgery, Inc., which had been spun off from Ethicon in 1992 to concentrate on endoscopic, or minimally invasive, surgical instruments. J&J also acquired Indigo Medical, which specialized in minimally invasive technology in urology and related areas, in 1996, and in 1997, it acquired Biopsys Medical, Inc., which specialized in minimally invasive breast biopsies. J&J made an enormously successful and strategically timely acquisition in 1996 when it spent almost $2 billion for Cordis Corporation, a world leader in the treatment of cardiovascular diseases using its stents, balloons, and catheters. Then, during 1997, J&J acquired the OTC rights to the Motrin brand of ibuprofen pain relievers from Pharmacia & Upjohn in exchange for several consumer products. Other important developments during this period included the 1995 introduction of an Acuvue disposable contact lens. This product was designed to be worn for just one day and was priced at a reasonable level. In that same year, the U.S. approved the antacid Pepcid AC, an OTC version of Merck's Pepcid that was developed through a Johnson & Johnson and Merck joint venture.

J&J continued its aggressive program of acquisitions during the late 1990s, starting with the 1998 purchase of DePuy, Inc. for $3.7 billion in cash. The DePuy purchase was J&J's largest acquisition up to that time. DePuy was a leader in orthopedic products such as hip replacement devices. This move made sense and was strategic because J&J already marketed one of the leading knee replacement devices in the United States. This resulted in a nice fit between the two companies. However, there were also some less positive events during this time period that J&J's leadership team would learn some valuable lessons from. One such event was J&J's restructuring in 1998 following several problems. J&J had been a pioneer in the market for coronary stents, devices used to keep arteries open following angioplasty, but its stent sales fell from $700 million in 1996 to just over $200 million in 1998 when competitors introduced second-generation stents and J&J did not. Also in 1997 and 1998, the firm's pharmaceutical operation saw nine drugs in the development pipeline fail in testing, fail to get government approval, or encounter a delay to market. During the late 1990s, J&J announced that it would reduce its workforce by 4,100 and close 36 plants around the world over a period of about one and a half years. J&J invested $697 million in restructuring and in-process research and development charges and was focused on cutting its costs between $250 million and $300 million per year through this effort.

In a move that strengthened its drug research and development area, J&J completed its first major pharmaceutical deal since the 1961 purchase of Janssen Pharmaceutica. In October 1999, J&J merged with a major biotechnology company, Centocor, Inc., in a $4.9 billion stock-for-stock transaction. This was the largest deal of this type in J&J's history. With Centocor and Ortho Biotech now part of J&J, J&J came to be recognized as one of the world's leading biotech firms. Not long after this merger, the Food and Drug Administration approved a key Centocor-developed drug, Remicade, for the treatment of rheumatoid arthritis. Centocor was also developing other pharmaceuticals for cancer, autoimmune diseases, and cardiology. Furthermore, J&J acquired the dermatological skin care business S.C. Johnson & Son, Inc. in 1999, which was primarily made up of the Aveeno brand, for an undisclosed amount. Finally, the company introduced Splenda, a no-calorie sweetener that would by 2003 assume the top position in U.S. retail sales of tabletop sweeteners. Despite its late 1990s troubles, J&J reported record results for 1999, earning $4.17 billion on revenues of $27.47 billion. Net earnings had nearly quadrupled since 1989, while net sales had nearly tripled over the same period, a remarkable comeback.

In the year 2000, J&J got off to a rough start and was forced to withdraw Propulsid, a prescription drug for heartburn, from the market. This prescription medication had been linked to 100 deaths and hundreds of cases of cardiac irregularity. Propulsid had generated nearly $1 billion in sales in 1999. By 2004, the number of persons who had allegedly died from using the drug had risen to more than 415, and more than 400 lawsuits representing the interests of about 5,900 plaintiffs had been filed against J&J's Janssen unit, the maker of Propulsid. In early 2004, Janssen reached an agreement to settle lawsuits involving approximately 4,000 plaintiffs whereby it would pay compensation totaling between $69.5 million and $90 million as well as administrative and legal fees amounting to $37.5 million. On a more positive note, J&J's pharmaceutical business was led in the early 2000s by a true blockbuster, Procrit (marketed as Eprex in Europe), an anemia medication licensed from Amgen, Inc. and introduced by J&J in 1991. Sales of Procrit exceeded $3 billion per year in the first years of the 21st century. The drug accounted for approximately 10% of J&J's total revenues, which surpassed the $30 billion mark for the first time in 2001 and reached $40 billion in 2003.

Meanwhile, Johnson & Johnson continued to expand and enhance its OTC pain reliever product line in 2000 by acquiring the St. Joseph brand, best known for its orange-flavored low-dose aspirin, which was in wide use as a doctor-recommended daily therapy. Several other key acquisitions followed. In June of 2001, J&J acquired ALZA Corporation in a $12.3 billion stock-swap transaction, the company's largest purchase yet. Based in Mountain View, California, ALZA was a leading developer of drug-delivery technologies such as time-release capsules and transdermal patches. Sales of the firm's two biggest-selling drugs, Concerta, a treatment for attention deficit/hyperactivity disorder, and Ditropan XL, a urinary incontinence remedy, were expected to surge based on J&J's worldwide marketing strengths. Moreover, in 2001, J&J's LifeScan unit was bolstered through the $1.3 billion purchase of Inverness Medical Technology Inc., producer of devices used by diabetes patients to monitor their blood-sugar levels.

As we discussed earlier, Johnson & Johnson's succession planning was a key strength largely because of the company's leadership development programs. Therefore, when Ralph Larsen retired from the company in early 2002, his successor as CEO and the sixth chairman in the history of Johnson & Johnson was William C. Weldon, who joined the firm in 1971 and had most recently served as head of the pharmaceuticals side since 1998. Weldon took over at a time when some of J&J's top-selling drugs, including Procrit, were faced with a drop-off in sales because of increased competition. One key achievement for J&J during 2003 was the receipt of FDA approval for Cordis' Cypher, a stent coated with a drug designed to reduce re-blockage of blood vessels. Although J&J succeeded in being the first to market with a drug-coated stent, and the product achieved strong first-year sales of $1.4 billion, Cypher quickly faced stiff competition from Boston Scientific Corporation's Taxus drug-coated stent. In the pharmaceuticals market, J&J continued its strategic initiatives to acquire other pharmaceutical companies with outstanding R&D programs. This maneuver would serve to bolster a somewhat lethargic drug-development pipeline. J&J also acquired Scios Inc. during April 2003. Scios, a biotech firm specializing in treatments for cardiovascular and inflammatory disease, brought the Natrecor treatment, which was touted as the first new treatment for congestive heart failure in 15 years. Sales of Natrecor rose to $384 million by 2004, but the potential blockbuster status of the drug came into question following reports that it was damaging patients' kidneys. In mid-2005, a panel composed of independent experts recommended that use of Natrecor be restricted to acutely sick hospitalized patients and endorsed J&J's plans for additional studies of the drug.

In 2004, J&J revenues reached $47.35 billion and increased for the 71st consecutive year. That year, J&J also continued its record of issuing dividends to shareholders every quarter since 1944, increased its dividend for the 43rd straight year, and achieved a double-digit increase in profits for the 19th consecutive year. The firm was now ranked as the fourth-largest pharmaceutical company in the world, trailing only Pfizer Inc., GlaxoSmithKline plc, and Sanofi-Aventis. It was also ranked as the number-two biotech company after Amgen. Johnson & Johnson also held sway as the largest manufacturer of medical devices and diagnostics tools in the world, a position it aimed to bolster by acquiring Indianapolis-based Guidant Corporation (and merging Cordis into it) in a deal announced in December 2004 that was initially valued at $25.4 billion. Guidant, with annual sales of about $3.8 billion, focused on implantable devices to treat abnormal heart rhythms, including implantable cardiac defibrillators and pacemakers as well as catheters and stents. The deal was expected to be completed in late 2005 but became questionable after Guidant was forced to recall tens of thousands of its defibrillators and pacemakers because of malfunctions. Further clouding Johnson & Johnson's future were reports that the drug-coated stents being produced by both J&J and Boston Scientific might pose a higher long-term risk of life-threatening blood clots than the old-fashioned bare-metal type. In both cases, J&J had to make some tough calls, but it continued to be guided by its Corporate Credo's core principles. Faced with one challenge after another, Johnson & Johnson continued to grow profitably through 2006. One piece of good news for Johnson & Johnson as well as other pharmaceutical companies was the unanimous decision reached by the Supreme Court in June 2005 that manufacturers of generic drugs are exempt from patent infringement considerations in early-stage research. This ruling was designed to protect pharmaceutical companies like J&J that prefer to launch research on developing generic forms of rival blockbuster drugs prior to the patent expiring. The ruling reinforces the Drug Price Competition and Patent Restoration Act passed in 1984.

Abertis Infraestructuras, S.A.

Abertis Infraestructuras, S.A., a company based in Spain, has achieved a remarkable record not only as the leading operator of toll roads in Spain but also as an international transportation infrastructure specialist. Abertis is Spain's leading operator of parking garages; it owns more than 90,000 car parking spaces in more than 35 cities. It is present in 25 cities in Italy, Portugal, Morocco, and Andorra through its Saba subsidiary. Abertis has also extended its infrastructure operations through its subsidiary Abertis Logistica to include CIM Vallés Logistics Park, the Ronda del Litoral and the Cilsa port operation in Barcelona, and two new logistics centers in Alava and Sevilla that will add some 500,000 square meters of warehouse space and 200,000 square meters of offices under the company's management.

In an effort to diversify its portfolio of businesses in another infrastructure extension, Abertis acquired control of the Tradia and Retevision radio and telecommunications transmission networks, which provide analog and digital transmission capabilities at more than 2,400 sites in Spain, during 2003. Abertis also manages the operations of Colombia's Eldorado airport. However, its core business of toll roads remains the company's largest operation, accounting for 84% of its revenues of nearly EUR 1.3 billion ($1.1 billion U.S.) in 2003. In Spain, the company's network (developed through the mergers of Acesa, Aurea, and Iberpistas) comprises some 68% of the country's toll road system. Spain also represents Abertis' primary market, with a market share of 94%. Abertis, however, has sought to broaden its international presence at the turn of the 21st century, and now it also directs toll road operations in Argentina and Puerto Rico and has stakes in a toll road operators company called Autostrade in Italy, Brisa in Portugal, and RMB in the United Kingdom. All told, the company directly controls 1,500 kilometers of motorways.

Formed through the merger of Acesa and Aurea and followed by the absorption of Iberpistas in 2003, Abertis represents the combination of nearly 40 years of road building in Spain. Acesa started out as Autopistas, Concesionaria Española SA and was founded in 1967 in order to build Spain's first toll road, the highway linking Montgat and Mataró. Based in Barcelona, Acesa became a major regional player and constructed nearly 550 kilometers of roadway, including the Jonquera-Salou segment, the Maresme coastal road, and the link through the Ebro corridor to Zaragoza. Abertis has been able to sustain consistent and profitable growth in this market and continues to thrive in the Value Zone.

Cintas

Cintas Corporation designs, manufactures, and implements corporate identity uniform programs. It also provides entrance mats, shop towels, restroom supplies, promotional products, first aid and safety products and services, and document management services. The company sells, leases, and rents uniforms and has 350 facilities across North America. In addition to offering shirts, jackets, slacks and footwear, the company also provides clean-room apparel and flame-resistant clothing.

Cintas was originally known for its uniform rental business in the Cincinnati area in the late 1960s, but since that time, it has expanded its product portfolio over the years into other areas such as entrance mats, cleaning supplies, and first aid kits and now sells these items to its customers in addition to renting them. The company provides its services in the U.S. and Canada to more than 700,000 businesses. It is headquartered in Cincinnati, Ohio, and employs about 30,000 people. Despite the many challenges faced by this midwestern company, Cintas was able to sustain solid and profitable growth all of those years. Let's see how the company did it.

The Cintas storyline is a literal rags-to-riches story. Its founder was Richard Farmer, who started out as a ragman. Along with his son Herschell, Richard built a thriving industrial linen business in the 1930s and 1940s. However, it was third-generation leader Richard T. Farmer who would guide the company into the uniform rental business in the late 1950s and lead a trend-setting consolidation of that industry in the 1980s and 1990s. His second-in-command called Richard T. Farmer a "visionary"; he pioneered new fabrics, instituted modern management and control systems, and expanded his target market from industrial to service businesses, among other innovations. During this process, he became one of Cincinnati's wealthiest and most influential businessmen.

Richard Farmer took his company public in 1983, selling a minority stake on the over-the-counter market at $17 per share. The equity sale signaled the beginning of a string of acquisitions that would catapult Cintas to the highest ranks of the uniform rental industry. Though some regional mergers and acquisitions had occurred before this time, the 1980s introduced an unprecedented consolidation of this service industry, which shrunk from about 1,600 mom-and-pop companies in 1981 to fewer than 800 companies by the early 1990s. Cintas was one of a handful of trend-setting companies including Unitog Co., UniFirst Corp., G & K Services, Inc., and the leader, Aramark Uniform Services Inc. (formerly Aratex, Inc.), a subsidiary of Aramark Corporation.

Throughout the course of the 1980s, Cintas expanded into 17 new geographic markets via savvy—and often small—acquisitions. Revenues doubled from $63 million in 1983 to $123.7 million in 1987 and then doubled again to $285 million by 1989. By the early 1990s, the company had a presence in three-fourths of the nation's 100 largest markets, and its market share had more than doubled from about 3.5% in 1983 to 10% in the early 1990s. Significantly, only about one-third of Cintas' growth during this period was generated by acquisitions, while the remainder came from organic growth.

In the latter half of the 1980s, Cintas spearheaded the uniform industry's expansion from a blue-collar base into more tailored uniforms for hotel and motel employees, restaurant workers, and even bank employees. Within its core airline constituency, for example, the company moved from coveralls for baggage handlers and mechanics to uniforms for pilots, flight attendants, and other customer service workers. By the mid-1990s, major national clients included Wal-Mart, Delta, Coca-Cola, Pepsi, Northwest Airlines, Chevron, Jiffy Lube, Sunoco, AAMCO, Safety Kleen, and Chemlawn.

From 1992 to 1997, Cintas added 70 new cities to its listing of service areas. As it grew, the company also focused on improving its productivity by committing millions of dollars to research and development each year. For example, Cintas executives had an automated manufacturing system installed and implemented. This system featured computerized design, cutting, and embroidery machines as well as electronic data interchange systems that used bar coding to manage inventory, processing, and distribution. This automation of laundering facilities cut staffing in half.

In 1995, Cintas began to expand globally with the acquisition of Toronto's Cadet Uniform Services Ltd. While geographic diversification such as this continued to be central to growth, the company also experimented with new product lines during this period. In 1997, Cintas acquired two new businesses that supplied OSHA-required first-aid kits to companies. With only $18 million in sales that year, this new business segment was little more than an interesting sideline at first. Cintas executives rapidly launched four major brands through acquisitions, and over the next three years, they picked close to 100 small first-aid companies.

In the mid-1990s, Richard Farmer developed an exit strategy for his retirement and initiated a management transition that led to Robert Kohlhepp, the longtime right-hand man of Richard Farmer, taking over as CEO. Farmer's strategy made use of a critical element involved in succession planning: turning the leadership reins to a trusted leader. In 1997, Richard's son Scott Farmer was promoted to president, setting up the fourth generation of Farmers to lead the company. Meanwhile, the elder Farmer concentrated on broad strategic initiatives with a view to capturing an ever-larger share of the latent market for uniforms.

Cintas continued to expand through acquisitions during the late 1990s and into the 21st century. Meanwhile, the uniform rental industry as a whole also continued to expand. According to Census Bureau statistics, the uniform rental industry grew at a rate of over 8% a year during the late 1990s, and Cintas executives believed that there were even more business opportunities for uniform rentals. Cintas had an impressive record of sustained growth in sales and profits, with growth in the double digits through the late 1990s. This served to improve Cintas' stock price, and the company was able to make many acquisitions by swapping its valuable shares. Between 1997 and 1999, the company acquired 65 companies. Most of them were small companies in the uniform rental business, but some provided first aid supplies and services, a growing new segment for Cintas. One example of a larger acquisition was the company Uniforms to You, which Cintas acquired in 1998. This private Chicago-based company had sales of around $150 million in 1998. Meanwhile, sales for Cintas in 1998 were over $1 billion. In 1999, Cintas made its largest acquisition up to that time, acquiring one of its top competitors, Kansas City-based Unitog Co. The transaction, which was paid for in Cintas stock, was valued at roughly $357 million. At the time, Unitog ran a uniform rental operation in 24 states and in Canada and had close to 60 plants. With this new acquisition, Cintas increased its market share to about 25%, becoming the largest company in the uniform rental industry and surpassing Aramark for the first time in its history. However, the integration of the new company did not go very smoothly; 75% of Unitog's sales force resigned. Cintas executive leaders apparently faced this challenge and reaped consistently positive results of sustained growth in revenues and profits.

By 1999, Cintas' operations had grown to over 200 uniform rental facilities across the United States. Cintas' manufacturing facilities increased from four to thirteen, it had six distribution centers, its clean-room business had grown to six facilities, and its first aid business now had thirty-two business centers. About four million people put on a Cintas uniform every day, yet the company executives still believed that there were more growth opportunities in the market. At that time, the uniform rental market as a whole was worth about $10 billion annually. Cintas management thought that that figure could still grow to around $31 billion. The company's research showed that some 37 million people worked in occupations where uniforms could or should be used. The company was successfully expanding into the ancillary area of first aid, too, assembling an array of small companies and unifying them into one brand, which it launched in 2000 as Xpect First Aid. The first aid division and other services outside of uniform rentals still accounted for less than 25% of the firm's revenues.

As Cintas became an emerging industry leader at the advent of the 21st century, its leadership team was very focused on growth and consolidation. In 2002, the company spent $22 million to acquire certain parts of the uniform manufacturing and marketing division of the Missouri-based laundry company Angelica Corp. One month after this acquisition was completed, Cintas acquired Omni Services, Inc., its largest acquisition, surpassing the Unitog deal completed two years earlier. Omni Services of Culpepper, Virginia was owned by the French company Filuxel, S.A. Omni had annual sales of around $300 million, with 90,000 customers in over 30 states. The merger increased Cintas' sales to around

$2.5 billion and clearly enabled Cintas to continue to lead the industry. The company recorded revenues of $3,067.3 million in the fiscal year ending in May 2005, an increase of 9% over fiscal 2004. Internal (organic) growth improved throughout fiscal 2005 and was 6.3% for the year.

McDonald's Corporation

Since its incorporation in 1955, McDonald's Corporation has not only become the world's largest fast-food restaurant organization, but it has literally changed the eating habits of Americans and non-Americans. On an average day, more than 46 million people eat at one of McDonald's' more than 31,000 restaurants, which span 119 countries and 6 continents. About 9,000 of the restaurants are company owned and operated; the remainder is run either by franchisees or through joint ventures with local businesspeople. System-wide sales (which encompass total revenues from all three types of restaurants) totaled more than $19 billion in 2004. Nine major markets—Australia, Brazil, Canada, China, France, Germany, Japan, the United Kingdom, and the United States—account for 80% of the restaurants and 75% of overall sales. The vast majority of the company's restaurants are of the flagship McDonald's hamburger restaurant variety.

McDonald's has a very interesting history of sustained growth and profitability. It all started in 1954 when Ray Kroc, a Multimixer milkshake machine salesman, learned that two brothers, Richard and Maurice (Dick and Mac) McDonald, were using eight of his high-tech Multimixers in their San Bernardino restaurant. With his curiosity piqued, Kroc went to San Bernardino to take a look at the McDonalds' restaurant.

The McDonalds had been in the restaurant business since the 1930s. In 1948, they closed down a successful carhop drive-in to establish the streamlined operation that Ray Kroc saw in 1954. Their menu was simple: hamburgers, cheeseburgers, French fries, shakes, soft drinks, and apple pie. The carhops were eliminated, enabling McDonald's to be a self-serve operation with no tables to sit at, no jukebox, and no telephone. The result was that McDonald's attracted families rather than teenagers. From Kroc's perspective, the most impressive aspect of the restaurant was the efficiency with which the McDonald's workers did their jobs. Mac and Dick McDonald had taken great care in setting up their kitchen. Each worker's steps had been carefully choreographed like an assembly line to ensure maximum efficiency. The savings in preparation time and the resulting increase in volume allowed the McDonalds to lower the price of a hamburger from 30 cents to 15 cents. Wow! That's better than the dollar menu bargain prices today. Indeed, times have changed.

Kroc believed that the McDonalds' formula was a sure winner and suggested that they franchise their restaurants throughout the country. The McDonalds were reluctant to take on this additional burden, so Kroc volunteered to do it for them. He returned to his home outside of Chicago with the rights to set up McDonald's restaurants throughout the country. The only exception was a handful of territories in California and Arizona already licensed by the McDonald brothers.

Kroc opened his first McDonald's restaurant in Des Plaines, Illinois, near Chicago, on April 15, 1955—the same year that Kroc incorporated his company as McDonald's Corporation. As with any new venture, Kroc encountered a number of speed bumps. The first challenge was adapting the McDonald's building design to a northern climate by installing a basement with a furnace. Another key factor was adequate ventilation—exhaust fans to transfer warm air in the winter and cool air in the summer. Another frustration was Kroc's initial failure to reproduce the McDonalds' delicious French fries. When Kroc and his team duplicated the McDonald brothers' method—leaving just a little peel for flavor, cutting the potatoes into shoestrings, and rinsing the strips in cold water—the fries turned into mush. After a number of telephone conversations with the McDonald brothers and several consultations with the Potato and Onion Association, Kroc pinpointed the cause of the soggy fries. The McDonald brothers stored their potatoes outside in wire bins, and the warm California breeze dried them out and cured them, slowly turning the sugars into starch. To get similar results, Kroc developed a system using an electric fan to dry the potatoes. He also experimented with a blanching process. Within three months, he had French fries that were, in his opinion, slightly superior in taste to the McDonald brothers' fries.

Kroc decided early on that it was best to first establish the restaurants and then to franchise them out so that he could standardize them. Early McDonald's restaurants were situated in the suburbs. Kroc preferred lots in the middle of blocks to accommodate his U-shaped parking lots. Since these lots were cheaper, Kroc could give franchisees a price break.

McDonald's grew slowly during its first three years; by 1958 there were 34 restaurants. However, during 1959, Kroc opened 67 new restaurants, bringing the total to more than 100. Kroc also made two strategic decisions:

1) He decided at the outset that McDonald's would not be a supplier to its franchisees—his background in sales warned him that such an arrangement could lead to reduced quality for greater profits; and

2) He also decided that the company should at no time own more than 30% of all McDonald's restaurants.

Kroc understood that his success was linked to the success of the franchisees; therefore, he was determined to assist them in any way that he could.

In 1960, the McDonald's advertising campaign "Look for the Golden Arches" gave sales a huge boost. Kroc believed that investing in advertising would bring great returns and in the end come back many times over. Advertising has always played a key role in the development of the McDonald's Corporation. McDonald's ads have been some of the most memorable over the years, with two notable changes:

1) In 1962, McDonald's replaced its "Speedee" the hamburger man symbol with its now world-famous Golden Arches logo, and

2) A year later, the company sold its billionth hamburger and introduced Ronald McDonald, a red-haired clown with particular appeal to children.

In the early 1960s, McDonald's' growth skyrocketed. Its growth dovetailed with the growth in the U.S. automobile industry and an increase in drivers due to the suburbanization of America. In 1961, Kroc bought out the McDonald brothers for $2.7 million. In 1965, McDonald's Corporation went public. Common shares were offered at $22.50 per share; by the end of the first day's trading, the price had shot up to $30. A block of 100 shares purchased for $2,250 in 1965 was worth about $1.8 million by the end of 2003 and after 12 stock splits (increasing the number of shares to 74,360). In 1985, McDonald's Corporation became one of the 30 companies that made up the Dow Jones Industrial Average.

McDonald's' success in the 1960s was mainly due to the company's skillful marketing and flexible response to customer demand. For example, the Filet-o-Fish sandwich, billed as "the fish that catches people," was introduced to McDonald's restaurants in 1965. In 1968, the now legendary Big-Mac made its debut, and in 1969, McDonald's sold its five billionth hamburger. In 1970, McDonald's launched the "You Deserve a Break Today" advertising campaign, and in that same year, McDonald's restaurants had reached all 50 states. Now that we've reviewed a little about the history of this remarkable company, let's jump to the 1970s, 1980s, the 1990s, and the 21st century.

McDonald's' spectacular growth continued during the 1970s. Americans were on the go more than ever before, and fast service was a priority. In 1972, the company passed $1 billion in annual sales; by 1976, McDonald's had served 20 billion hamburgers, and system-wide sales exceeded $3 billion. McDonald's pioneered breakfast fast food with the introduction of the Egg McMuffin in 1973, a move which was based on market research indicating that a quick breakfast would be welcomed by consumers. Five years later, the company added a full breakfast line to the menu, and by 1987, one-fourth of all breakfasts eaten out in the United States came from McDonald's restaurants.

Kroc was a firm believer in giving "something back into the community where you do business." In 1974, McDonald's acted upon that philosophy in an original way by opening the first Ronald McDonald House, which was located in Philadelphia, to provide a "home away from home" for the families of children in nearby hospitals. Twelve years after this first house opened, one hundred similar Ronald McDonald Houses were operating throughout the United States.

In 1975, McDonald's opened its first drive-thru window restaurant in Oklahoma City. This service gave Americans a fast, convenient way to purchase a quick meal. The company's goal was to provide service in 50 seconds or less. Drive-thru sales eventually accounted for more than half of McDonald's system-wide sales. In the meantime, the Happy Meal, a combo meal for children featuring a toy, was added to the menu in 1979.

During the late 1970s, competition from other hamburger chains such as Burger King and Wendy's began to heat up. Experts felt that the fast-food industry had grown as large as it ever would, so the companies would now have to fight for market share. Thus, a period of aggressive advertising campaigns and price slashing began in the early 1980s, leading to the legendary "burger wars." Burger King suggested that customers "have it their way"; Wendy's offered itself as the "fresh alternative" and asked of other restaurants, "where's the beef?" However, McDonald's sales and market share continued to grow. Consumers seemed to like the taste and consistency of McDonald's best.

During the 1980s, McDonald's persisted in diversifying its menu based on evolving consumer tastes. For example, Chicken McNuggets were introduced in 1983, followed by ready-to-eat salads in 1987 meant to lure more health-conscious consumers. With solid business results in the suburbs, McDonald's began to focus in urban areas, introducing new architectural styles. Even though McDonald's restaurants were no longer identical in terms of looks, the food quality and service remained consistent. The result was sustained and profitable growth.

In spite of the industry analysts' assertions that the fast-food industry was saturated, McDonald's continued to increase its markets. With the first generation raised on restaurant food now in its adult years, eating out had become a way of life. With this in mind, McDonald's relentlessly continued its aggressive advertising campaigns and marketing programs to improve sales. Innovative marketing campaigns, such as the "when the U.S. wins, you win" giveaways during the Olympic Games in 1988, were a smashing success.

McDonald's' growth during the 1990s was quite robust, with an increasing percentage of its revenue and profits coming from outside the United States. By 1992, about two-thirds of the company's system-wide sales were from the U.S. By 1997, however, that figure dropped to more than one half. In the United States, the number of units grew from 9,000 in 1991 to 12,500 in 1997. Although the additional units increased market share in some markets, a number of franchisees complained that new units were taking sales from existing ones. Same-store sales for outlets open for more than one year were flat in the mid-1990s, a reflection of the mature nature of the U.S. market.

McDonald's 1997 Teenie Beanie Baby promotion was tremendously successful, with about 80 million of the toys/collectibles given away in record time. McDonald's also began to benefit from a ten-year global marketing partnership with Disney that began in 1996. Disney movies promoted by McDonald's included *101 Dalmatians, Flubber, Mulan, Armageddon,* and *A Bug's Life.* Another significant change in its marketing strategy occurred in 1997, when McDonald's named BDD Needham as its new lead ad agency. Needham was McDonald's' agency in the 1970s and was responsible for the hugely successful "You Deserve a Break Today" campaign. In 1997. McDonald's launched the Needham-designed "Did Somebody Say McDonald's?" campaign, a very successful campaign.

In May 1998, McDonald's named a new president and CEO of McDonald's Corporation. He was an executive who had joined the company only four years earlier from Pizza Hut and who replaced a McDonald's veteran executive as president of McDonald's Corporation U.S.A. This was a shift for McDonald's, where executives typically were long-timers. Another first was McDonald's' announcement of its first job cuts, which eliminated 525 employees from its headquarters staff. In the second quarter of 1998, McDonald's took a $160 million charge in relation to the cuts. As a result, the company recorded a decrease in profits for the first time since it went public in 1965, from $1.64 billion in 1997 to $1.55 billion in 1998.

McDonald's also began to strategically diversify its portfolio through a number of acquisitions. For example, during 1999, the company acquired Aroma Café, a U.K. chain of 23 upscale coffee and sandwich shops. Later that year, McDonald's added Donatos Pizza Inc., a midwestern chain of 143 pizzerias based in Columbus, Ohio. Also in 1999, McDonald's opened its 25,000th restaurant and named Jim Cantalupo company president. Cantalupo, who had joined the company as controller in 1974 and later became head of McDonald's International, had been vice-chairman, a position he retained. In May 2000, McDonald's completed its largest acquisition up to that time, buying the bankrupt Boston Market chain for $173.5 million in cash and debt. At the time, there were more than 850 Boston Market outlets specializing in home-style meals, with rotisserie chicken as the lead menu item. Revenue at Boston Market in 1999 was $670 million. McDonald's rounded out its acquisition spree in early 2001 by buying a 33% stake in Pret A Manger, an upscale urban-based chain specializing in ready-to-eat sandwiches made on the premises. There were more than 110 Pret shops in the United Kingdom and several more in New York City.

As McDonald's continued to search for new areas of growth, its core businesses were experiencing some major problems. For example, the launch of the "Made for You" system was not working well in many franchises. Although the franchisees believed that this system succeeded in improving the quality of the food, it also increased service times and was very labor-intensive. Some franchisees reportedly complained that the actual cost of implementing the system was much higher than the corporation's estimates. The bottom line was that "Made for You" was failing to reverse the company's lethargic growth in sales. Growth in sales at stores open for more than a year (known as same-store sales) fell in both 2000 and 2001. During the latter part of 2001, the company launched a restructuring that involved the elimination of about 850 positions, 700 of which were in the United States, and the closure of some units.

Some other troubling areas for McDonald's were a variety of lawsuits. For example, McDonald's was sued in 2001 after for adding a small amount of beef extract to the vegetable oil used in cooking the French fries. The company had claimed in ads that it used 100% vegetable oil. McDonald's soon apologized for any "confusion" that had been caused by its use of the beef flavoring, and in mid-2002, it reached a settlement in the litigation, agreeing to donate $10 million to Hindu, vegetarian, and other affected groups. Also in 2001, more embarrassment to its brand occurred when 51 people were charged with conspiring to rig McDonald's game promotions over a period of several years. It was revealed that $24 million of winning McDonald's game tickets had been stolen as part of the scam. Fortunately for McDonald's, the company was not implicated in the scheme, which centered on a worker at an outside company that had administered the promotions.

Perhaps the most devastating issues for the McDonald's brand and image were the increasing charges that the company was a purveyor of fatty, unhealthy food. Consumers began filing lawsuits contending that years of eating at McDonald's had made them overweight and unhealthy. McDonald's' response was to begin introducing low-calorie menu items and changing to a more healthful cooking oil for its French fries. McDonald's franchises overseas also became a favorite target of people and groups expressing anti-American and/or anti-globalization sentiments. One example of this occurred during August 1999, when a group of protesters led by a farmer destroyed a half-built McDonald's restaurant in Millau, France. The protest was against U.S. trade protectionism. McDonald's was also one of three multinational corporations (along with Starbucks Corporation and Nike, Inc.) whose outlets in Seattle were attacked in late 1999 by some of the more aggressive protesters against a World Trade Organization (WTO) meeting taking place there. In the early 2000s, McDonald's pulled out of several countries, including Bolivia and two Middle Eastern nations, at least in part because of the negative brand image in these regions.

Despite the introduction of a low-cost Dollar Menu, sales remained anemic during 2002. This situation forced Jim Cantalupo, a McDonald's veteran executive, out of retirement to become chairman and CEO at the beginning of 2003. Cantalupo started his tenure by announcing a major restructuring that involved the closing of approximately 700 restaurants (mostly in the United States and Japan), the elimination of 600 jobs, and charges of $853 million. The charges resulted in a fourth-quarter 2002 loss of $343.8 million. This was the first quarterly loss in McDonald's' 38 years as a public company. Cantalupo moved away from the company's traditional reliance on growth through the opening of new units to a focus on increasing sales from existing units. To that end, several new menu items were successfully launched, including entree salads, McGriddles breakfast sandwiches (which used pancakes in place of bread), and white meat Chicken McNuggets. Some stores began test-marketing fruits and vegetables as Happy Meal options. Shoring up the new products was the launch in September 2003 of an MTV-style advertising campaign featuring the new tag line, "I'm lovin' it." This was the first global campaign in McDonald's history, as the new slogan was to be used in advertising for more than 100 countries. It turned out to be the first truly successful ad campaign in years; sales began rebounding, boosted also by improvements in service. In December 2003, for instance, same-store sales increased 7.3%. Same-store sales rose 2.4% for the entire year after falling 2.1% in 2002. This was certainly an example of strategic initiatives being used to sustain financial performance.

Some other key strategic moves made by McDonald's during 2003 included focusing on its core hamburger business by downsizing its other ventures. For example, McDonald's sold some of its acquisitions and discontinued its development of non-McDonald's brands outside of the United States. This included

Boston Market outlets in Canada and Australia and Donatos units in Germany. McDonald's kept its minority investment in Pret A Manger, but McDonald's Japan was slated to close its Pret units there. These moves would enable McDonald's to focus on its efforts to enhance its international markets while reducing the non-hamburger brands in the United States to Chipotle and Boston Market, both of which were operating in the black.

McDonald's continued its strategy to curtail store openings in 2004 and to focus on building its core business at existing restaurants. In fact, it budgeted more than $1.5 billion for capital expenditures in 2004 to be used for remodeling existing restaurants. McDonald's also aimed to pay down its debt by $400 million, leaving a balance of $700 million, and to return approximately $1 billion to shareholders through dividends and share repurchases. Cantalupo also set several long-term goals such as sustaining annual system-wide sales and revenue growth rates of 3% to 5%. In a move to both simplify the menu and make its offerings less fattening, McDonald's announced in March 2004 that it would phase out Super Size French fries and soft drinks by the end of the year.

Each of the companies discussed in this chapter provided great examples of sustained financial performance and consistent and profitable growth. These companies were able to navigate themselves through the turbulent years of 1981 through 2005 and achieve their remarkable results. They well represent their peers, the other companies included in the Value Zone Hall of Fame (for the years 1981 through 2005). The next Value Zone element that we will examine is market growth and expansion. In the next chapter, we will learn about companies that were able to achieve remarkable growth on a global scale.

Chapter Eight
Continuous Expansion into New Markets

Market expansion is another core element of the Value Zone, and our research has shown example after example of companies that sustain consistently positive business results by paying constant attention to market expansion initiatives. In this chapter, we will look at a few examples of companies that have achieved remarkable results through market expansion. Perhaps there is no better example in this area than Wal-Mart. Up until last year, Wal-Mart enjoyed the distinction of being not only the largest retailer in the world, but also the largest company in the world in terms of revenue growth. So how did Wal-Mart do it? Let's take a look at this astounding company's history and see what we can learn.

Wal-Mart Stores, Inc.

As the 21st century was ushered in, the dynamics of the global marketplace changed drastically. One market area that experienced sensational growth was retail, and one of the companies that was rapidly expanding into emerging markets worldwide was Wal-Mart. Its founder Sam Walton dreamed that Wal-Mart would become the largest retailer in the world, but if he were still alive today, Mr. Walton would be astounded to see that his Arkansas-based retail chain had grown to become the largest company in the world for a short period. Only the combined revenues of Exxon-Mobil now eclipse Wal-Mart in revenues worldwide. Wal-Mart looks like a behemoth compared to its nearest competition, generating three times the revenues of the world's second-largest retailer, France's Carrefour SA. In the U.S. alone, for example, Wal-Mart has more than 1.2 million workers, making it the nation's largest single nongovernmental employer. Its U.S. operations include 1,478 Wal-Mart discount stores (located in all 50 states) and 1,471 Wal-Mart Supercenters, which are combined discount outlets and grocery stores, thus making Wal-Mart the country's top food retailer. Wal-Mart also owns 538 Sam's Clubs, the number-two U.S. warehouse membership club chain, trailing only Costco Wholesale Corporation. There are also 64 Wal-Mart Neighborhood Markets, which are smaller food and drug outlets that offer a variety of general merchandise.

If we peer into the company's international operations, we will see that Wal-Mart began expanding into global markets in 1991. This initial foray into international markets included Wal-Mart discount stores in Canada and Puerto Rico; Wal-Mart Supercenters in Argentina, Brazil, China, Germany, Mexico, Puerto Rico, South Korea, and the United Kingdom; and Sam's Clubs in Brazil, China, Mexico, and Puerto Rico. In Mexico, Wal-Mart also operated Bodegas discount stores, Suburbia's specialty department stores, Superamas supermarkets, and Vips restaurants. Furthermore, Wal-Mart runs Todo Dias supermarkets in Brazil, Neighborhood Markets supermarkets in China, ASDA combined grocery and apparel stores in the United Kingdom, and Amigo supermarkets in

Puerto Rico. Wal-Mart has a 36% stake in The Seiyu, Ltd., a leading Japanese retailer. Overall, more than 25% of Wal-Mart's stores are located outside the United States, and international operations generate about 18.5% of total revenues. So let's learn how this remarkable achievement was reached.

It all started back in the late 1940s with a young college graduate who served in the Armed Forces during WWII. Sam Walton had earned a degree in economics and was a management trainee with the J.C. Penney Company before he served in the military. Upon his return to civilian life, he chose to use his savings and a loan to open a Ben Franklin variety store in Newport, Arkansas. By the late 1950s, Sam and his brother J.L. (Bud) Walton owned nine Ben Franklin franchises.

It was during the early 1960s that Sam Walton took what he had learned from studying mass-merchandising techniques around the country to make a mark in the retail market. Sam Walton's key strategic initiative to promote market expansion was to target small-town populations. He believed that these towns would welcome large discount shopping stores and that these stores would in turn become quite profitable. Sam's concept was simple: slash prices and sell large volumes. He approached the Ben Franklin franchise owners with his proposal, but they were not willing to let him reduce merchandise as low as he insisted it had to go. The Walton brothers thus made the decision to go into that market themselves and opened their first Wal-Mart Discount City in Rogers, Arkansas in 1962. In those days, the Waltons generally opened their department-sized stores in towns with populations of 5,000 to 25,000, and the stores tended to draw customers from a large radius. "We discovered people would drive to a good concept," Walton later stated in a 1989 article in *Financial World*.

Walton's "good concept" involved large stores that offered customers a wide variety of name-brand goods at deep discounts. This was part of an "everyday low prices" strategy. Walton was able to keep prices low and still turn a profit using sales volume and a very low-key and unique marketing strategy. Wal-Mart's advertising costs generally amounted to one-third that of other discount chains; while most competitors were putting on sales and running 50 to 100 advertising circulars per year, Sam Walton kept his company's prices low and ran only 12 promotions a year.

By the beginning of the 1970s, the Walton brothers had opened 18 Wal-Mart stores in addition to their 15 Ben Franklin franchises throughout Arkansas, Missouri, Kansas, and Oklahoma. These ventures became incorporated as Wal-Mart Stores, Inc., in October 1969. Because expansion was one of Walton's key drivers, Wal-Mart expanded rapidly. To drive this growth, Walton implemented a warehouse distribution strategy. Walton built his own warehouses so he could buy in volume and store the merchandise, and he then proceeded to build stores throughout 200-square-mile areas around the distribution points. This "best practices" strategic initiative reduced Wal-Mart's costs and provided more control over operations. This approach meant that merchandise could be restocked as quickly as it sold, and advertising was specific to smaller regions and cost less to distribute—very brilliant.

In 1970, Wal-Mart went public, and in 1972, the company was listed on the New York Stock Exchange. By the mid-1970s, Walton had phased out his Ben Franklin stores so that the company could put all of its expansion efforts into the Wal-Mart stores. A new strategic approach to help speed up expansion was acquisitions. In 1977, Wal-Mart made its first significant acquisition, buying 16 Mohr-Value stores in Missouri and Illinois. Also in 1977, based on data from the previous five years, *Forbes* ranked Wal-Mart first among the nation's discount and variety stores in return on equity, return on capital, sales growth, and earnings growth. By 1979, there were 276 Wal-Mart stores in 11 states. Sales had gone from $44 million in 1970 to $1.25 billion in 1979. Wal-Mart distinguished itself by reaching the $1 billion mark faster than any other retail company.

Wal-Mart's sales growth continued into the 1980s, and it opened its first three Sam's Wholesale Clubs in 1983. During this time, it also began to expand into the big-city markets. Business at the 100,000-square-foot cash-and-carry discount membership warehouses yielded very positive business results, so by 1991, Wal-Mart owned 141 clubs and changed their name to Sam's Clubs.

During 1987, Wal-Mart acquired 18 Supersaver Wholesale Clubs, which were converted to Sam's Clubs. However, a more significant event during that year was the launch of a new Wal-Mart merchandising concept: a center that combined a grocery store, a general merchandise market, and a variety of service outlets like restaurants, banks, shoe shine kiosks, and videotape rental units in a space that covered an area larger than six football fields. As part of this concept, prices were reduced as much as 40% below full retail level and sales volume averaged $1 million per week (sales volume average was $200,000 for a conventional-sized discount store). Walton called these stores Hypermarts.

The key to making these large stores successful was to make customers feel at home in such a large-scale shopping facility, a task that required inventiveness. One example of how this was done was seen in the Dallas store, where phone hotlines were installed in the aisles for customers who needed directions. Furthermore, Hypermart floors were made of a rubbery surface for ease in walking, and the stores offered electric shopping carts for the handicapped. To entertain children, there was a "ball pit" or playroom filled with plastic balls, an idea the company got from Swedish furniture retailer Ikea.

However, there were some speed bumps along the way, including the problem of air conditioning and heating these gigantic spaces and dealing with the higher-than-expected traffic congestion and limited parking. Customers were complaining about the grocery section and stating that it was not as well stocked or maintained as it should be in order to compete against nearby grocery stores. Wal-Mart began addressing these problems by redesigning the grocery section of these stores. During 1988, Wal-Mart continued its expansion, opening five smaller "Supercenters" that averaged around 150,000 square feet. These Supercenters featured a large selection of merchandise and offered well-stocked grocery sections without the outside services such as restaurants or video stores. This store format proved much more successful than the Hypermart format, which was eventually abandoned. Hundreds of Supercenters were subsequently opened during the 1990s.

Suppliers, and especially the suppliers' sales representatives, did not like Wal-Mart's buying practices. Wal-Mart was known for controlling its suppliers, a practice which resulted in a public information campaign staged by 100,000 independent manufacturers' representatives making the assertion that their elimination jeopardized a manufacturer's right to choose how it sells its products. But despite this effort, Wal-Mart's revenues kept growing; the company achieved 12 consecutive years of 35% annual profit growth from 1975 through 1987. By 1988, Wal-Mart had 1,182 stores, 90 wholesale clubs, and two Hypermarts in 24 states concentrated in the Midwest and the South. During this time, David D. Glass emerged as a key reason for Wal-Mart's growth and was named president and CEO in 1988.

To improve its supply-chain relationships, Wal-Mart sent an open letter to U.S. manufacturers in March 1985 inviting them to take part in a "Buy American" program. Wal-Mart offered to work with its suppliers to produce products that could compete against imports. In April 1988, Sam Walton made the following statement: "Our American suppliers must commit to improving their facilities and machinery, remain financially conservative and work to fill our requirements, and most importantly, strive to improve employee productivity."

During weekly management meetings, Wal-Mart agenda items included product conversions and making arrangements to buy competitively priced U.S.-made goods in place of imports. According to one Wal-Mart executive, Wal-Mart cut imports by approximately 5% between 1985 and 1989. However, business analysts still estimated that Wal-Mart bought approximately 25% to 30% of its goods from global suppliers.

Another sore spot for Wal-Mart executives was the criticism about Wal-Mart's impact on small-town America during the 1990s. The bottom line was that independent store owners were often driven out of business when Wal-Mart came to town because they were unable to compete with the superstore's economies of scale. Interestingly enough, Iowa State University economist Kenneth Stone conducted a study on this phenomenon and made the following commentary in the April 2, 1989 issue of *New York Times Magazine*: "If you go into towns in Illinois where Wal-Mart has been for 8 or 10 years, the downtowns are just ghost towns." He found that businesses suffering the most were drug, hardware, five-and-dime, sporting goods, clothing, and fabric stores. Major appliance and furniture businesses continued to grow along with restaurants and gasoline stations, which grew because of increased traffic.

Meanwhile, Wal-Mart began to create a record of community service. For example, Wal-Mart began awarding scholarships to high school students in each community in which Wal-Mart had a presence. During 1990, Wal-Mart became the number-one retailer in the United States, passing both Sears, Roebuck and Co. and Kmart. Meanwhile, stores were added in California, Nevada, North Dakota, Pennsylvania, South Dakota, and Utah. Late in 1990, Wal-Mart acquired the Temple, Texas-based McLane Company, Inc., a distributor of grocery and retail products, for about $275 million. Wal-Mart also opened twenty-five Sam's Clubs, four of which were 130,000-square-foot prototypes incorporating space for produce, meats, and baked goods. During the mid-1990s, the company continued its aggressive expansion campaign, acquiring Western Merchandise, Inc., of Amarillo, Texas, a supplier of music, books, and video products to many of the Wal-Mart stores. Still another example of Wal-Mart's ambitious expansion efforts occurred early in 1991. In a $162 million transaction, The Wholesale Club, Inc. of Indianapolis merged with Sam's Clubs, adding 28 stores that were to be integrated with Sam's by the year's end.

Wal-Mart's expansion efforts continued, and by 1992, the company opened about 150 new Wal-Mart stores and 60 Sam's Clubs, bringing the total to 1,720 Wal-Mart stores and 208 Sam's Clubs. Some of these stores represented a strategic change in expansion target regions because they opened near big cities with large populations. The company instituted another important policy change when it publicly announced that it would no longer deal with independent sales representatives.

In 1991, for the first time in the company's history, Wal-Mart ventured outside the United States, entering into a joint venture with Cifra, S.A. de C.V., Mexico's largest retailer. The venture developed a price-club store called Club Aurrera that required an annual membership of about $25. Shoppers had a choice of over 3,500 products to buy. Within one year, the joint venture operated three Club Aurreras, four Bodegas discount stores, and one Aurrera combination store. Meanwhile, expansion in the United States was still on the rise; 161 new Wal-Mart stores opened between 1992 and 1993. Another 48 Sam's Clubs and 51 Bud's Warehouse Outlets also opened. By 1993, Wal-mart's 2,138 stores included 34 Wal-Mart Super Centers and 256 Sam's Clubs.

Wal-Mart founder Sam Walton passed away on April 5, 1992. However, there was a smooth transition of leadership through well-conceived succession planning on the part of Mr. Walton. He had already handpicked his successor, David Glass, who had served as CEO since 1988; and S. Robson Walton, his eldest son, was named chairman of the board.

Without any warning, the Wal-Mart brand was tarnished during January 1993 when NBC-TV's *Dateline* news program reported on child laborers in Bangladesh who produced merchandise for Wal-Mart stores. The program showed children working for five cents an hour in a country that lacked child labor laws. The program further alleged that items made outside the United States were being sold under "Made in USA" signs as part of Wal-Mart's "Buy American" campaign. David Glass appeared on the program and said that he did not know of any "child exploitation" by his company, but he did apologize about some of the signs incorrectly promoting foreign-made products as domestic items.

During 1993, Wal-Mart launched another private label called "Great Value." The label was initially used for a line of 350 packaged food items for sale in its Supercenters. The proceeds from the company's other private label, Sam's American Choice, were to be channeled into the Competitive Edge Scholarship Fund, which Wal-Mart launched in 1993. Also during that year, Wal-Mart spent $830.5 million to purchase 91 Pace Membership Warehouse clubs from Kmart, which had decided to shut down the Pace chain. Wal-Mart subsequently converted the new units into Sam's Clubs. The Sam's Club chain was thereby bolstered, especially in California, where it opened 21 new stores. The financial performance for 1993 was solid; Wal-Mart posted profits of $2.33 billion on revenues of $67.34 billion. The company workforce now exceeded half a million people.

In the mid-1990s, Wal-Mart continued to grow in the United States, but less rapidly. The company had always posted double-digit, comparable-store sales increases, but starting in fiscal 1994, these sales increases had fallen to levels closer to the retail industry average, which was roughly between 4% and 7%. Furthermore, overall net sales had typically risen 25% or more per year in the 1980s and early 1990s. For fiscal years 1996, 1997, and 1998, however, net sales increased 13%, 12%, and 12%, respectively. Wal-Mart appeared to be reaching the limits of expansion in the U.S. market. This was reflected in Wal-Mart's decision to scale back its discount store chain, which reached a peak of 1,995 units in 1996 before being reduced to 1,921 units by 1998. Wal-Mart staked its domestic future on expanding from 34 units in 1993 to 441 units in 1998. Most of the new Supercenters, some 377 in total, were converted Wal-Mart discount stores, converted because the company sought the additional per-store revenue that could be gained by selling groceries. Meanwhile, the Sam's Club chain was struggling and was not as profitable as the company overall. As it attempted to turn this unit around, Wal-Mart curtailed its expansion in the United States; there were only 17 more Sam's Clubs in 1998 than there were in 1995.

In an effort to leverage another avenue for expansion, Wal-Mart entered into another NAFTA market in 1994 when it purchased 122 stores in Canada from Woolworth Corporation in a $335 million deal. During the next few years, Wal-Mart entered Argentina, Brazil, and China through joint ventures. Furthermore, during 1997, Wal-Mart set up several joint ventures with its Mexican partner, Cifra. That same year, these joint ventures were merged together and then merged into Cifra. Wal-Mart then took a controlling, 51% stake in Cifra for $1.2 billion. The company thus held a majority stake in the largest retailer in Mexico, whose 402 stores included 27 Wal-Mart Supercenters, 28 Sam's Clubs, and 347 units consisting of several chains, including Bodegas discount stores, Superamas grocery stores, and Vips restaurants.

In December 1997, Wal-Mart made a major foray into Europe for the first time when it acquired the 21-unit Wertkauf hypermarket chain in Germany for an estimated $880 million. The Wertkauf format was similar to that of the Wal-Mart Supercenter. The profitable Wertkauf chain had annual sales of about $1.4 billion and was the eighth-largest hypermarket operator in Germany. Also during December 1997, Wal-Mart bought out the minority partner in its Brazilian joint venture, which by that time ran five Wal-Mart Supercenters and three Sam's Clubs. By early 1998, the company also operated nine Wal-Mart Supercenters and five Sam's Clubs in Puerto Rico. Later that same year, Wal-Mart announced plans to triple its retail base in China by the end of 1999, aiming for a total of nine stores. Moreover, in July 1998, the company announced that it had purchased a majority stake in four stores and six additional development sites in Korea, thereby extending its expansion in Asia. Around this same time, however, Wal-Mart's expansion into the troubled nation of Indonesia under a franchise agreement failed.

During fiscal 1997, Wal-Mart's international operations were profitable for the first time, and in 1998, international sales had reached $7.5 billion. This was very impressive because Wal-Mart had begun its foreign expansion only in 1991. However, this figure represented just 6.4% of overall sales. Although growth in sales at home was slowing down, Wal-Mart managed to exceed the $100 billion mark in overall revenues for the first time during fiscal 1997, and the company also gained further prestige that year when it was selected to be one of the 30 companies on the Dow Jones Industrial Average. (It was a replacement for Woolworth's, which was in a terrible tailspin.) At the same time, Wal-Mart became the largest nongovernmental employer in the United States, with 680,000 domestic workers.

In late 1998, Wal-Mart began testing a new format, the Wal-Mart Neighborhood Market, as another possible way to strengthen its number-one position in retailing in the United States and increase sales as it neared the saturation point for its Supercenters. In an attempt to compete directly with traditional supermarkets and convenience stores, Wal-Mart introduced this new concept that included a 40,000-square-foot store offering produce, deli foods, fresh meats, other grocery items, and a limited selection of general merchandise. The new store also featured a drive-through pharmacy. Company executives hoped that the Neighborhood Market would allow Wal-Mart to penetrate markets unable to support the huge 100,000-square-foot Supercenters, such as very small towns and certain sections within metropolitan areas.

Another major milestone for Wal-Mart occurred in 1999, when Wal-Mart became the world's largest retailer (and the largest nongovernmental employer in the world, with 1.14 million employees). It was also the leading retailer in both Mexico and Canada. However, Europe was at the forefront of the corporation's international expansion during the late 1990s. In December 1998, Wal-Mart strengthened its German operations through the acquisition of 74 Interspar hypermarkets from SPAR Handels AG. In July 1999, Wal-Mart entered the U.K. market for the first time by acquiring ASDA Group PLC for about $10.8 billion. ASDA was the third-largest supermarket operator in the U.K., operating 229 stores at the time of its acquisition and generating approximately $13.2 billion in annual revenues. These stores were run in a similar way as that of the Wal-Mart Supercenters, with large-format units offering food, apparel, and general merchandise at everyday low prices; an emphasis on private-label brands; and an avoidance of promotions. The stores acquired in the United Kingdom continued to use the ASDA name, whereas the German units were eventually rebadged as Wal-Mart Supercenters.

In January 2000, H. Lee Scott, Jr., a 20-year company veteran, was promoted from chief operating officer to president and CEO, succeeding Glass, who remained on the board of directors as chairman of the executive committee. Scott had played an important role in reversing the declining results of Wal-Mart's domestic operations. One important turnaround point was the adoption of a more aggressive approach to controlling excessive inventories at the stores and warehouses. Leveraging technology led both to significant decreases in inventory levels and to improved performance in keeping store shelves well stocked. Also during 2000, Wal-Mart spent $587 million to purchase another 6% of Cifra, which was subsequently renamed Wal-Mart de México S.A. de C.V. Wal-Mart had a stake of approximately 62% in this subsidiary.

Another interesting milestone for Wal-Mart occurred during 2001 when its grocery sales reached $56 billion, making it the largest food retailer in the United States. This milestone was reached mainly through the aggressive rollout of the Wal-Mart Supercenter formats. By early 2002, there were about 1,050 Supercenters in the United States, while the number of Wal-Mart discount stores had declined to fewer than 1,650. In fiscal 2002 alone, 178 Supercenters were opened, and there was a net reduction in discount units of 89, with 121 being converted to Supercenters. Also during this time, the Wal-Mart Neighborhood Markets format grew to include 31 stores, providing a further base for the ever-rising grocery revenue.

In spite of the problems it encountered penetrating the very difficult German retail market, Wal-Mart was relentless in its international market expansion efforts. For example, the first Wal-Mart Supercenter in Puerto Rico opened for business in 2001. The company then paid approximately $242 million for Supermercados Amigo, Inc., the leading supermarket chain in Puerto Rico, which had 37 outlets in December 2002. Wal-Mart had Japan next on its market expansion radar screen. During May 2002, Wal-Mart acquired a 6.1% interest in The Seiyu, Ltd. for about $51 million. Seiyu operated about 400 stores in Japan; it had various formats, but they were mainly of the food-and-clothing variety. Seiyu was Japan's fifth-largest supermarket chain. In December 2002, Wal-Mart invested another $459 million to expand its stake in Seiyu to 35%, with rights to increase it to nearly 67% by 2007. By 2003, Wal-Mart had more than 330,000 workers outside the United States, and its international operations rang up $40.7 billion in sales that year, representing a solid 15% increase over the preceding year. International operating profits for 2003 catapulted almost 56%, hitting $2.03 billion. In an effort to focus solely on retailing, Wal-Mart sold its McLane wholesale distribution subsidiary to Berkshire Hathaway Inc. for $1.5 billion in May 2003.

Wal-Mart achieved something quite remarkable during fiscal 2003. With revenues reported at $244.52 billion, Wal-Mart Stores, Inc. became the world's largest corporation. Wow! Sam Walton would be amazed and no doubt very proud. What an astounding accomplishment. The fact that Wal-Mart became the first non-manufacturing company to top the Fortune 500 was fitting, as the company increasingly had become an icon of both the good and bad aspects of the

U.S. economy during the early part of the 21st century. In an October 6, 2003 article titled "Is Wal-Mart Too Powerful?," *Business Week* suggested a number of ways in which to view the power of Wal-Mart, such as:

- its aim to drive costs and prices down, thus influencing in part the low rate of inflation in the late 20th and early 21st centuries;
- its cost-cutting focus, also an important factor in the shifting of factories outside the United States;
- and its 2002 imports from China of $12 billion, representing 10% of total U.S. imports from that country.

Another consideration was Wal-Mart's hard line on labor costs and its vigorous resistance of efforts to unionize its workforce. Two consequences of this were its extraordinarily high turnover rate of 44% per year for its hourly workers and the fact that in 2001, the average Wal-Mart sales clerk made less than the federal government poverty income level. Offering a somewhat different perspective related to the power of Wal-Mart, *Fortune* magazine in a March 3, 2003 issue estimated that the company's share of the U.S. Gross National Product (GNP) in 2002 was 2.3%. This approached the levels reached by General Motors Corporation (3% in 1955) and U.S. Steel Corp. (2.8% in 1917) when those firms were at their respective peaks. *Fortune* estimated that Wal-Mart's share of the nation's economy would become its biggest ever by around 2006, assuming that its current growth rate was sustainable.

Sustaining outstanding performance is not easy, and Wal-Mart had some major challenges during the mid-2000s. For one thing, it was under relentless criticism about its business practices. To counter this, Wal-Mart launched a public relations campaign. Wal-mart was also faced with a number of potentially damaging lawsuits, including a host of class-action lawsuits involving claims that employees were asked to work off the books and not to take scheduled breaks. In another case, 1.5 million current and former female employees accused Wal-Mart of engaging in a pattern of discrimination against women in pay and promotion as part of a sex discrimination lawsuit. To add to all of this, a federal investigation was launched during the fall of 2003 into Wal-Mart's use of a cleaning contractor that employed illegal immigrants.

Despite its legal and image troubles, Wal-Mart continued to expand its markets. For example, during 2004, the company planned to open at least 220 new Supercenters, and its discount stores were reduced by approximately 90 units. What this meant was that for the first time in its history, Wal-Mart would have more Supercenters than Wal-Mart discount stores in the United States. Meanwhile, the Neighborhood Market chain was scheduled to grow by 25 to 30 units, and Sam's Club would add about 15 stores. The international store count would likewise increase by about 100 units. It seems clear that Wal-Mart intends to become the largest retailer of all time.

Family Dollar Store

Quite amazingly, while Wal-Mart was expanding its markets at a record-breaking pace, Family Dollar also continued to thrive through the early 1980s. Furthermore, Family Dollar had a nine-year run of earning remarkable profits. Between 1982 and 1987, Family Dollar opened more than 100 new stores a year. Apparently, however, company executives were not keeping their eyes on the ball and failed to recognize the enormous threat posed by Wal-Mart. Without warning, sales growth in recently-opened stores began slipping from 9% in 1984 to a dull 2% in 1985. Growth then came to a screeching halt in 1986 and dropped 10% in 1987.

So what happened? Well, to begin with, Family Dollar shoppers were and had always been families that made less than $25,000 a year. Most stores were built in rural areas, usually in small towns with populations of less than 15,000, and the stores were typically within walking distance or a very short drive from customers' homes. The average Family Dollar customer shopped there at least once a week and spent approximately $8 on average. Family Dollar stores were about one-tenth the size of a Wal-Mart or Kmart. This meant that product lines had to be carefully managed. Despite the fact that the bigger stores could offer more merchandise, the draw of Family Dollar stores was frequently location. Wal-Mart stores were typically planted outside or on the edge of town, while Family Dollar stores were downtown. During this time, Family Dollar business leaders were preoccupied with expansion and had stopped checking on the competition's pricing. When sales slipped enough to get their attention, Family Dollar executives learned that Wal-Mart was pricing its products as much as 10% below Family Dollar. Wal-Mart was typically cutting prices on such things as health and beauty products that Family Dollar was advertising as on sale.

To stop the bleeding that began in 1987, Family Dollar instituted a new pricing policy: simply put, they flat-out would not be undersold. Within two months, same-store sales rose by 10%. While the lower prices would mean slimmer margins, Family Dollar compensated by scaling back expansion. At the time, the chain had been expanding as far north as Michigan, as far west as Texas, and even right into Sam Walton's Wal-Mart territory. In 1986, there were 1,107 Family Dollar stores in 23 states. Meanwhile, Wal-Marts were invading Family Dollar's key territory, the rural Southeast. To sustain its performance, Wal-Mart was using its buying power to drive prices down, while Family Dollar countered by using its profits to open more stores.

In the midst of the challenges posed by Wal-Mart, Family Dollar faced another problem: a management shakeup. In the mid-1980s, Leon Levine was the company's chairman and chief executive; Leon's first cousin, Lewis E. Levine, served as president and chief operating officer; and Leon's son Howard Levine was senior vice-president of merchandising. Around September 1987, as Family Dollar reported its fourth consecutive quarter of lower earnings, Lewis Levine abruptly resigned, and Howard Levine also left. Lewis had been with the company for 17 years and was reportedly upset by salary differentials (CEO Leon Levine made an estimated $1.84 million in 1986, while Lewis made slightly more than $260,040). Leon and Lewis also disagreed on strategy, as Lewis felt that Leon was not making the changes necessary to compete more effectively against Wal-Mart. The bottom line was as simple as this: Lewis desired more control, which resulted in the board asking for Lewis' resignation. Leon served as president until a successor was named, capping his own salary at $350,000 for 1987 and 1988. Leon's son and the heir apparent, Howard Levine, left the company for what seemed to be more personal reasons.

With the battle lines clearly drawn, the war with Wal-Mart got hot. Family Dollar's new "everyday low price" strategy was still hard on the margins. During 1987, Family Dollar was spending $2 million to renovate its 1,272 stores and make the most of their compact size. Notably, when Family Dollar first began matching or beating Wal-Mart on prices for items like health and beauty aids and automotive supplies, same-store sales rose 9% for a few months but then fell back to the levels of the year prior. Family Dollar executives felt that they had two huge strategic advantages: 1) They could squeeze into urban store spaces without the fear of a large Wal-Mart moving in next door; and 2) Family Dollar was still debt-free.

Leon Levine appointed Ralph Dillon as the new president and CEO of Family Dollar in 1987. Dillon was formerly the head of Coast American Corporation, a Denver retail franchise. Family Dollar now had a new leader at its helm and rising sales resulting from the new store expansions. However, the profits were flat. Dillon's solution for this problem was simple; he went back to the basic reason for Family Dollar's original success, its low pricing practices. Strategically, the company continued its aggressive markdowns, and a policy was instituted that required any item tagged at more than $15 to be approved by top management.

To improve its margins, Family Dollar started stocking more of its generic label products, as well as manufacturer's overruns and closeouts. (These former "best practices" had been scaled back in the 1980s when Family Dollar had tried to upscale its merchandise.) The company also began stocking irregular brand-name goods like jeans and sweaters that were slightly flawed. Other high-margin goods, such as seasonal candies and costume jewelry, were also pushed. These strategies dovetailed with an advertising campaign that stressed the chain's return to "everyday low prices," and Family Dollar executives felt confident of a comeback. Although these cuts would hurt the company's overall margin for a few years, Family Dollar executives believed that, due to Family Dollar's healthy cash flow and minimal debt, the company could ride out the recession and get through these difficult times.

Indeed, despite the tough economic climate of the late 1980s, Family Dollar rode out the turbulent times and began to thrive again. In fact, executives reported another record year in 1991. Same-store sales were up, overall sales exceeded the $1 billion mark for the first time, and revenues increased 18% in 1992 alone. Also in that same year, Family Dollar opened 150 new stores. Most of them were in New England, where existing store sales were above average. By the end of 1992, Family Dollar had opened 175 new stores and closed 25.

Meanwhile, Family Dollar Store executives were now focused on improving gross margins. They launched a new point-of-sale (POS) system that provided detailed information on the apparel styles, colors, and sizes that were selling well in each store. The POS system also helped stores track their competition on a region-by-region basis in specific product lines. Also at this time, Peter Hayes was named the new president for Family Dollar.

In 1992, Wal-Mart had captured 26% of the discount store market and forced many smaller discounters into bankruptcy. However, Family Dollar survived by concentrating on its core strengths of convenience, solid stock, and low prices. Family Dollar stores were generally within three miles of consumer's homes and were about one-tenth the size of Wal-Mart stores. Moreover, because Family Dollar stocks were smaller per store, the prices of basic items such as toothpaste and laundry detergent at Family Dollar were often slightly more than those at Wal-Mart. Despite this, many customers were willing to pay slightly higher prices in exchange for a convenient location and easy in-store maneuverability. Family Dollar had faced the superstore threat head-on and was posting a better net margin than Wal-Mart by 1992.

In the mid-1990s, apparel accounted for approximately 0.5% of the Family Dollar inventory, while "hard" goods made up the remainder. Family Dollar aggressively searched for merchandise, taking advantage of downtime in factories and contracting them to manufacture merchandise at cut rates during slow periods. Roughly 10% of Family Dollar's business was from private-label sales, and most store merchandise was priced lower than $18. Family Dollar also enhanced its distribution system, adding a building in Memphis, Arkansas of more than 550,000 square feet, which totaled approximately 1.3 million square feet of space when combined with the North Carolina center. Both centers were fully automated.

In 1994, having recaptured their company's sales strength, Family Dollar executives fine-tuned their strategy, which was to center Family Dollar as a neighborhood convenience store with low prices. They also began to eliminate low-margin items like tools, paints, and motor oils and replace them with more popular, higher-priced items like toys and portable stereos. Family Dollar's pricing policy now allowed for items up to $25. Executives also stayed focused on expansion, another key strategic area; thus, it was not surprising to see them add another 165 new units in both 1993 and 1994. One major external economic factor helping them to successfully expand was the rash of bankruptcies among regional discount chains.

In the spring of 1994, Hayes resigned as president and chief operating officer of Family Dollar and was replaced by John Reier, who had been with the company since 1987 as senior vice-president in charge of Family Dollar's merchandising and advertising. Leon Levine remained board chair and CEO. Given the highly competitive nature of the industry, Family Dollar sales and profits failed to meet expectations in 1994. However, Levine remained optimistic in the 1994 annual report, noting that the company would continue its aggressive expansion plans and price reductions.

The major focus for Family Dollar continued to be store growth throughout the late 1990s. Howard Levine returned to the company in 1996 and became president in 1997. He led Family Dollar toward aggressive expansion efforts, and as a result, the company opened its 3,000th location in 1998. Family Dollar next began to focus on the western U.S., moving into Arizona in March 1999. One *Discount Store News* article reported, "Family Dollar stores have been opening at a steady, methodical pace in recent years, quietly cropping up in cities and rural towns across the country." Family Dollar's aggressive growth and sound financial results were quite remarkable, making it a formidable competitor.

Due to increased demand for its products, Family Dollar opened one new distribution center in Virginia in 1998 and an additional center in Oklahoma in 1999. In 1999, Family Dollar celebrated its 40th anniversary by posting record sales and profits.

Family Dollar entered the 21st century with an excellent record of growth and financial performance. It now focused strategically on putting additional brand names on its shelves and cutting back on its apparel line. Apparel was now only 15% of its product mix. Also in the new millennium, it hit another huge milestone, breaking the $3 billion mark in sales. By 2001, the 4,000th Family Dollar store had opened its doors. Family Dollar's success caught the attention of industry observers, and in 2002, the firm was included in the Fortune 500 list.

Family Dollar's successful business strategy was paying huge dividends. By fiscal 2003, the Family Dollar had achieved 30 consecutive quarters of record sales and earnings. Now that is sustaining value and getting remarkable business results! During this time, Howard Levine, who was named CEO in 1998, took on the additional role of chairman in 2003. Under his leadership, Family Dollar continued its growth streak, expanding to its 5,000th store on August 28, 2003, in Jacksonville, Florida.

During 2004, Family Dollar continued its aggressive expansion efforts, opening more than five hundred new stores and eight new distribution centers. Its focus also remained on strengthening its supply chain, improving the quality of its product offerings, and bolstering its brand-name product line. Although this company had indeed come a long way from its start in 1959, the company's leaders sustained growth and excellent financial results expansion each year. Levine firmly believed in Family Dollar's ability to succeed in the future, a belief which was evident in the theme of the company's 2003 annual report— "We've still got a long way to grow!"

Both Wal-Mart and Family Dollar competed with each other and, despite fierce competition, both have been able to excel in the Value Zone through their expansion strategies, thereby achieving remarkable business results and consistent outstanding financial performances. In both cases, these companies were also innovators that leveraged technology to help them reach solid business outcomes. Innovation is imperative for a business's survival in the 21st century. We will learn why in the next chapter.

Chapter Nine
Creative and Imaginative Innovation

There have been many mass extinctions throughout the history of our Earth. There is little doubt that the single most famous extinction is that of the dinosaurs, whose reign on the Earth ended 65 million years ago. Their fossils only represent a remnant of what they were. Scientists believe that fossil fuels were formed from prehistoric plants and animals that lived hundreds of millions of years ago.

Let's relate this to the times when corporate dinosaurs like US Steel, Bethlehem Steel, RCA, Eastern Airlines, and TWA once dominated the business world. Yet all of these corporation giants are no longer relevant in our business world today. Their extinction is both puzzling and troublesome. Why are they either extinct or facing extinction? What led to their downfall? Simply put, they failed to innovate!

Current reports show that operating profits for Toyota are at about $2000 per vehicle, while GM reports $18 per vehicle and Ford reports $200 per vehicle. This gap has resulted in GM and Ford losing significant market share while engaged in mass restructuring, including plant closings and the layoff of thousands of employees. Meanwhile, Toyota is expanding and in fact has reportedly reached a worldwide market share of 10%. Toyota executives recently reported that their goal is now to achieve a 15% worldwide market share, which would make them the number-one automaker in the world. You have to ask, "WHY?" Both GM and Ford were innovators during the most of the 20th century. Why did they stop? Why did they become so complacent and unwilling to be creative, innovative, and daring?

Recent business history strongly suggests that the failure to innovate led the U.S. steel and electronics industry to become virtually extinct, and now it is happening again in the automotive industry. The message is quite clear: "INNOVATE OR BECOME EXTINCT." That is, large corporate conglomerates that do not create a culture of creativity, imagination, entrepreneurial spirit, risk-taking, and vision face certain extinction. Thus, they are destined like their predecessors to become extinct and eventually to become fossil fuel, mere remnants of what they were.

"Ready or not," we have entered the dawn of a new age: the Age of Innovation, which contains a plethora of new challenges. New technologies, global warming, natural disasters caused by unexpected and unusual weather patterns, globalization, terrorism, unstable economies, skyrocketing energy costs, healthcare crises in country after country, depletion of natural resources, exponential population growth, and much, much more have catapulted our world into an age of unprecedented change. As our world rapidly accelerates through the 21st century, we are witnessing the birth of a new age. As we peer outside our time capsule called Earth as it hurtles through space, we are beginning to experience the emergence of the Innovation Age. This new age of innovation emerges from the enormous creative explosion of its predecessor the Information Age. Yes, boundless knowledge has unleashed innovation with unlimited opportunities. The choice is clear for all types of enterprises, whether they are businesses, governmental organizations, healthcare providers, or educational institutions: INNOVATE OR FACE EXTINCTION! Yes, today more than ever before, public and private sector executives must recognize the very sobering reality that if their enterprises are to going survive during the 21st century, they must become innovators. They have to find new and, more importantly, innovative ways to add more value for their customers, investors, and organizations.

This means a clear recognition that business as usual will "not cut it" any more. Resources will have to be reallocated towards creativity, imagination, and risk-taking, something foreign to many Industrial Age enterprises. It is imperative that senior leaders and their teams dedicate key resources to relearning, rethinking, imagining, and creating nascent products and services. This means that leaders must invest in strategic innovative initiatives and, more importantly, work hard at creating a culture in their organizations that rewards creativity and encourages thoughtful risk-taking. It means that large enterprises may have to radically transform their cultures into ones that function in a boundless world of creative imagination and entrepreneurship. A good example of this is Disney's Circle of Creativity innovation model. It consists of three phases: the dreamer, the realist, and finally, the critic. The dreamer uses imagination to come up with new ideas and is an integral part of the planning process. The realist develops the detailed plan that is required to execute the innovative ideas. The critic plays "devil's advocate" and discovers what's wrong with the innovation, its execution plan, and the customer value proposition. Some excellent examples of this process in action are innovations by Apple Computers and Progressive Insurance.

Consider, for example, Apple's introduction of something radically different from its personal computer lines—namely, the iPod technology, the new frontier of innovation in digitized portable music. This kind of thinking is a perfect example of "outside the box" thinking and creative imagination with its associated risks. The bottom line is that it is working, and iPod sales are "off the charts." To stay way ahead on the innovation curve, new iPods are able to download both radio and television programs as well as movies.

Progressive Insurance also leveraged radical innovation in its claims adjustment business model by sending its claims adjusters to accident scenes in mobile offices. In many cases, adjusters have arrived within minutes after the accident occurred. The bottom line is that Progressive's business increased by a factor of four. Fraudulent cases were drastically reduced, and customer satisfaction ratings improved dramatically.

In both of these cases, there was risk, yet a culture that is innovative accepts risk as a fact of life and not as an impediment to creative imagination. The late Peter Drucker pointed out that innovators "create new and different values and new and different satisfactions..." and engage in "the purposeful and organized search for changes...the opportunities such changes might offer for economic or social innovation." This type of business model leads to innovative ways of reaching out for new opportunities. In the cases of both Apple and Progressive Insurance, their innovative business models did not require decades of dedicated research and development investments. The radical innovation in both of these cases had to do with creating new value for customers. This in turn created new value and growth opportunities for both of these companies. The two examples that we have just discussed clearly illustrate that while innovation is a management dilemma for many companies, the business leaders at Apple and Progressive Insurance understood that they needed to address their core cultures and radically adopt a commitment to disruptive technology growth through radical innovation. These companies are innovators and will not face extinction. What about your organization? What is in your company's future? INNOVATE OR FACE EXTINCTION; the choice is yours. For this reason, innovation is a critical and core element of the Value Zone.

Our research has shown example after example of companies that sustain consistently positive business results by being innovative, as shown in the previous examples. In this chapter we will look at some examples of companies that have achieved remarkable growth through innovation. Two Value Zone Hall of Fame companies we have researched that have proven to be innovative companies are Walgreen and Comcast. Let's explore why and how these companies are innovators.

Walgreen Corporation

Walgreen is currently the largest drugstore chain in the United States in terms of revenues; more than 60% of its revenues result from retail prescriptions. Amazingly, Walgreen reported that it filled 400 million prescriptions in 2003, a figure which represents about 13% of all retail prescriptions in the U.S. Walgreen currently operates more than 4,400 drugstores in 44 states and Puerto Rico. About 80% of these drugstores are freestanding locations, and at least 75% have drive-through pharmacies. Also, almost 50% of these outlets offer one-hour photofinishing. Walgreen also runs Walgreen's Health Initiatives, a prescription benefit manager that provides services for small and medium-sized employers and managed care organizations. Walgreen has historically been known for its explosive growth, which has been fueled mainly by the opening of new stores. This is in sharp contrast with its key competitors, CVS Corporation and Rite Aid Corporation, both of which have historically grown through consolidation and acquisitions. In fact, by 2004, more than 50% of Walgreen drugstores were less than five years old.

This company started out in 1901 when Charles R. Walgreen bought the drugstore on the South Side of Chicago at which he had been working as a pharmacist. He bought a second store in 1909; by 1915, there were five Walgreen drugstores. He made numerous improvements and innovations in the stores, including the addition of soda fountains and a lunch service. Walgreen also began to make his own line of drug products; by doing so, he was able to control the quality of these items and offer them at lower prices than competitors. Charles Walgreen was truly an innovator.

By 1916, there were nine Walgreen drugstores, all on Chicago's South Side, reporting annual revenues of $270,000. In 1916, these stores were consolidated as Walgreen Co. in order to assure economy of scale. To continue the company's growth pattern, Walgreen expanded to 20 stores in 1919; 19 were on Chicago's South Side while the other was on the Near North Side. In an innovative move, Walgreen opened its first photo finishing studio, which promised faster service than most commercial studios.

As the Roaring Twenties rolled in, Walgreen exploded in terms of growth and innovation. For example, in 1922, Walgreen stores introduced the malted milkshake at their fountain counters. To meet the growing demand for its ice cream and to assure the ice cream's quality, Walgreen established its own ice cream manufacturing plants during the 1920s. Meanwhile, Walgreen kept expanding, and by mid-1925, there were 65 stores with total annual sales of $1.2 million. Fifty-nine of these stores were in Chicago and its suburbs, while others were opened in other cities including Milwaukee, Wisconsin and St. Louis, Missouri. Before the year was out, Walgreen also expanded into Minneapolis and St. Paul, Minnesota.

Walgreen opened its first East Coast store in New York's theater district in 1927 and went public in that same year. Despite the Great Depression of 1929, Walgreen continued to grow, operating 397 Walgreen stores in 87 cities, achieving annual sales of $47 million, and reporting net profits of $4 million. In 1930, Walgreen grew modestly to $52 million in sales. Also during that same year, Walgreen opened a 224,000-square-foot warehouse and a research laboratory in Chicago's Southwest Side. Early in the 1930s, Walgreen expanded on a project begun in 1929 that involved developing an agency system by which independent drugstores could sell Walgreen products.

By 1934, 600 Walgreen agency stores were operating in 33 states, mainly in the Midwest. Most stores were located in communities with a population of less than 20,000. In 1932, Walgreen finally felt the sting of the Depression, and its sales dropped to $47.6 million. As a consequence, it experienced its first major wage cuts. However, Walgreen also instituted a benefit fund to assist retirees and needy families inside and outside the company. Walgreen continued its marketing activities, and during 1931, it became the first drugstore chain in the United States to advertise on radio. Now that's innovation!

In 1934, Walgreen opened its first Walgreen Super Store in Tampa, Florida. At 4,000 square feet, the store's format was nearly double the size of the typical store, and it had a much larger fountain and more open displays of merchandise than the average drugstore. Other Walgreen Super Stores soon followed in Salt Lake City, Utah; Milwaukee, Wisconsin; Miami, Florida; and Rochester, New York. Also in 1934, Walgreen's stock began trading on the New York Stock Exchange. Walgreen's business recovered during the mid-to-late 1930s, and it reported sales totaling $69 million during 1938. Charles Walgreen, Senior resigned for health reasons in 1939, and his son succeeded him.

After World War II, Walgreen continued to expand its operations. More Walgreen Super Stores were opened in the late 1940s, including one on Chicago's Michigan Avenue. In 1948, the company expanded its corporate headquarters in Chicago and reported sales of $163.6 million. Also in that year, because it was an innovative company, Walgreen began advertising on television.

More innovation flowed during the 1950s. Walgreen began developing strategic initiatives to launch self-service stores. The first self-service Walgreen opened its doors on Chicago's South Side in June 1952, and the second followed shortly thereafter at Evergreen Plaza, Chicago's first major shopping center. The self-service stores offered lower prices than the traditional stores. By the end of 1953, there were 22 self-service stores. Self-service continued to grow throughout the 1950s as Walgreen built many new self-service units and converted conventional ones. Sales jumped from $163 million to $312 million over the course of the 1950s, largely due to the increased size and wider selection of the self-service stores. In fact, by the end of 1960, self-service units outnumbered traditional ones. Another major event of 1960 was the opening of the first Walgreen in Puerto Rico.

In 1962, Walgreen entered the discount department store business by buying out United Mercantile Inc. for about $3 million. United Mercantile Inc. owned three large Globe Shopping Center Stores and seven smaller Danburg Department Stores located in Houston, Texas. Walgreen expanded the Globe chain throughout the South and Southwest, and by 1966, there were 13 Globe stores generating annual sales of more than $120 million. This gave Walgreen the opportunity to run larger stores, resulting in the opening of more large stores under the Walgreen name. The first Walgreen Super Center opened in 1964 in the Chicago suburb of Norridge, and by 1969, there were 17 Super Centers around the U.S.

A third-generation Walgreen, C.R. (Cork) Walgreen III, assumed the company presidency in 1969. This made Walgreen one of the few companies headed by second- and third-generation descendants of the founder, though the Walgreen family no longer owned a controlling share of company stock. In 1974, the company opened its first Wag's restaurant. Wag's restaurants were freestanding family restaurants, many of which were open 24 hours a day. Also during 1974, Walgreen continued to expand by acquiring the Liggett chain of 29 Florida drugstores. In 1975, to continue its long history of being innovative, Walgreen completed the first phase of a new drug and cosmetics laboratory in Kalamazoo, Michigan; expanded its distribution center in Berkeley, Illinois; and modernized its plastic container plant and photo-processing studio. In 1975, for the first time in its tenure, Walgreen surpassed the $1 billion mark in sales.

In 1980, Walgreen continued to expand its drugstore business, acquiring the Madison, Wisconsin-based Rennebohm chain. Rennebohm had 17 drugstores, two clinic pharmacies, two health and beauty aid stores, a card shop, and six cafeterias. That next year, Walgreen acquired 21 Kroger SuperX drugstores in Houston, Texas. Meanwhile, Walgreen continued to be an innovative company with the addition of new services to its drugstores, such as next-day photo finishing. These services were made available chain-wide. Moreover, in 1983, Walgreen continued to be innovative by completing a chain-wide launch of its newly developed Intercom computerized pharmacy system. By the end of the 1980s, its Intercom connected each store in the chain via satellite to a mainframe computer in Des Plaines, Illinois. This system enabled its customers to have their prescriptions filled at any Walgreen in the country. This system was an innovation that enabled Walgreen to provide its clients with sustained value.

Walgreen opened its 1,000th store, which was on the Near North Side of Chicago, in 1984. Walgreen continued expanding and focusing on the drugstore business as its core competency. Because of its concentrated efforts in the drugstore business, it divested its other businesses, including its interest in Sanborn. When it moved into the New England markets, Walgreen acquired 66 Medi Mart stores. This was its largest single acquisition. That same year, Walgreen also acquired 25 stores from the Indiana chain Ribordy and opened 102 new stores, making 1986 Walgreen's biggest year for expansion.

Walgreen continued to focus on the drugstore business by selling its 87 freestanding Wag's restaurants to Marriott Corporation. In 1989, the company opened four mini-drugstores called Walgreen RxPress. These drugstores offered a full-service pharmacy and popular non-prescription items in areas where full-sized store locations were difficult to find. By the mid-1990s, these 2,000-square-foot units, some of which offered one-hour photo finishing services, also featured convenient drive-through pharmacies. There were 25 RxPress locations by 1996.

For Walgreen, the 1990s were dominated by an unprecedented rate of expansion. Walgreen ended the 1980s with 1,484 units, and by mid-1997, the company had more than 2,200 units (an increase of almost 50%) and was aiming for the 3,000 mark by the 21st century. For the pharmacy industry as a whole, the 1990s were a decade of remarkable change. There were growing numbers of people over the age of 50, a demographic reality that resulted in more prescriptions being filled each year. This made the pharmacy business a hot commodity. This also resulted in fierce competition when aggressive chains such as Wal-Mart Stores, Inc. challenged Walgreen's leading position in prescription drugs. Furthermore, managed care health plans grew increasingly important as the decade progressed. This served to put pressure on drugstores to lower their prices on prescriptions, a practice which resulted in slimmer margins. Walgreen responded to these challenges by being innovative and investing heavily in technology. It launched new initiatives aimed directly at taking advantage of the trend toward managed care.

In a demonstration of its capacity for innovation, Walgreen improved its inventory management capabilities by developing and launching a point-of-sale scanning system in 1991. In 1994, it completed and implemented a new system called SIMS (Strategic Inventory Management System). This system was an innovation that integrated all elements of the purchasing-distribution-sales cycle. In 1997, Walgreen launched a second-generation Intercom Plus system that performed more than 200 functions, enabling customers to order prescription refills using the keys on a push-button phone. This system also cut the time customers had to wait to receive their prescriptions by 50%. These are excellent examples of innovations that provided Walgreen clients with sustained value.

Still another example of Walgreen's innovation was its response to the managed care boom in the form of cost-effective mail-order pharmacies. Walgreen formed a subsidiary, Healthcare Plus, in 1991 that offered managed care providers a pharmacy mail service. Healthcare Plus was launched in Orlando, Florida, with a mail service facility capable of handling 5,000 prescriptions a day. Healthcare Plus added a second facility in late 1994 in Tempe, Arizona, which had a capacity of 7,500 prescriptions per day. Mail service sales were expected to hit $500 million by 1998. During the fall of 1995, Walgreen expanded Healthcare Plus into WHP Health Initiatives, Inc., a pharmacy benefits manager. This enabled Walgreen to offer additional products and services to managed care providers, including long-term care pharmacies, durable medical equipment, and home infusion services. WHP was aimed at small and medium-sized employers and HMOs in Walgreen's top 28 retail markets.

Meanwhile, Walgreen continued to grow during the 1990s. It opened two more distribution centers, one in Lehigh Valley, Pennsylvania, in June 1991, and the other in Woodland, California, in July 1995, bringing the total up to eight centers. The Woodland center was particularly important, as it supported aggressive expansion in California as well as the opening of the first Walgreen in Portland, Oregon. Walgreen also expanded into several other new markets in the mid-1990s, including Dallas/Fort Worth, Detroit, Kansas City, Las Vegas, and Philadelphia. Throughout the expansion efforts of the 1990s, Walgreen concentrated on opening freestanding stores; these were considered more convenient than mall stores. The first freestanding store opened in 1992, and by 1996, more than half of all Walgreen stores were freestanding. Another example of Walgreen's innovativeness was its drive-through prescription service, which was offered in more than 700 stores and which greatly enhanced Walgreen's image of convenience. In addition to all the store openings, including 210 during 1996 alone, Walgreen also refurbished or closed some of its older stores. As a result, the average age of a Walgreen store was 7.4 years in 1996. It reported 1996 net sales of $11.78 billion, more than double that of 1989.

In the late 1990s and into the early years of the 21st century, Walgreen achieved a remarkable record of sustained growth and profitability. As revenues more than doubled from $15.31 billion in 1998 to $32.51 billion in 2003, profits increased at a similar pace, jumping from $511 million to $1.18 billion. Moreover, the results for 2003 marked the company's 29th consecutive year of record sales and earnings. Walgreen added about 350 stores per year in this period, opening its 3,000th store in Chicago in March 2000 and its 4,000th store in Van Nuys, California in March 2003.

Walgreen achieved growth by developing organically, selecting its own sites for new stores rather than settling on stores with undesirable locations or store formats that were representative of the typical large acquisition targets. This strategy allowed for a faster transition of store bases that fit Walgreen's preferred format of freestanding stores generally located near high-traffic corners and equipped for drive-through pharmacies. By the beginning of 2004, there were 4,227 company drugstores, 3,363 of which were freestanding units and 3,280 of which had drive-through pharmacies. More than half of the stores were less than five years old. Another key strategy that resulted in more value for Walgreen's customers was the creation of outlets that were open 24 hours a day, almost all of which offered one-hour photo finishing services.

Continuing its quest to be an innovative company, Walgreen launched a comprehensive online pharmacy in 1999 that enabled customers to order prescriptions for in-store pickup or mail delivery and also offered access to the health and wellness content of the Mayo Clinic Health Information Center. At the turn of the century, the Walgreen portal expanded to include front-of-the-store merchandise like nail polish and shampoo. During its anniversary year, another leader emerged. David Bernauer, a former pharmacist and lifelong Walgreen employee, was named CEO. To support its rapid expansion, Walgreen opened several new distribution centers in Jupiter, Florida and Dallas, Texas (both in 2002); in Perrysburg, Ohio (2003); and in Moreno Valley, California (2004), bringing the total number of such facilities to 11. Late in 2003, Walgreen ended 17 years of no acquisitions by purchasing 11 stores and the pharmacy files of five others. These stores were located in the Portland, Oregon, and Vancouver, Washington, metropolitan areas.

Despite the pharmaceutical industry's fierce, combative, and competitive environment, Walgreen continued its steady growth. An aging U.S. population and the introduction of innovative new drugs acted as driving forces for prescription growth, enabling Walgreen to be even more profitable. Revenue growth for Walgreen surged from less than 50% in 1996 to 62% by 2003. Walgreen continued to expand, seeking to add a net 365 stores during 2004 and aiming toward a long-term goal of 7,000 stores by 2010. A key market earmarked for future expansion is New York City, where Walgreen has only a small presence.

Comcast Corporation

Comcast Corporation is a leading cable, telecommunications, and entertainment firm and the fourth-largest cable company in the United States, with 4.4 million customers in 21 states. Comcast Cellular provides services for 783,000 cellular telephone customers in Pennsylvania, New Jersey, and Delaware. Comcast holds a 57% stake in QVC, Inc., the leading cable television shopping channel; has a controlling interest with the Walt Disney Company in E! Entertainment Television, a cable channel devoted to entertainment and celebrity programming; and holds a majority interest in the Philadelphia 76ers NBA basketball team and the Philadelphia Flyers NHL hockey team.

Comcast began in the early 1960s as American Cable Systems, Inc., a small, innovative cable operation serving Tupelo, Mississippi. At that time, American was one of only a few community antenna television (CATV) services in the nation. The CATV business was founded on the fact that rural areas did not receive good service with commercial television stations, which catered to large metropolitan areas. Without CATV's huge antennas pulling in distant signals, rural consumers had little use for television. Even though CATV customers had to pay for services, they considered the access to commercial television stations worth the cost.

It was during 1963 that Ralph and Joe Roberts sold their interest in Pioneer Industries, a men's accessories business in Philadelphia, and were searching for new investment areas. After doing extensive research, they learned that the owners of American Cable Systems wanted to sell their CATV business. The Roberts brothers, along with some other experts in the area of investments, saw the value in CATV. They agreed that while the system carried only five channels and served only 1,500 customers, the upside investment potential was very attractive, so they bought the company.

Despite the fact that CATV was innovative, especially in rural areas, and provided consumers with access to television, growth was lethargic and slow. In fact, the Robertses even had to sell door-to-door to grow their business. Despite this setback, they continued to make acquisitions, buying additional franchises in Meridian, Laurel, and West Point, all in eastern Mississippi. That next year, American acquired more franchises in Okolona and Baldwyn, Mississippi. Despite increasing subscribers, the Robertses failed to have much market penetration.

The Robertses next turned their attention to larger markets like Philadelphia. The brothers successfully went after cable franchises in Abington, Cheltenham, and Upper Darby, all in the northern suburbs of Philadelphia. They next acquired the Westmoreland cable system that served four other communities in western Pennsylvania, thus achieving better economy of scale. After establishing a strong foothold in suburban Philadelphia, the Robertses extended their company's presence into six additional local communities. The brothers continued to expand their company, building additional cable systems in the Florida cities of Sarasota and Venice. In 1968, to add some limited diversification in this business, the Robertses purchased a large franchise to provide a subscription "elevator music" service in Orlando, Florida.

The Robertses made a key strategic move in 1969 when they decided to change their company's name. In a pronounced effort to adopt a more technological brand identity, they took portions of the words "communication" and "broadcast," created Comcast Corporation, and reincorporated the company in Pennsylvania. The company now expanded into Dallas, Texas; San Diego, California; Detroit, Michigan; and Hartford, Connecticut.

With the company possessing a little over 40,000 customers and still struggling to grow, the Robertses decided to take the company public in 1972, offering shares on the OTC market. In 1974, Comcast acquired a cable franchise for Paducah, Kentucky, followed by 1976 acquisitions in three Michigan cities: Flint, Hillsdale, and Jonesville. By this time, cable had become much more than an antenna service. For several years, cable operators included local access and special programming channels as well as programming from large independent stations such as WGN in Chicago and WTBS in Atlanta. The U.S. government restricted cable television programming, often blocking access to programs that customers clearly wanted. Dan Aaron, a manager with Comcast, was active in the National Cable Television Association (NCTA) and lobbied effectively for the relaxation of programming and other restrictions. Then during 1977, while chairman of the NCTA, Aaron brought many of the industry's efforts to fruition. As the cable industry was allowed to mature, additional cable-only stations were added, making the service available within metropolitan areas that were well-served by broadcasters.

Comcast made an important strategic move in 1983 when, in partnership with British gambling and entertainment enterprise Ladbroke, it won a license to establish a cable television system in the residential suburbs of London. Most cable licenses in the United States had been taken, and the remaining ones were expensive or only marginally profitable. However, the industry was still in its infancy in the United Kingdom, and Comcast executives believed that British viewers would appreciate cable's selection because Britain only had about five stations offering mostly government-supported programming.

In 1984, an important change took place in the telecommunications industry that would have a deep and lasting impact on the cable industry. After a half-century of antitrust litigation, the U.S. government finally broke up the Bell System; as a result, AT&T and its long-distance operations became 22 local Bell companies. Each of these Bell companies was organized into one of seven companies that saw cable television as the next logical course of progression for its telephone networks. The U.S. Congress, however, had already enacted legislation that would prevent telephone companies from taking over the still-fragile cable industry. The Cable Act, which was written primarily to guarantee fair pole attachment rates to cable companies, had the effect of keeping telephone companies out of the cable business.

Because telephone companies were being kept out of the cable business, Comcast was able to continue its growth through acquisitions. In 1985, after purchasing cable operations in Pontiac/Waterford, Michigan; Fort Wayne, Indiana; and Jones County, Mississippi, Comcast won the right to serve the densely populated northeast Philadelphia area, a major win. During 1986, Comcast took over a cable system serving Indianapolis and purchased a 26% share in Group W, one of the country's largest cable companies. This brought Comcast's subscribers to more than one million customers. The following year, Comcast acquired a cable system in northwest Philadelphia from Heritage Communications, thus solidifying its position in suburban Philadelphia.

Focusing more on investments in other cable companies than on actual franchises, Comcast purchased a 20% share of Heritage Communications and a 50% share of Storer Communications in 1988. The Storer acquisition brought the number of Comcast subscribers to more than two million customers and made Comcast the fifth-largest cable company in the United States. The company consolidated its partnerships and took full control of Maryland Limited Partnership, Comcast Cablevision of Indiana, and Comcast Cable Investors.

To continue its aggressive strategic growth as an innovative company, Comcast moved into the cellular service industry in 1988 by purchasing American Cellular Network, or Amcell, a cellular telephone business serving New Jersey. Cable and telephone companies, prevented from competition in landline services, were facing off in the cellular telephone business for the first time. Also for the first time, a cable company was able to offer telephone customers an alternative to the telephone company.

In 1990, a year after Comcast relocated its corporate offices to Philadelphia, Ralph Roberts named his 30-year-old son Brian his successor as president of the company, while Ralph Roberts remained as chairman. Brian Roberts had exceptional academic credentials and was, like his father, a very effective manager. Also in 1990, after having purchased an interest in an additional franchise serving suburban London, the company's newly formed international unit won more British franchises, allowing the company to serve Cambridge and Birmingham. Comcast now had more than one million customers in Britain alone. Comcast's smaller companies, such as Amcell, were beginning to experience lackluster growth. Through the use of a well-thought-out strategy, Comcast completed a deal in 1991 with the Metromedia Company in which it purchased that company's Metrophone cellular unit for $1.1 billion. This joint venture resulted in a new alliance company, which was established in 1992, and quadrupled Comcast's potential market to more than 7.3 million customers.

Later that year, the company's offices at One Meridian Plaza in Philadelphia were destroyed by a fire. In a demonstration of remarkable resiliency, the company reestablished new offices four blocks away at 1234 Market Street only eight days later, and with this temporary location, the company's 250 employees were once again in business.

In an extraordinarily innovative move during September 1992, Comcast staged a five-way international telephone call using the Comcast network and a long-distance carrier. This call demonstrated that the company could handle telephone calls and completely bypass the local telephone network. While the demonstration was intended to raise investors' interest in such bypass operations, it also succeeded in creating quite a stir in the telephone industry by creating a case for permission to offer cable television services. Comcast continued to strengthen its position in the bypass business in 1992, when it gained a 20% interest (later reduced to 15%) in Teleport Communications Corporation. Teleport was the operator of a fiber-optic-based bypass telecommunications network that was serving more than 50 major markets nationwide by the mid-1990s.

The mid-1990s also saw an escalation of activity throughout the cable and telecommunications industries. This increased activity was driven by deregulation that increasingly brought cable and telephone companies into competition as well as partnership with each other. This same time period saw a flurry of acquisitions, mergers, and system swaps in the cable industry as companies sought to build networks of contiguous systems to improve efficiency. Comcast was in the middle of all of this activity, making aggressive and innovative moves into the area of programming content.

Another key innovation strategy for Comcast occurred during 1992, when Comcast began testing a forerunner of what eventually became known as the Sprint PCS (personal communications services) digital cellular technology. This new cellular technology delivered crisper sound and more security than analog cellular phone technology and provided more value for customers. In 1994, Comcast entered into an alliance that formed the Sprint Telecommunications Venture, which was renamed Sprint Spectrum LP in 1995. The alliance partners were Sprint Corp., which owned 40% of the venture; Tele-Communications Inc., which owned 30%; and Comcast and Cox Communications Inc., which owned 15% each. This was a key strategy in innovation because during the early part of 1995, Sprint Spectrum was the biggest winner in the Federal Communications Commission (FCC) auction of PCS licenses. It gained the rights to wireless licenses in 31 major U.S. markets that, when combined, covered a population of 156 million. The venture was soon renamed Sprint PCS, and the four partners spent millions of dollars building a wireless network. In 1997, Comcast's cellular operations in Pennsylvania, New Jersey, and Delaware were converted to the digital technology, but by then the company considered Sprint PCS, which faced tough competition from cellular veterans such as AT&T Corp., a drag on earnings. Then, in May 1998, the Sprint PCS partners announced that they planned to sell 10% of the venture to the public through a public offering. Sprint PCS was set up as a tracking stock under Sprint's corporate domain (shareholders of tracking stocks have very limited voting rights). This move was considered the first step toward the possible exit of Comcast, Cox, and TCI from the joint venture. While this was going on in January 1998, Comcast acquired GlobalCom Telecommunications, a regional long-distance service provider. Along with the company's other operations, the addition of GlobalCom (renamed Comcast Telecommunications after the acquisition) enabled Comcast to offer a full range of telecommunications services.

In 1994, Comcast continued its acquisition activities in the cable industry when it acquired Maclean Hunter's U.S. cable operations for $1.27 billion, gaining an additional 550,000 customers. Two years later, in November of 1996, Comcast acquired the cable properties of E. W. Scripps Co in a $1.575 billion stock swap. Scripps's 800,000 customers brought Comcast's cable holdings to more than 4.3 million customers in 21 states, making them the fourth-largest cable system in the United States. In February 1998, the company sold its underperforming U.K. cable operations to NTL Inc. for $600 million in stock plus the assumption of $397 million in debt. Three months later, Comcast announced that it would spend $500 million over the next several years to take over the 30% interest in Jones Intercable Inc. held by the Canada-based BCI Telecom Holding Inc. This was a strategic innovation initiative because Jones had a technologically advanced, one-million-customer cable system, much of which was in the suburbs of Washington, D.C. and contiguous to some of Comcast's main markets.

Comcast's innovation moves were also driving the company to become a major provider of entertainment content. It held a 13% stake in QVC, Inc., the number-one cable-based shopping channel, and during July 1994, company executives planned a merger between QVC and CBS Inc. by offering to pay $2.2 billion for a controlling interest in QVC. CBS, refusing to engage in a bidding war, immediately retreated, leaving Comcast to increase its QVC interest to 57%. In early 1996, Comcast paid $250 million to acquire a 66% stake in a new venture, Comcast-Spectacor, L.P. Most of the remaining ownership interest was held by Spectacor, which owned the Philadelphia Flyers NHL hockey team and two sports arenas in Philadelphia. Comcast-Spectacor was set up to own and operate the Flyers, the Philadelphia 76ers NBA basketball team, and the two arenas. Comcast then established Comcast SportsNet, a 24-hour regional cable sports channel, which debuted in the fall of 1997 and featured telecasts of Flyers, 76ers, and Philadelphia Phillies (major league baseball) games, in addition to other sports programming. In March 1997, Comcast partnered with the Walt Disney Company to acquire a majority interest in E! Entertainment Television, a 24-hour cable network devoted exclusively to entertainment and celebrity programming. E! was available in more than 45 million homes in more than 120 countries around the world.

Recognizing that Comcast was a leading innovator in the cable television industry, Microsoft Corporation announced in June 1997 that it would invest $1 billion in Comcast in return for an 11.5% nonvoting interest. Microsoft's motivation was that it wanted a cable partner for testing interactive television and high-speed computer services. It chose Comcast because the latter company's cable system was one of the most technologically advanced in the country. Continuing its tradition of being a leading innovator in the cable television industry, Comcast had converted about 70% of its customers to a new hybrid fiber-coaxial technology by the end of 1997 that was more reliable, offered improved signal quality, and had the capacity to deliver more services. The company was also a partner with a 12% interest with At Home Corporation. In December 1996, that Comcast leveraged its partnership with Microsoft to launch high-speed interactive services provided 24-hour unlimited Internet access for its customers. This partnership with Microsoft was clearly positioning Comcast for promising involvement in future innovative technologies and services and transforming the company into an important innovator in the technology-rich world of the 21st century.

So far, we have learned about companies like Walgreen and Comcast that have successfully launched strategic "best practices" initiatives that enabled them to achieve remarkable business results with sustained value for their customers. It is equally important for companies to leverage strategic "best practices" that help their operations to be more efficient and effective. The next chapter will illustrate how some companies in the Value Zone Hall of Fame have been able to streamline their operations and eliminate waste and redundancies.

Chapter Ten
Building and Sustaining Efficient Businesses

Since the late 1980s, businesses have been streamlining their business processes by eliminating waste, getting rid of redundant business processes, and leveraging innovative technologies to enhance their performance. It should always be the goal of any for profit or not-for-profit organization to strive to be efficient by "doing things right" and effective by "doing the right thing." Building and sustaining an efficient business is an essential element of the Value Zone. In this chapter, we will learn about how some of the Value Zone Hall of Fame companies were able to build and sustain efficient and effective business practices consistently for the past 25 years.

Family Dollar Stores

We have already discussed the remarkable success of Family Dollar Stores, and so it is not surprising that we find ourselves admiring them in this area as well. Another ingredient in Family Dollar's success has been its efficient distribution system handled entirely out of Charlotte, from which the company was able to make bulk deliveries to its stores. In 1980, the size of the distribution center was increased twofold to enable the company to take further advantage of discounts on single, bulk deliveries and open new stores without concern about stock shortages.

To offset the effects of the economic downturn during the 1970s, Family Dollar Store began to focus on shoring up some of its weaknesses and looking for ways to improve its marketing and merchandising. It also changed its policy of pricing all merchandise at $3 or less, which, despite its appeal to shoppers, had proven too hard on store margins. To improve its efficiency in inventory management, it also tightened inventory controls, adding an electronic data processing system. Although the economy continued to be unstable in the late 1970s, Family Dollar was able to exceed $100 million in sales in fiscal year 1978 and hit a record $151 million in sales in 1979, with same-store sales remaining fairly flat during this period.

By 1992, Wal-Mart had captured 26% of the discount store market, and many smaller discounters were forced out of business. Family Dollar survived by focusing on its core strengths: convenience, solid stock, and low prices. Family Dollar stores were usually within three miles of shopper's homes and were about one-tenth the size of Wal-Mart stores. Moreover, because its inventory was smaller per store than Wal-Mart, the prices of essential household items such as toothpaste and laundry detergent at most Family Dollar stores were slightly more than one might pay at Wal-Mart. However, the key to the company's success was that many customers seemed willing to pay slightly higher prices in exchange for a convenient location and a smaller, easy-to-navigate store. Family Dollar had faced the superstore threat head-on and was, by 1992, even posting a better net margin than Wal-Mart.

During the early 1990s, apparel represented about 45% of the Family Dollar stock, while "hard" goods made up the remainder. Family Dollar Store widened its search for merchandise and took advantage of downtime in factories, contracting them to manufacture merchandise at cut rates during low production periods. Roughly 10% of Family Dollar Store's overall business came from private-label sales, and most store merchandise was priced lower than $18. It significantly enhanced its distribution system, installing a building in Memphis, Arkansas of more than 550,000 square feet, which, when combined with the North Carolina center, totaled about 1.3 million square feet of space. Both of these centers were fully automated. To keep up with product demand, Family Dollar Store opened a new distribution center in Virginia in 1998, and an additional facility went online in Oklahoma in 1999. Also during 1999, Family Dollar Store celebrated its 40th anniversary by posting record sales and profits.

Family Dollar's 2005 Annual Report said that the company's mission was the determination to provide exceptional value to the people who are the most important to it: its shareholders, its customers, and its associates. To further improve the company's efficiency and effectiveness, Family Dollar announced during 2005 that it would continue to make significant investments in its business to create greater value for its market and non-market stakeholders. To sustain its financial performance through growth and profitability, it invested in four strategic initiatives in 2005:

- The Cooler Initiative reformatted stores to provide value and convenience to customers by expanding the food assortment and adding refrigerated coolers for those frequent "milk and eggs" fill-in trips. Family Dollar also offered family staples in both perishable and non-perishable foods, providing incentives for customers to make repeated trips to the store.
- The Urban Initiative addressed the opportunities and challenges of operating in urban markets. Better customer service and store presentation standards, a more organic organizational structure, and improved processes drove higher financial performance and created value for all of the company's stakeholders.
- The Treasure Hunt Initiative offered Family Dollar Store customers the opportunity to receive exceptional value with exciting and unique Treasure Hunt items as well as everyday home and family items. The addition of the Treasure Hunt merchandise produced great results with customers who were delighted to find unexpected holiday "treasures" at Family Dollar.
- The New Store Initiative allowed Family Dollar Store to expand into new areas and increase its presence in existing markets. The company opened new stores in order to provide more value and neighborhood convenience to one of the fastest-growing, yet vastly under-served, consumer segments. During 2005, Family Dollar Store continued its ambitious store expansion program by opening 500 new stores, thus

enabling the company to more efficiently accelerate its growth in the future.

In an effort to improve its efficiency and provide exceptional value to its customers, Family Dollar Store stated in its 2005 Annual Report that its most valuable asset is its employees. The company views these employees as talented and dedicated associates. In the report, Family Dollar officials restated their commitment to provide these associates with the skills and development tools to build, not just a job, but a career with Family Dollar Store. Part of this effort includes building Family Dollar's management team with strong talent to support its growth. Its executives believe that their recruiting efforts have resulted in the addition of excellent new players to their existing talented team. Family Dollar has also realigned its senior management structure to provide better support for its cross-functional strategic agenda.

Longs Drug Stores Corporation
Longs Drug Stores Corporation was incorporated in Maryland on May 24, 1985, as a successor to Longs Stores, incorporated in 1946 in California. The company specialized in the retail drugstore industry since its founding in 1938. In 1975, Joseph Long credited the company's practice of spreading its wealth among its employees with a great deal of its success. Such a strategy, which improved efficiency through the decentralization of power, created wealth for the company's investors and also a sense of purpose and solid financial rewards for its employees. For example, store managers were paid quarterly bonuses proportional to their unit's profits, and the bonus system extended down through the half-dozen assistant department managers that any specific store might employ. By one estimate, a Longs store manager in the late 1980s might have made $80,000 per year. For that time period, such as salary was a remarkable achievement.

Longs expanded conservatively and with exceptional due diligence, thoroughly investigating potential locations. Another key area of efficiency was Longs' lack of liabilities. Longs Drug Stores preferred to purchase property beneath its stores. It did no business on credit. In the early 1970s, Longs opened about six stores a year. Many of these stores were located in upper-middle-income areas where retail sales were high. Longs opened outlets mostly in northern California, where there were not that many competitors. In the tougher retail market of Southern California, Longs eschewed highly competitive Los Angeles for its affluent suburbs. Despite the tightening economy, Longs increased expansion to about ten stores annually in the mid-1970s. During this time, Longs' high earnings financed much of its expansion initiatives. The key in terms of financial efficiency was that Longs carried no debt and took out no loans, so rising interest rates did not affect its growth rate.

The financial results for Longs during the period of general economic decline in the 1970s were very positive. For example, during 1975, each Longs store averaged $4 million in annual sales, versus a figure of $500,000 for the industry. Its $250-per-square-foot sales far exceeded the industry average of $100. Its gross margin was less than 25% in an industry where it was typically 33% at that time. Longs stores did about twice the business of competing stores. The use of decentralized pricing gave Longs an advantage in the inflationary economy of the 1970s, enabling its managers to raise prices according to local costs instead of waiting for the word from the central office. Its decentralized acquisition of store stock also gave its managers the ability to negotiate in a tough economy. Warehousing costs were nil because Longs did not maintain a central warehousing system. Most of its stock was purchased at the store level from direct manufacturers or local wholesalers and jobbers. Merchandise was stored in the retail unit, but just briefly, because Longs turned over its inventory eight times a year, about twice the industry standard. The stores in general avoided costly items. Any given store might sell such an item, but it would only stock a few of that item until the item proved to be a big seller. This way, each store avoided being saddled with merchandise that did not sell well in an economic downturn.

Longs experienced declining profits during the early 1990s despite consistent revenue growth. The early 1990s recession hit Longs especially hard because so many of its stores were located in California, which suffered a more severe recession. Growing pressures from competition with huge discounters such as Wal-Mart and Costco also hurt profits. In an effort to adapt to change, Longs executives re-thought their company's decentralized strategy and moved towards a strategy of centralization. In 1992, Longs began installing point-of-sale scanning systems into its stores in order to more efficiently control inventory and cut purchasing costs. The next year, Longs started centralizing its over-the-counter drug business. It also began to establish chain-wide pricing, breaking with its tradition of store managers setting prices.

In their 2006 Annual Report, Longs executives felt that their company was operating in an environment of changes including escalating competition, industry consolidation, pricing pressures via third party health plans, growing use of generic drugs, and significant fuel costs. To address these challenges, they had announced (three years prior to their annual report) five broad categories of strategic initiatives to become more competitive and profitable. These categories were:

- Supply chain
- Front-end sale
- Pharmacy profitability
- Customer service
- Operational processes

In the executives' report on the progress made in these initiatives, they discussed the company's supply chain technology improvements, including the implementation of a new distribution management system in Longs' front-end California distribution centers, a new retail merchandise system implemented across all of its stores, and a new procurement and allocation system that was integrated with both its distribution management system and its retail merchandise system. In fiscal 2007, Longs will implement a new system for store ordering, receiving, and inventory management. Also during 2007, the company will build a new front-end distribution center in California to increase its self-distribution.

The executives have shifted the company's front-end merchandise mix to include categories of health, wellness, beauty, and convenience. This strategic move will, in their view, differentiate Longs from its competitors and will improve its profitability. They have also continued to centralize Longs' merchandising and promotions. This enables the company to continue to develop its private brand of merchandise and enhance its ability to self-distribute its front-end merchandise.

Longs also reported completing the remodeling of 41 stores during fiscal 2006 and anticipates remodeling 40 more during fiscal 2007. Thus far, approximately 25% of the company's stores have been remodeled and made significantly more efficient and convenient for customers. A key goal in Longs' remodeling efforts is to make more productive use of its stores' non-selling floor space by utilizing diagnostic labs, classrooms, and walk-in clinics.

Longs has taken a number of steps to improve its pharmaceutical profitability in anticipated third-party pricing pressures. Some steps it has initiated include: improved buying, a growth in generic usage, an upgraded pharmacy technology environment, and expanded mail order and central fill capabilities. The goal here, according to Longs executives, is to sustain progress in pharmaceutical procurement, inventory management, in-stock position, and workflow efficiencies.

Other strategic initiatives include the strengthening of Longs' RxAmerica capabilities. This initiative significantly improves Longs' benefit services subsidiary in two important ways: 1) it prepares the company for its new Medicare prescription drug plan offerings, and 2) it enables Longs to go after new growth areas in its pharmacy benefit management business. The key goal here is to drive RxAmerica growth.

Home Depot

Back in the 1980s, Home Depot's founders built their sales staff from both dedicated do-it-yourselfers and professional tradespeople, hiring most employees in as full-time workers. During this time, approximately 10% of Home Depot's sales personnel was part-time. Whenever possible, each store had a licensed plumber and electrician on staff, and customers were urged to call the Home Depot store in their area if they had any problems or questions while they were doing their home repair or improvement projects. This strategic initiative was clearly both efficient and effective, and it also sustained real value for Home Depot's customers. Other effective strategic initiatives that achieved great results were the scheduled in-store instructional workshops for customers conducted by experts such as local contractors. These strategic initiatives generated solid results that were shown by Home Depot's 1986 sales of $1 billion and its growth to 50 retail outlets.

During the late 1980s, Home Depot's sales continued to rise. However, for the first time in its history, the cost of sales also increased. For example, the company's earnings declined 42% in 1985 because of the ever-increasing costs of opening new outlets. These costs were huge—more than $8 million per store—and drove up Home Depot's long-term debt from $4 million to $200 million in just two years. Rising costs also forced its stock price to fall. The message was loud and clear for Home Depot executives: they needed to develop other strategic initiatives to drive down costs and become more efficient. These changes would mean sustained value for their customers and would enable Home Depot to continue to grow and prosper.

One strategic initiative that Home Depot executed during this time was slowing down expansion projects. For example, Home Depot only opened ten new stores in 1986. All of these new stores were opened in existing and established markets. The company also issued a stock offering of 2.99 million shares at $17 per share, resulting in reduced and restructured debt. Home Depot also installed a computerized inventory control system and enhanced the company's management training programs.

Home Depot's strategic decision to grow more conservatively and to more efficiently manage its debt was working; in 1989, it surpassed Lowe's Companies in sales to become the largest home-repair chain in the United States. By the end of 1989, almost all outlets were using the company's new satellite data communications network. This system linked its stores and provided a fast and accurate exchange of information between stores. This system facilitated continued growth by enhancing Home Depot's responsiveness to market changes. The satellite system also served as a platform for the Home Depot television network, a network that produced and transmitted live programming by top management to each outlet. Home Depot's profits rose 46% in 1990, and a three-for-two stock split occurred that same year. Sales increased by 38% in 1989. With the trend for continued growth in the do-it-yourself market shown by a 33% increase in the number of customer transactions logged by the company in 1990, as well as an increase of 4% for the average customer sale, Home Depot was an emerging giant in the U.S. retail marketplace.

Home Depot's strategic vision during the early 1990s was materializing: the company had reached more than $10 billion in sales from 350 locations by the mid-1990s. Part of this strategy was a 75-store expansion into the northeastern United States, one of Home Depot's strongest markets despite the region's economic problems. Home Depot executives believed the area's dense population and large number of older homes would generate great results.

Throughout the 1990s, Home Depot developed a number of strategic initiatives that were designed to determine where new business growth would occur. For example, during 1991, Home Depot sampled customer interest in an installation program for items like carpets, doors, and windows. The program was successful, and Home Depot adopted it throughout its stores in the U.S. Other strategic initiatives included a bridal registry, a drive-in lumberyard, and a delivery service. Home Depot also established an environmental marketing department to help educate consumers about what product choices were more environmentally friendly. Over 70 hardware products, from light bulbs to paint, were identified for customers via in-store flyers and posters. Home Depot continued to focus on efficient and effective ways to sustain value for its customers. One way that it did this was by measuring customer satisfaction. To do this, the company developed a program called S.P.I. (store productivity improvement) in which cleaning, restocking, and other routine tasks were scheduled after store hours. In 1995, Home Depot opened its first 24-hour store and even published a book on home repair. This 480-page book was entitled *Home Improvement 1-2-3*.

Under the leadership of Bob Nardelli, Home Depot has emerged as a technology leader in retail. For example, to improve the efficiency of its operations during fiscal 2005, Home Depot continued to improve its technology capabilities by opening a second technology center in Austin, Texas. This center enabled growth and expansion. It currently houses engineers, software developers, and computer operation staff.

Home Depot also completed the rollout of back-end scanned receiving to all U.S. and Canadian stores, a process that allowed the company to simplify, standardize, and automate its product receipt procedure. It has also begun to certify vendors for receiving and has implemented self-checkout registers, which, as of the end of fiscal 2005, were in 1,272 stores. It has also expanded centralized automatic replenishment to 20% of store sales, implemented a Special Order Services Initiative pilot in 285 stores, and introduced new mobile cart functionality in all stores.

While Home Depot's technology investments have been mainly focused in its stores, it has also invested in technology improvements in other areas. For example, it launched a new financial system in 2005 for its Mexico retail operations, upgraded its call centers, improved its websites, and launched several new direct-to-consumer brands.

Home Depot leveraged several mechanisms to decrease distribution costs and increase efficiency. One example of this strategy is the use of import distribution centers to process globally sourced merchandise. By the end of 2005, Home Depot had 16 import distribution centers located in the U.S. and Canada and 30 lumber distribution centers in the U.S. and Canada to support the lumber demands of its stores and its ten transit facilities. At its transit facilities, Home Depot receives merchandise from manufacturers and immediately transfers these products onto trucks for delivery to its stores. Home Depot executives believe that the transit facility network will have provided service to approximately 80% of their stores in the U.S. by the end of 2006. The company also operates other specialty distribution centers for specific merchandise needs. The distribution centers and transit facilities allow Home Depot to provide high service levels to its stores at relatively low costs. By the end of 2005, approximately 40% of the merchandise shipped to Home Depot's stores was processed through its network of distribution centers and transit facilities. As its networks continue to evolve, Home Depot anticipates an increase in the percentage of merchandise processed by its facilities. The remaining merchandise will be shipped directly from its suppliers to its stores.

In addition to replenishing merchandise supplies at its stores, Home Depot also provides delivery services directly to its customers. Its executives continually assess opportunities to improve the company's distribution network so that Home Depot can better satisfy the needs of its stores and customers and keep driving down costs. Home Depot has made and will continue to make significant technology investments both in its stores and in its administrative functions. Its technological strategic initiatives are designed to streamline its operations and enable its associates to continue to provide high-quality service for their customers and provide these customers with a better in-store experience.

Pall Corporation

Pall Corporation is the largest manufacturer of filtration, separation, and purification products in the world. It markets its products in four major industries: healthcare, pharmaceutical, fluid processing, and aerospace. According to Pall Corporations reports, fluids are processed by a Pall product over 60 million times each day across the globe. Approximately 40% of company sales come from Pall's European operation.

Pall Corporation began through the formation of the Micro Metallic Corporation by David Pall in 1946. During World War II, Pall, a Canadian-born chemist, worked on the Manhattan Project, a covert operation in which the American government sought to develop the first atomic bomb. Pall, who was 27 years old at the time, helped design a filter to separate uranium-235 from uranium-238. He and his colleagues developed the filter to separate the raw uranium material from the heavier, less stable uranium. Pall and his company, which was renamed the Pall Corporation in 1957, remained focused on developing filters for special tasks and, as technology in other fields emerged, new markets opened up for the company's filters.

In 1958, Pall began developing filters for the aircraft industry. Pall's first filters were made for the American Airlines fleet of Boeing 707s because pilots were being forced to operate landing gears manually due to impurities that were causing the hydraulic landing gear systems to malfunction. Following this, Pall developed a filter for purifying jet fuel. The company soon became the leading supplier of aircraft filters, and in the 1960s and 1970s, Pall filters were used on most major military aircraft, including helicopters and fighter jets.

By the late 1970s, Pall had become very dependent on military and defense industries, and it began to seek new markets for its fine filter technology. During this time, Pall was able to provide the emerging semiconductor and bio-technical industries with the fine filters required for their manufacturing processes.

During the late 1980s, Pall executives focused on niche markets with very specialized and challenging manufacturing needs. Accordingly, Pall avoided producing filters that were widely used by individual consumers. (Such filters would include gasoline or oil filters for cars.) In fact, once Pall's development of a certain technology was complete, the company usually dropped its business in that area. One example of this occurred during 1988, when Pall sold its compressed air dryer business and the facility that produced gas mask filters once they both became technologically and financially mature product lines.

During the late 1980s, Pall Corporation began a special succession planning strategic initiative because it recognized that it could not rely solely on the genius of one person, David Pall; thus, it began to focus on building a research and development team. In fact, one Pall senior executive once commented in reference to David Pall that a good manager can be succeeded but pure genius cannot be succeeded. This provided incentive for Pall to assemble an impressive array of scientists who would help develop fluid clarification products. Pall efficiently managed its costs, spending only approximately 4% of its sales on research and development. By comparison, some of its chief competitors reportedly allotted more than 7% of sales to research and development. Pall was able to keep its costs down by sticking to its core competency of fluid clarification; its competitors, on the other hand, had diversified their interests and therefore required a wider array of researchers.

Another organizational strategy of Pall's was leveraging a team of scientists known collectively as the company's Scientific Laboratory Services, or SLS, to help test, advise, and communicate with researchers. According to one senior Pall executive, this provided a conduit between "best practices" customers and the company's own marketing and research teams.

Another area in which Pall was very efficient and effective was worldwide pricing. In order to ensure that supplies and prices remained consistent globally, manufacturing for each of Pall's product lines took place in at least two Pall facilities. The size of each facility was limited to no more than 450 employees, thus fostering a sense of team spirit and familiarity.

A significant part of the sustained growth that Pall experienced through the 1980s and into the 1990s, which averaged approximately 17% annually, was accomplished through internal growth rather than through acquisitions. Pall focused on building new plants and creating subsidiaries throughout the world. Pall faced global competition by maintaining its edge in several markets, and it continued to dominate almost every niche market that it carved out for its subsidiaries.

During the early 1990s, Pall's healthcare products division was its fastest growing segment. In fact, during 1992, this division posted sales of $331.6 million, which represented almost half of Pall's sales and 60% of its operating expenses. This division produced filters for direct use with hospital patients to provide protection against contamination and infection through blood, breathing, or IVs. Blood filters were an especially high growth area in the first part of the 1990s, with sales estimated to reach $260 million, or 26% of total sales, by 1995. For example, Pall's leukocyte filters treated with gamma rays were used to filter out white blood cells that caused the rejection of platelets during the multiple transfusions necessary for organ donors and recipients, AIDS patients, and patients undergoing chemotherapy. David Pall himself reportedly led the team that developed the blood filter, which proved a vital part of the system used for processing whole blood at blood collection sites.

Some other Pall healthcare products included filters used in diagnostic devices and filters used in the manufacture of contamination-free pharmaceuticals and biopharmaceuticals. Moreover, Pall produced electronic instruments for testing the filters before and after their use. It also produced food, beverage, and household water filters in its healthcare segment. Products in this market included filters for the final filtration process of beer, wine, and bottled water and filters used in the production of high-fructose corn syrup.

By the end of fiscal year 1992, Pall reported sales of $204.7 million in its Aeropower division. This division produced fluid clarification filters used to clean hydraulic, lubricating, and transmission fluids for both military and commercial aircraft. Other industrial customers included manufacturers and end users of fluid power equipment and bearing lubrication systems for steel, aluminum, and paper mills; manufacturers in the automobile and aerospace industries; and manufacturers of on- and off-road vehicles, construction equipment, and machinery for moving earth. The filters had additional applications in agriculture machinery, oil drilling and exploration, mining, metal cutting, and electric power generation.

Military sales were only 10% of Pall's sales in 1990, down from 25% ten years earlier. However, during the Persian Gulf crisis involving Operation Desert Shield and Operation Desert Storm, military sales shot up as Pall reportedly supplied $26 million worth of filters to keep sand out of helicopter engines. Furthermore, Pall entered into an agreement with FMC Corporation, a defense and military systems contractor, to provide an industrial air purification method (called Pressure Swing Absorption or PSA) to FMC for many military applications in North America, including foreign military sales. Pall anticipated that this would build a strong base for military sales, which the company expected to steadily increase despite the downsizing of the military that occurred in the early 1990s.

Pall's international operations provided about two-thirds of its revenues in the early 1990s. Its success in running international operations was based on three key rules: retain, use, and listen to competent locals. In 1991, Pall's sales growth in Europe was at 18% and its growth in Asia reached 31%, while its growth in the United States that year was only 8%. By 1993, Pall was generating about two-thirds of its revenues from foreign markets and had subsidiaries in Brazil, Spain, Germany, France, Singapore, Canada, Japan, Korea, and other nations. Pall was also considering further expansion in Japan and the rest of the Pacific Rim. Pall forecasted that by 1995, as much as 75% of its sales would be generated from foreign markets.

In 1993, Pall's international growth was concentrated in the high-tech areas of ultrafiltration (molecular separation) and dynamic microfiltration. To fuel this growth, Pall formed alliances with global operations instead of acquiring them.

According to a senior official at Pall, a company must have globalization strategy to survive as a business.

Pall focused on expansion and diversification in the mid-1990s. It made several key acquisitions and launched several new products as part of its growth strategy. In 1995, Pall announced the development of a filter used in HIV-related blood filtration. In 1999, Pall secured a $6 million water purification contract with the Pittsburgh Water and Sewer Authority. During that same year, the United Kingdom began to require the removal of white blood cells—leukocytes—from all blood and blood products after nearly 30 people died from mad cow disease. Shortly thereafter, Austria, France, Ireland, Malta, Norway, Poland, and Canada adopted the requirement that blood products go through a process called leukocyte reduction. In 2000, Germany followed suit, a move that resulted in Pall landing a $6 million blood filtration contract from the German Red Cross Transfusion Center.

Pall entered the 21st century with an excellent outlook on growth based on three strategic initiatives as foundational cornerstones: alliances, acquisitions, and research and development. During this time period, Pall began to make some internal changes to improve its efficiency. One example of this was Pall's adoption of the CoRe Cost Reduction program, which was expected to generate savings of nearly $20 million in 2005. Pall also realigned its business segments in 2004, restructuring them into three operating companies: Pall Life Sciences, which included the medical and biopharmaceuticals business; Pall Process Technologies, which combined microelectronics and general industrial interests; and Pall Aeropower, which integrated the company's aerospace holdings with its machinery and equipment holdings.

By 2005, it was apparent that Pall was a truly remarkable company that clearly qualified for inclusion in the Value Zone Hall of Fame. Its strategic initiatives have consistently resulted in remarkable business results. In 2004, Pall's founder David Pall, who personally held 181 U.S. patents, died, leaving behind a legacy that was far different from the small firm he founded in a New York garage in the 1940s. Indeed, with nearly 60 years of history under its belt, Pall has emerged as a formidable competitor in the purification, filtration, and separations industries.

In this chapter, our focus has been on efficiency, a Value Zone element that has helped Family Dollar Stores, Longs Drug Stores Corporation, Home Depot, and Pall Corporation sustain value for their customers. This has resulted in each of these companies consistently sustaining solid business performance for a period of 25 years. They have accomplished this through efficiency by "doing things right" and effectiveness by "doing the right thing." These firms have each demonstrated that building and sustaining an efficient business is an essential element of the Value Zone. Along with efficiency, another key element in the Value Zone is quality. We will next examine some exceptional examples of companies with high-quality products and services.

Chapter Eleven
Building and Sustaining Quality in Products and Services

Members of today's business world determine quality based on a concept called Six Sigma. For many businesses, Six Sigma simply means a measure of quality that aims for near perfection. Six Sigma is a disciplined, data-driven approach and methodology for eliminating defects (driving towards six standard deviations between the mean and the nearest specification limit) in any process, whether that process is manufacturing or transactional, a product or a service. From a statistical perspective, Six Sigma describes quantitatively how a process is performing. To achieve Six Sigma, a process must not produce more than 3.4 defects per million opportunities. A Six Sigma defect is defined as anything outside of customer specifications. A Six Sigma opportunity is then the total quantity of chances for a defect. In this chapter, we will discuss a core element of the Value Zone: quality. In the simplest terms, quality involves meeting or exceeding customer expectations in terms of products and/or services received. As we discussed before, quality is measured in terms of Six Sigma in today's business world. There are six key concepts of Six Sigma:

1) Critical to Quality: what attributes are most important to the customer
2) Defect: failing to deliver what the customer wants
3) Process Capability: what your process can deliver
4) Variation: what the customer sees and feels
5) Stable Operations: how you ensure consistent, predictable processes to improve what the customer sees and feels
6) Design for Six Sigma: how you design to meet customer needs and process capability

We look at product quality in eight dimensions: performance, features, flexibility, durability, conformity, serviceability, aesthetics, and perceived quality. We look at service quality in six dimensions: timeliness, courtesy, consistency, convenience, completeness, and accuracy. The challenge for businesses is to sustain product or service quality for a period of five years or more. Our research involving Value Zone Hall of Fame companies has provided strong evidence that companies known for products and services of exceptional quality have typically institutionalized quality as core to their cultures. In essence, quality is pervasive throughout the organization and practiced diligently by employees, managers, executives, suppliers, and business alliance partners. Let's now look at several companies that have institutionalized quality as a core competency and have a historical record that demonstrates a commitment to quality.

Cintas Corporation
Cintas Corporation is the leading supplier of rental uniforms in the United States, with a market share of approximately 25%. It provides products and ser-

vices for approximately 500,000 customers in North America. Cintas primarily rents its uniforms and then provides laundry service, pick up and delivery, and related services. The company also provides entrance mats, sanitation supplies, and clean-room supplies. Through its Xpect First Aid division, the company also sells first aid kits and safety devices and trains workers in first aid and Occupational Health and Safety Administration (OSHA) compliance. Cintas also sells uniforms and accessories such as hats and belts. The company runs 13 garment manufacturing plants and hundreds of laundry facilities and has a fleet of approximately 3,000 delivery trucks. The company is highly automated; it uses state-of-the-art manufacturing and distribution facilities that allow for rapid order turnaround. Cintas grew quickly through acquisitions in the 1990s and absorbed a large competitor, Omni Services, Inc., in 2002. The company is publicly traded, but over 20% of its shares are in the hands of Chairman Richard Farmer.

Cintas is a literal rags-to-riches story. The company's founder, Richard Farmer, started out as a ragman and, with his son Herschell, built up a thriving industrial linen business in the 1930s and 1940s. However, it was the third-generation leader Richard T. Farmer who guided the company into uniform rental in the late 1950s and led a trend-setting consolidation of that industry in the 1980s and 1990s. The latter Farmer was called a "visionary." He pioneered new fabrics, instituted modern management and control systems, and expanded his target market from industrial to service businesses, in addition to introducing other innovations that significantly improved the quality of the firm's products and services.

Cintas experienced significant growth as a company during the late 1950s under the leadership of Richard T. Farmer, a grandson of the company's founder. As we mentioned before, it was Farmer who went after the uniform rental business. Within a few years after entering into the uniform rental business, the firm grew to such an extent that it changed its name to the more inclusive Acme Uniform & Shop Towel Supply Co. During 1962, it was reported that Acme's revenues increased by a factor of six in just five years. By leveraging a key innovation process during the 1960s, Farmer enhanced the quality of the firm's uniforms by developing easy-care poly-cotton blends comprised of 65% cotton and 35% polyester; the fabric resisted wrinkling while holding a crease. Uniforms using the new blend could last at least twice as long as cotton ones. Farmer drew up exclusive contracts with the developers of this new material and invested in the conversion of their plant from soap-and-water laundering to dry cleaning, the ideal care for the new blend. By 1966, Acme was laundering about 80 tons of uniforms a week and making annual revenues of $1.8 million.

Knowing that he planned to take the family company public in the future, Farmer formed a holding company, Satellite Corp., in the late 1960s. Funded with $400,000 in equity raised by Farmer and the controller Robert Kohlhepp, Satellite established several uniform plants throughout the Midwest. When Satellite and Acme merged in 1972, the unified company's name was changed to Cintas.

Because he was a "visionary," Farmer tapped the "corporate identity" segment of the uniform market in the late 1960s and early 1970s, breaking into this market by persuading companies to take advantage of the benefits of uniformed employees in the workplace. As noted writer Susan Avery of the trade magazine *Purchasing* stated in 1994, "Employees in uniform are perceived to be trained, competent, and dependable. ... [They] also help convey images of cleanliness, safety, and security." Acme designed uniforms especially for each segment, incorporating corporate logos and signature colors in highly functional clothing tailored for each particular work environment. Working with national companies forced Cintas to grow geographically in order to service its new customers. By 1972, Cintas had established offices throughout Ohio and in Chicago, Detroit, and Washington, D.C. By 1973, sales surpassed the $10 million mark, and within two years, Cintas was operating in 13 states.

Cintas went public in 1983 and thus began a string of acquisitions that would catapult this firm to the highest ranks of the uniform rental industry. The 1980s witnessed an unprecedented consolidation of this service industry; it shrank from about 1,600 mom-and-pop companies in 1981 to less than 800 by the early 1990s. During the rest of the 1980s, Cintas expanded into 17 new geographic markets. Cintas' revenues doubled from $63 million in 1983 to $123.7 million in 1987 and then doubled again to $285 million by 1989. By the early 1990s, the company had a presence in three-fourths of the nation's 100 largest markets, and its market share had more than doubled from about 3.5% in 1983 to 10%. Importantly, only about one-third of Cintas' growth during this period was generated by acquisitions—the remainder came from organic growth.

During the late 1980s, Cintas pioneered the uniform industry's expansion from a blue-collar base to more tailored uniforms for hotel and motel employees, restaurant workers, and even bank employees. Within its core airline constituency, for example, the company moved from coveralls for baggage handlers and mechanics to uniforms for pilots, flight attendants, and other customer service workers. By 1995, other national clients included Wal-Mart, Delta, Coca-Cola, Pepsi, Northwest Airlines, Chevron, Jiffy Lube, Sunoco, AAMCO, Safety Kleen, and Chemlawn. Clearly, the quality of Cintas' uniforms and services was attracting new clients.

By 1997, Cintas had expanded to 70 new cities, and as it grew, it focused on improving productivity and committing millions of dollars to research and development each year. One example of this focus was the introduction of automated manufacturing systems featuring computerized design, cutting, and embroidery machines and electronic data interchange systems that used bar-coding to manage inventory, processing, and distribution. Modernization of Cintas' laundering plants helped reduce staffing by 50%, thereby significantly reducing the company's operating costs.

Cintas began to expand globally with the 1995 acquisition of Toronto's Cadet Uniform Services Ltd. While geographic diversification such as this continued to be a key strategic initiative for growth, the company also tried out new product lines during the late 1990s. For example, during 1997, Cintas acquired two businesses that supplied OSHA-required first-aid kits to companies. With $18 million in sales that year, this new business segment quickly grew to four major brands through the acquisition, and over the next three years, Cintas acquired over 100 small first aid companies.

In the mid-1990s, Richard Farmer initiated a succession planning strategic management transition that would end with his exit from Cintas. In 1995, he turned over the chief executive office and presidency to his longtime right-hand man, Robert Kohlhepp. In 1997, Richard's son Scott Farmer was promoted to president, setting the stage for the fourth generation of Farmers to lead Cintas. Meanwhile, Richard Farmer concentrated on broad strategic initiatives with a view to capturing an ever-larger share of the latent market for uniforms.

Cintas continued to expand through high-quality acquisitions during the late 1990s and into the 2000s. The uniform rental industry as a whole continued to expand during this period, and Census Bureau statistics showed that the uniform rental industry was growing at a rate of over 8% a year during the late 1990s. This led Cintas management to believe that there were many more business sectors left that would benefit from uniforms. Cintas achieved an impressive record of rising sales and profits, and its growth was in the double digits through the late 1990s. This served to increase Cintas' stock price, and the company was also able to make more acquisitions by swapping out its valuable shares. In just two years during the late 1990s, Cintas acquired 65 companies. The quality of its due diligence in these acquisitions was quite remarkable. Most of the acquired companies were in the uniform rental business; some provided first aid supplies and services, a growing segment for Cintas. Some of these companies were rivals like Uniforms to You and Kansas City-based Unitog Co. The Unitog transaction, which was paid for in Cintas stock, was valued at roughly $357 million. Unitog ran a uniform rental operation in 24 states and in Canada, and it had close to 60 plants. With this new acquisition, Cintas' market share rose to about 25%. During this time, Cintas became the largest company in the uniform rental industry, surpassing Aramark for the first time.

By 1999, Cintas' operations had expanded to close to 200 uniform rental facilities across the United States. Cintas also increased its manufacturing facilities from four to 13, expanded to six distribution centers, grew its clean-room business to six facilities, and grew its first aid business to 32 business centers. During this period, Cintas reported that approximately 4 million people wore Cintas uniforms every day. Despite this remarkable market growth, Cintas still saw more growth in the future. The uniform rental market in total was worth about $10 billion annually during the late 1990s, but Cintas executives believed that that figure could still grow to around $31 billion. The company's research showed that some 37 million people worked in occupations where uniforms could or should be used. Cintas appeared to be successful in expanding into the ancillary area of first aid, too, assembling an array of small companies and unifying them into one brand, which it introduced in 2000 as Xpect First Aid.

As the industry leader, Cintas was still intent on growing and consolidating through more acquisitions. An example of this occurred during 2002, when Cintas spent $22 million to acquire certain portions of the uniform manufacturing and marketing division of the Missouri-based laundry company Angelica Corp. Then, in what was its largest acquisition, it purchased Omni Services, Inc. This deal surpassed the Unitog deal of two years earlier. The French company Filuxel, S.A, owned Omni Services of Culpepper, Virginia. Omni reported annual sales of around $300 million and had 90,000 customers in over 30 states. The merger was expected to bump Cintas' sales to around $2.5 billion. Clearly, Cintas will continue to lead the industry for years to come.

Johnson Controls, Inc.

Johnson Controls, Inc. is a diversified company made up of two main business groups:

1) automotive systems, which include seating, overhead and instrument panels, floor consoles, door systems, engine electronics, and batteries; and
2) building management and control systems.

It is the world's largest independent maker of automotive seating and interior systems and the leading supplier of automotive batteries for the original equipment and replacement markets in North America, South America, and Europe. Johnson Controls is number one worldwide in building control systems, services, and integrated facility management. It provides these products and services for schools, hospitals, office buildings, airports, and other nonresidential buildings. Johnson Controls' Automotive Systems Group generates nearly 75% of the company's revenues, and its Controls Group is responsible for the remaining 25%. The percentage of sales generated outside North America has increased to about 40%. Over the course of more than a century, Johnson Controls has had an impressive track record of providing high-quality products and services, a practice which has resulted in the consecutive payment of dividends since 1885 and 57 straight years of sales increases through 2003. This is a remarkable achievement; therefore, we have included Johnson Controls in the Value Zone Hall of Fame's Ring of Honor along with Johnson & Johnson.

Warren Seymour Johnson, the founder of Johnson Controls, was born in Rutland County, Vermont and grew up in Wisconsin. Johnson worked as a printer, surveyor, schoolteacher, and school superintendent before he was appointed a professor at the State Normal School in Whitewater, Wisconsin in 1876. Although known as an excellent teacher, Johnson's main interest was his laboratory, where he conducted experiments in electrochemistry. In 1883, he produced the first Johnson System of Temperature Regulation, an electric thermostat system that he installed at the State Normal School. Johnson received a patent for the electric telethermoscope, which was the first room thermostat, and also persuaded Milwaukee, Wisconsin hotelier and heir to the Plankinton Packing Company William Plankinton to become his financial backer in producing the device. He formed a new partnership with Plankinton, and they formed the Milwaukee Electric Manufacturing Company. As a result, Johnson resigned his professorship so he could devote all his time to his inventions. On May 1, 1885, the company was reorganized as the Johnson Electric Service Company, a Wisconsin corporation, in Milwaukee.

Johnson, who was affectionately called "The Professor," continued to invent additional control devices while also designing a variety of other products such as chandeliers, springless door locks, puncture-proof tires, thermometers, and a hose coupling for providing steam heat to passenger railcars. His inventions were quite novel and received a great deal of recognition. One such invention was the Professor's impressive tower clock. Johnson, who was only interested in developing products of high quality, invented a system powered by air pressure that increased the reliability of such clocks. The company built its first big clock in 1895 for the Minneapolis courthouse and built the clock for the Milwaukee City Hall tower a year later. Johnson's largest tower clock was installed in the Philadelphia City Hall. A giant floral clock for the 1904 Saint Louis World's Fair received international notoriety and enhanced the growing reputation of the company. The clock's success clearly showed off the usefulness of the pneumatic operations the company was employing in its control applications. Thus, from the very beginning of his company, "The Professor" institutionalized product quality as a foundational cornerstone for the company's culture.

At the 1900 Paris World's Fair, Johnson's wireless-communication exhibit won second prize. In the same competition, Guglielmo Marconi, developer of the wireless telegraph, placed third. Company directors elected Johnson president of the company in 1901, and a year later, the firm's name was changed to Johnson Service Company. Under Johnson's leadership, more than 50 patents for technology that harnessed power generated by fluid, air, or steam pressure were assigned to the Johnson Service Company. Johnson died in 1911. Harry W. Ellis was elected president in 1912. Ellis, a former manager of the Chicago branch office, decided to focus on opportunities for growth in the controls field. He sold all of the company's other businesses, improved the efficiency of factory operations in Milwaukee, and introduced a modern accounting system.

"The Professor," who had an eye for high quality, insisted that only trained Johnson mechanics install his company's devices. Ellis reinforced this policy; he insisted that the Johnson Service Company was to serve not just as a producer of regulation equipment but also as a single source for design, installation, and service, which in his mind guaranteed the highest quality. Johnson's temperature-control business grew and fit in well with the country's building boom. Skyscrapers became popular as structural steel replaced iron. During World War I, the company's temperature-control business was classified by the War Industry Board as nonessential to the war effort because it was seen as a means of providing comfort. Johnson contracts dropped off as civilian construction projects were sharply reduced. The firm looked to government buildings for business and began seeking contracts to retrofit old buildings with new temperature-control systems.

In 1919, the company's new contracts exceeded $1 million. By 1928, the company's new contracts passed the $4 million mark. However, the Great Depression of 1929 led to a serious setback to the construction industry, and most new building control installations in the 1930s focused on cost reductions. Projects in schools and government buildings that were assigned by the Public Works Administration also had fuel savings as a goal. Johnson's new Dual Thermostat, which allowed a building to save fuel by automatically lowering temperatures at times when the building was unoccupied, was in demand.

Joseph A. Cutler, a former engineering professor at the University of Wisconsin, was elected the third president of the company in 1938, and his presidency, like Ellis', would last almost 25 years. Cutler led the first public listing of Johnson's stock, which began trading over-the-counter on the NASDAQ in 1940. After the United States entered World War II, Johnson was classified as part of an essential industry, a move that showed evidence of change in the public perception of building controls. Johnson's contributions to the war effort included installing high-quality temperature and humidity control systems in defense facilities and engineering special military products. The company also made leak detectors that were used to test barrage balloons used over military installations, ships, and landing barges; developed the radiosonde to help combat pilots encountering unknown flying conditions to gather weather data; and manufactured echo boxes used for testing radar sets.

After World War II ended, civilian construction skyrocketed, leading to a large number of new contracts. Along with this new business came an interest in air conditioning. In mid-1950s, Johnson began to build and install high-quality pneumatic control centers that allowed a single building engineer to monitor panels displaying room temperatures, ventilating conditions, water temperatures, and outdoor temperatures. To ensure high quality via a steady and reliable source of customized control panels for these centers, Johnson acquired a panel-fabrication company in Oklahoma in 1960 and continued with the help of its other expansion projects to produce highly innovative products with consistent quality.

Richard J. Murphy became Johnson's president in 1960, the year the company celebrated its 75th anniversary. Mr. Murphy had started with the company as a timekeeper in 1918 and had moved up through the ranks; therefore, he thoroughly understood Johnson's culture of high-quality products and services. Although his tenure was relatively short, lasting only six years, Mr. Murphy was responsible for many innovations. For example, the Systems Engineering and Construction Division was established in 1961, which provided equipment for all 57 Air Force Titan II launch complexes and most other major missile programs. The National Aeronautics and Space Administration contracted with Johnson Controls throughout the 1960s for mission-control instrumentation for the Apollo-Saturn program, again because of Johnson's precise and high-quality instruments.

With an eye on global growth, Mr. Murphy established an international division with subsidiaries in England, France, Australia, Belgium, Italy, and Switzerland. Each international office was managed as a virtually independent business, as were operations in the United States and Canada. During 1964, construction of the first foreign manufacturing plant began in Italy.

Since World War II, Johnson had enjoyed an excellent reputation for its work in atomic research plants and other installations requiring exceptional levels of reliability. However, Johnson and its main competitors Honeywell and Powers Regulator were charged in 1962 with a federal antitrust suit for price-fixing related to the sale of pneumatic temperature control systems. The suit's resolution in a consent decree, along with new competitors entering the controls market, meant that the market was growing increasingly competitive and forcing Johnson to make little or no profit. Despite this setback, Johnson managers recognized that electronics technology could be used to control all aspects of maintaining a building and therefore put strategic initiatives in place to improve Johnson's in-house electronics capability. As part of its increasing involvement in projects requiring exacting quality standards and high-quality components, Johnson acquired Associated Piping & Engineering Corporation and Western Piping and Engineering Company in 1966. These companies fabricated high-quality expansion joints and piping for nuclear and fossil fuel generating plants and many other industrial applications.

Fred L. Brengel became the sixth Johnson president in 1967. Mr. Brengel joined Johnson as a sales engineer in 1948, served as manager of the Boston branch office, and served as sales manager of the New England and Midwest regions before becoming vice-president and general sales manager in 1963. It was apparent that Mr. Brengel understood as well as his predecessors did that quality was an essential element of this company. Mr. Brengel became president just as Johnson introduced the T-6000, a solid-state, digital data logger that used a "management by exception" system that announced when its variables were outside specified limits so an engineer's attention was only called for when required. Not only did the T-6000 perform heating, ventilating, and air conditioning functions; it also monitored fire and smoke detection, security, and emergency lighting systems. Without question, this product had to be extremely reliable and of the highest quality.

One year after Mr. Brengel became president, Johnson acquired Penn Controls, Inc., a 50-year-old company that manufactured controls for original equipment manufacturers (OEMs), distributors, and wholesalers. With its Penn Controls acquisition, Johnson bolstered its competitive edge by gaining its own supply of electrical products for installation projects. Penn Controls also had manufacturing plants and subsidiaries in Canada, the Netherlands, Argentina, and Japan that helped Johnson expand its international markets. The year it acquired Penn Controls, the company's sales rose approximately 20% to $155 million. Meanwhile, during 1972, Johnson introduced the JC/80, the industry's first minicomputer system that managed building controls. One of the many advantages of the JC/80 was only a minimal amount of technical training was needed to operate the system. The JC/80, which could cut fuel requirements by as much as 30%, was introduced at an extremely important time—just a year before international embargoes on oil would change the way the world viewed energy consumption. Virtually overnight, the world would become interested in reducing energy costs.

In 1974, the company adopted its present name, Johnson Controls, Inc., and by 1977, it had captured approximately 35% of the estimated $600 million market for commercial building control systems. Also during this time period, Johnson Controls had 114 branch offices in the United States and Canada and more than 300 service centers staffed by 10,000 engineers, architects, designers, and service technicians. In spite of a worldwide recession, the company's sales rose to almost $500 million that year.

Despite this enormous success, Johnson Controls faced increasing competition as new companies began to crowd the building controls field. To diversify itself further, Johnson Controls merged with Globe-Union Inc., the country's largest manufacturer of automotive batteries, in 1978. This merger was completed with a lot of due diligence on the part of both companies. Johnson Controls' emphasis on a culture of exceptional quality was also shared by Globe-Union. Originally founded in Milwaukee in 1911, the Globe Electric Company had as its original aim the fulfillment of the battery needs of streetcars, rural light plants, and switchboards. All of these products called for high reliability and quality. In 1925, Globe's treasurer Chester O. Wanvig entered into an agreement with Sears, Roebuck and Co. President General Robert Wood to produce automobile replacement batteries for the company. However, Globe shareholders declined the opportunity, forcing Mr. Wanvig to form a new company, the Union Battery Company, to serve Sears. In 1929, Globe Electric and Union Battery consolidated with Mr. Wanvig as president. By the late 1930s, Globe-Union had expanded to ten manufacturing plants across the United States. In the late 1950s, Globe-Union's latest innovation was the thin-wall polypropylene battery container, a major technological breakthrough that won the company a leadership position in the industry. The thickness of the battery walls was reduced and the container was lighter and stronger than the traditional hard-rubber cases. In 1967, Sears used this technology in its Die Hard battery, which was made by Globe-Union. By 1971, Globe-Union had become the largest U.S. manufacturer of automotive replacement batteries, and its sales climbed past $100 million that year. Globe-Union turned to non-automotive battery applications in 1972 when it formed an industrial products division. One of its notable innovations was the Gel/Cell, a line of sealed, portable lead acid units for the standby power needs of security and telecommunications applications that required high reliability.

The result of the merger with Johnson Controls was immediate, doubling Johnson's sales, broadening its financial base, and giving it leadership in a new field. By 1980, sales surpassed $1 billion. During the early 1980s, Johnson Controls took a leadership position in the development of controls for "intelligent buildings," buildings that featured state-of-the-art technology to manage energy, comfort, and protection needs. Again, these systems required the most reliable and highest quality products. Despite the increase of new competitors in this market, Johnson remained a leader in the field. During the late 1980s, Johnson Controls announced a joint venture with Yokogawa Electric Corporation to manufacture control instrumentation and to integrate and service industrial automation systems for the North American market.

Johnson Controls made a huge foray into the automotive business in 1985 when it acquired Hoover Universal, Inc., a major supplier of seating and plastic parts for automobiles and a new entrant in the plastic-container industry. At the time of the purchase, Hoover was transitioning from providing seating components to building completely assembled automotive seating. The company had an excellent reputation for its just-in-time delivery system, which meant that the company supplied its automotive customers with needed parts and components exactly when they required them, thus reducing customer storage charges.

Those acquisitions and expansions efforts into the auto industry earned Johnson Controls the reputation of being a parts supplier that could design, engineer, assemble, and deliver modular systems to its customers' plants "just in time." Furthermore, Johnson Controls also supplied components to the major North American carmakers; several of the U.S. operations of Japanese auto manufacturers, including Toyota, Honda, and Nissan; and a Toyota-General Motors joint venture.

With James H. Keyes now at the helm, Johnson Controls expanded its plastics business in 1988 with the acquisition of the Apple Container Corporation and the soft drink bottle operation American National Can Company. By mid-1989, Johnson Controls also acquired Pan Am World Services, Inc., a leading provider of high-tech and other facility management services for military bases, airports, and space centers. This $167 million acquisition was intended to strengthen Johnson's nascent business in providing engineering and protection services for commercial buildings.

Johnson Controls' controls business had established an international presence concentrated in Europe and the Far East since the 1960s, and during the mid-1980s, it also began to expand its plastic-container and seating businesses into Europe. This aggressive expansion was facilitated primarily through acquisition, and by 1990, Johnson Controls had achieved leadership positions in both markets. One move that led to this leadership position was Johnson Controls' acquisition of Varta Ltd., the largest automotive battery maker in Canada. During that same year, the battery division unveiled the Ever Start, a new automotive battery that carried its own emergency backup power system. It was called the first real breakthrough in battery technology in decades.

One key challenge threatening Johnson Controls' position as a leader in producing quality products that were highly reliable was its resistance of hostile takeovers. The company's management was committed to thwarting all such attempts; President Keyes told *Forbes* in a March 1989 interview that "It depends on whether you take a short-term view and want to improve returns immediately, or you take a long-term view and seek to maintain market leadership. We've chosen the latter approach."

During the 1990s, Johnson Controls' automotive businesses became its most important business sector. However, to bolster its original core competency of control systems, Johnson Controls introduced the Metasys facility management system in the early 1990s. Under development for three years at a cost close to $20 million, Metasys was a breakthrough system designed for buildings as small as 50,000 square feet that tied together the entire control system through a distributed computer-controlled network.

In 1991, a significant event occurred when the U.S. Supreme Court settled Johnson Controls' involvement in a landmark sex discrimination lawsuit. During the 1980s, Johnson Controls had switched from a voluntary to a mandatory policy barring women of childbearing age from jobs involving exposure to high levels of lead at its 15 car battery plants. The company's key concern was that pregnant women exposed to a potentially harmful substance might sue if the exposure resulted in birth defects. However, The United States Supreme Court said in a 6-3 ruling that decisions about the welfare of future children "must be left to the parents who conceive, bear, support, and raise them rather than to the employers who hire those parents." The Court ruled that Johnson Controls' policy was discriminatory against women and therefore had to be removed.

Out of all of Johnson Controls' diversified operations, its battery business was the least profitable. The reasons for this were because prices for batteries remained flat for a decade and also because the unit's unionized plants had to compete with nonunion plants of other companies. During the mid-1990s, Johnson Controls attempted to sell its battery division but failed to do so. This problem was exacerbated by the loss of its contract to supply Die Hard batteries to Sears in late 1994. Since that time, however, Johnson Controls has signed or renewed contracts with such retailers as AutoZone and Wal-Mart, and it has also remained a supplier of the largest battery distributor in the U.S., Interstate Battery System of America. During October 1997, a new contract was signed to supply Sears with Die Hard Gold batteries, the top of that product line. This Johnson Controls division remained aggressive in its expansion efforts, opening a plant in Mexico in 1994, forming a joint venture in China in 1996 to make batteries for Volkswagen, and creating another joint venture in 1997 with Varta Battery AG of Germany to make batteries in South America.

While offering high quality and reliable products remained a core element of its culture, Johnson Controls also continued to make a number of significant automotive systems acquisitions during the mid-1990s. This move greatly increased sales in the company's automotive segment by a whopping 94% from 1995 to 1998 alone. One example of this expansion was Johnson Controls' purchase of a 75% interest in Roth Frères SA, a Strasbourg, France-based major supplier of seating and interior systems to the European auto industry, in 1995. Johnson Controls also paid about $1.3 billion for the Prince Automotive unit of Prince Holding Corporation in 1996, the largest acquisition in Johnson Controls history. Based in Holland, Michigan, Prince Automotive was an innovative supplier of automotive interior systems and components such as interior ceilings, overhead consoles and switches, door panels, armrests, and floor consoles. This acquisition meant that Johnson Controls could now make virtually all major interior auto components and could offer its customers complete seating systems.

Furthermore, the company expanded into the Asia-Pacific region in 1996. Some examples of this expansion were a joint venture in China with Beijing Automotive Industry Corp. to run a car seating and interior system factory; another joint venture in India to supply seats and trim for Ford Escorts built there; and the purchase of Aldersons, a unit of Sydney, Australia-based Tutt Bryant Industries PLY Ltd. that supplied interior systems to Australia's four major automakers. It was not surprising that during 1996, Johnson Controls revenues exceeded the $10 billion mark for the first time.

Joint ventures and acquisitions continued in 1998 with Johnson Controls' announcement of the formation of a venture with Recaro North America Inc. (a unit of German seat manufacturer Recaro GmbH & Company) in which Johnson Controls would supply brand-name specialty seats for the first time under the Recaro brand. In July 1998, Johnson Controls acquired Sterling Heights, Michigan-based Becker Group, Inc., a supplier of interior systems in both North America and Europe, for $548 million and the assumption of $372 million in debt. The addition of Becker made Johnson Controls the number-one supplier of interior systems in Europe. To help pay down additional debt taken on to purchase Becker, Johnson Controls divested two more non-core units. It sold its plastics machinery business to Cincinnati Milacron Inc. for about $190 million in September 1998, and it sold its industrial battery division to C&D Technologies Inc. in March 1999 for approximately $135 million.

Johnson Controls entered into further joint ventures to make automotive batteries in Mexico and South America. Early in 1999, Johnson Controls regained its position as the sole supplier of batteries to Sears. In the controls side of its business, Johnson Controls spent about $41 million in November 1998 to buy Cardkey Systems, a maker of electronic access and security management systems based in Simi Valley, California. In 1999, its Automotive Systems Group began entering into partnerships with a host of electronics firms in order to start integrating electronics into every aspect of vehicle interiors. Early results of these partnerships included integrated hands-free cellular car phone functions, in-car DVD players, and a computer-controlled car seat that automatically adjusted several pressure points to combat driver fatigue.

From the late 1980s to the early 2000s, Johnson Controls' sales came increasingly from global markets largely because of the international nature of its acquisitions. Revenues streaming in from outside of North America increased from 30% to 40% during this period. The acquisitions made between 2000 and 2003 continued this trend. One example of this growth was Johnson Controls' acquisition of its first major automotive asset in Asia through the purchase of a controlling 90% stake in Ikeda Bussan Co. Ltd. for about $90 million in 2000. Ikeda was the primary supplier of automotive seating to Japanese automaker Nissan. At the end of 2000 came Johnson Controls' acquisition of Gylling Optima Batteries AB, a Swedish maker of high-performance, leak-resistant lead-acid batteries marketed under the Optima brand name. This was significant in that it was the first battery brand owned by Johnson Controls, as Johnson had previously produced only original-equipment and private-label batteries. This Swedish product met Johnson Controls' standards for high quality.

Johnson Controls significantly bolstered its automotive electronics capabilities via the October 2001 $435 million buyout of Sagem SA. Sagem's strength was in interior electronics such as instrument panels; however, the French firm was also a supplier of fuel injectors and engine controllers, which were new products for Johnson Controls. Another deal concluded that same month was the purchase of Hoppecke Automotive GmbH & Co. KG, based in Germany. Hoppecke specialized in batteries designed for the emerging market in 36/42-volt automotive electrical systems; these batteries promised to provide more power and to help cars weigh less and achieve better mileage because the wires in such systems were smaller. The battery operation of Johnson Controls was strengthened during October 2002 when Johnson acquired the automotive battery division of Germany's Varta AG for about $310 million. Germany's Varta AG produced original equipment batteries for several European automakers and also made after-market batteries for a number of customers, including hypermarket chains and wholesalers. This acquisition provided Johnson Controls with a leadership position in the European automotive battery market ahead of competitors like Exide Technologies.

Johnson Controls was faced with still another challenge during June 2002 when workers at four of its parts plants in the United States went on strike. The work stoppage lasted only two days, however, because Johnson Controls' management agreed to give the workers higher wages and benefits and, perhaps most importantly, the right to organize workers at another 26 company plants in the United States that were suppliers to the Big Three U.S. automakers. Johnson Controls' workforce had largely been nonunion, but the company believed that it had to become more of a unionized supplier in order to secure major outsourcing contracts from the Big Three U.S. automakers, its three largest customers. The issue of outsourcing had become a growing area of contention between these automakers and their largely unionized workforces. Meanwhile, in the fiscal year ending in September 2002, Johnson Controls' revenues surpassed $20 billion for the first time in its history. These revenues represented a fourfold increase in sales over a ten-year period, and Johnson's net income hit a record $600.5 million. During this time, seasoned veteran Mr. Barth was named president and CEO, while Mr. Keyes remained chairman.

During mid-2003, Johnson Controls greatly strengthened its automotive electronics operations by acquiring Borg Instruments AG for EUR 117.5 million in cash. Based in Germany, Borg specialized in high-end instrument clusters and other information displays. It was also the producer of the Quo Vadis navigational system and an electronic parking assistance system providing an electronic signal to a driver whose vehicle is about to bump another vehicle. During this time, Johnson Controls announced that Mr. Keyes would retire at the end of 2003 and Mr. Barth would take on the additional post of chairman. Mr. Keyes left behind a company with an enviable record of achievement, particularly during the uncertain political and economic climate of the early 2000s. Fiscal 2003 results showed that Johnson Controls had achieved its 57th consecutive year of sales increases (reaching $22.65 billion), its 13th consecutive year of increased earnings ($682.9 million), and its 28th consecutive year of dividend increases. Over the previous ten years, sales had grown at an average annual rate of 14%, while net income had increased by 17% per year. Johnson Controls had clearly been served well by its diversified operations in high-quality controls and automotive systems and by its ever-growing capabilities within these two areas.

Tesco plc

Tesco plc is one of the largest retailers in the world, operating more than 2,300 supermarkets and convenience stores and employing 326,000 people. Tesco's core business is in Britain, where the company ranks as the largest private sector employer and food retailer in the United Kingdom, operating nearly 1,900 stores. Tesco also operates in the Czech Republic, Hungary, Poland, the Republic of Ireland, Slovakia, and Turkey. In Asia, the company operates in Japan, Malaysia, South Korea, Taiwan, and Thailand. Through Tesco.com, the company is recognized as the largest online supermarket in the world. Tesco also offers financial services through Tesco Financial Services, which controls 4.6 million customer accounts divided between credit cards and car insurance policies. Tesco's more than 100-unit Tesco Express chain is the largest provider of gasoline in the United Kingdom. Tesco is known for its high-quality, service-oriented stores.

Tesco's tradition of high-quality, service-oriented stores began with its founder John Edward (Jack) Cohen. In 1919, Cohen invested his £30 stipend from his World War I service as a member of the Royal Flying Corps in stock for his small grocery stall in the East End of London, thus beginning his career as a market trader. Cohen soon became a successful trader in other London markets outside of the East End and also branched out into wholesaling for other market traders. In 1932, Cohen officially founded Tesco Stores Limited. The name was originally that of a private-label brand of tea Cohen sold and was created from the initials and the first two letters of the name of T.E. Stockwell, a merchant from whom he bought tea.

Over the next eight years, Tesco's growth was rapid; it expanded to more than 100 small stores, most of which were in the London area. In 1935, Cohen was invited to the United States by several major American suppliers. He quickly became an enthusiastic student of the American food retailing system. World War II temporarily impeded his vision of taking the American self-service supermarket concept back to the United Kingdom. Nevertheless, Cohen's dream became a reality in 1947, the same year that shares in Tesco Stores (Holdings) Limited were first offered for sale to the public and Tesco opened its first self-service store in St. Albans, Hertfordshire. Despite the fact that the St. Albans store closed in 1948 after failing to capture the interest of British shoppers, it reopened one year later to a much warmer reception.

During the next two decades, Tesco expanded rapidly across the United Kingdom. This growth was accomplished mainly through the acquisition of smaller grocery chains, including the 19-store Burnards chain in 1955, the 70-store Williamsons Ltd. in 1957, the 200-branch Harrow Stores Ltd. in 1959, the 97-unit Charles Phillips & Company Ltd. in 1964, and the 47-store Adsega chain in 1965. In 1956, the company opened its first supermarket in Maldon, Essex. It carried fresh foods in addition to Tesco's traditional dry goods. In 1960, Tesco established a special department in its larger stores called "Home 'n' Wear" to carry higher-margin, nonfood merchandise such as apparel and household items. In 1967, Tesco completed construction on a 90,000-square-foot warehouse in Westbury, Wiltshire. The very next year, Tesco opened its first 40,000-square-foot superstore at Crawley, Sussex. The term "superstore" referred not only to the store's size but also to its vast selection of inexpensive food and nonfood items.

By 1976, Tesco was running about 900 supermarkets and superstores using the "pile it high, sell it cheap" formula that Cohen had gleaned from his studies of American retail markets. The firm's management found that the effectiveness of this strategy decreased over time, leaving Tesco with uncomfortably slim margins and a serious image problem among consumers. While Tesco had been preoccupied with opening as many stores as possible and loading them with merchandise, the company had missed some important signs that its market was changing and that its customers had come to value merchandise quality versus quantity.

The task of turning the company was given to Ian MacLaurin, who had risen through the Tesco ranks to become managing director in 1973. In the first phase of his recovery plan, Tesco discontinued the use of Green Shield trading stamps (which had been introduced in 1963), an action that major stores in the United States had also taken. This was followed in 1977 by a questionable tactic, Operation Checkout, in which Tesco cut prices across the board in an attempt to increase sales and market share during a period when consumers were spending less money on food purchases. Despite the fact that the company accomplished its key objective and increased its market share from 7% to 12% in the span of a year, Operation Checkout did little to improve Tesco's declining image among consumers. The problems faced by Tesco were enormous; stores were cramped, difficult to operate, and very difficult to staff. Customer service was poor and merchandise selection in many outlets was limited. Tesco also touched off a price war with J. Sainsbury plc, one of its major rivals, which ended up driving a number of smaller retailers and independent grocers out of business or making them acquisition targets of larger companies when they found themselves unable to compete with the prices offered by the two warring retailers.

To create a high-quality, service-oriented image and to reposition itself, Tesco embarked upon a massive modernization program intended in part to improve its market share. Tesco closed 500 unprofitable stores and extensively upgraded and enlarged others, installing enhanced lighting and widening its aisles. Tesco pursued the superstore concept much more aggressively than it had in the past in order to compete more successfully with other major retailers and be more responsive to consumers who preferred to shop where parking was convenient and the selection of goods was broad. Tesco made a significant investment not only in improving the physical appearance of its stores but also in providing the higher quality merchandise that consumers wanted. Superstores were also seen as the key to generating a higher volume of business at increased margins while lowering overhead. At their beginning, the superstores averaged 25,000 square feet, but they eventually grew as large as 65,000 square feet. Each superstore functioned as a self-service department store coupled with a supermarket. Tesco placed a heavy emphasis on having a varied selection of fresh, high-quality foods available in addition to a wide range of general merchandise such as household items and clothing that was designed to appeal to more high-end market tastes.

To improve the high-quality, service-oriented image of these stores, Tesco introduced its own private-label product lines that had been developed through an extensive research and development program. Tesco also restructured and computerized its distribution system, opening its own centralized warehouses for storing inventory that could then be supplied to its stores as needed instead of having to rely on manufacturers' delivery schedules.

During the latter part of 1981, food sales were slumping, placing additional pressure on Tesco's bottom line. To counteract this slump and to revitalize consumer activity, Tesco launched Checkout '82, cutting prices between 3% and 26% on approximately 1,500 food items. This strategy was similar to the strategy employed in 1977, but Tesco now operated in an environment of slimmer profit margins. Checkout '82 rekindled the price wars between Tesco and its chief competitor, J. Sainsbury, in which each chain devoted all of its energies to outdoing the other to gain and sustain customer loyalty.

In 1983, the company changed its name to Tesco plc and joined forces with Marks & Spencer, an upscale British variety store, that following year to develop shopping centers in areas outside the United Kingdom's major cities. Their first joint venture, which became a model for subsequent centers, was established at Brookfield Centre near Cheshunt. Located there was a 65,000-square-foot Tesco superstore next to a 69,000-square-foot Marks & Spencer department store. To help sustain high-quality customer service, the Tesco store was supported by 42 computerized checkout counters and 900 employees. This Tesco store offered a variety of food and nonfood departments in addition to a variety of services including a bank, a gas station, a baby-care facility, and a consumer advisory kitchen staffed by home economists. The Marks & Spencer store featured mostly nonfood merchandise but had a small amount of space devoted to the popular specialty food items it marketed under its own St. Michael label.

In 1985, Ian MacLaurin assumed the role of chairman of Tesco, and in that same year, the company opened its 100th United Kingdom superstore in Brent Park, Neasden. This outlet was a source of contention between the company and the local government from the date Tesco first acquired the 43-acre site in 1978. The local government council made a number of objections to the proposed development, maintaining that the store did not fit the planning needs of the area and did not make sufficient allowances for future warehousing requirements. The council's greatest concern was that this Tesco store would pose a threat to incumbent shopping centers and local merchants. However, once Tesco's store finally opened for business, it became London's largest food store.

To enhance the quality of the products and services it offered, Tesco launched a major capital spending program in 1985 to support aggressive store and warehouse expansion and provide more efficient technology in existing stores. These technology upgrades were implemented at the checkout counters, in the back offices, and in the distribution centers. Tesco's investment in the development of a sophisticated distribution system, together with other facility improvements, enabled the company to incorporate its 1987 acquisition of the 40-store Hillards plc chain easily. This expansion also gave Tesco increased visibility in many key regions throughout the United Kingdom. In 1988 and 1989, the company spent £500 million to build 29 new stores. In the late 1980s, Tesco also introduced a composite six-warehouse distribution system to serve its stores, resulting in increased efficiency and improved service.

By the early part of the 1990s, Tesco had 371 stores in England, Scotland, and Wales, 150 of which were superstores. This moved Tesco up in its industry, and thus it became one of the United Kingdom's top three food retailers. The early 1990s also saw Tesco's fight for market share, which was fueled in part by a two-year, £1 billion development program launched in 1990 that added about 60 new stores and approximately 2.3 billion square feet of additional store space. By 1991, Tesco had become the largest independent gasoline retailer in Great Britain. In 1995, Tesco reached the number-one spot among food retailers in terms of market share. This achievement was due in part to the 1992 introduction of the Tesco Metro format, which had its debut at Covent Garden, London. The Metro stores were smaller outlets with about 10,000 square feet or so of floor space and were designed for urban areas. They offered a few thousand product lines tailored specifically for the local market. Tesco had typically concentrated its stores in suburbia, but the Tesco Metro stores targeted city neighborhoods and were intended to compete squarely with Marks & Spencer's successful urban food-only stores. By 1997, Tesco had opened 40 Tesco Metro units.

However, more significant for Tesco in the long term was the company's aggressive 1990s push outside of Great Britain. In 1993, Tesco paid £175 million ($282 million US) to purchase Catteau S.A., a 92-store grocery chain in northern France. This first foray into other regions in Europe proved ill-founded, however, as Catteau struggled to compete against discounters and larger chains such as Promodes and Carrefour. Lacking the critical mass needed to compete successfully, Tesco decided to exit from France four years after it had entered the country by selling Catteau to Promodes in December 1997 for £250 million ($416.9 million US).

Despite the setback in France, other Tesco expansion moves in the 1990s were more successful. For example, in August 1994, the company acquired William Low, gaining 57 stores in Scotland and northern England for £247 million. Also in that same year, Tesco moved into the burgeoning central European market for the first time through the £15 million purchase of a 51% stake in Global, a supermarket chain in northwest Hungary with 43 stores. The following year, Tesco acquired the 31-store Savia chain in Poland for £8 million. In 1996, the company spent £79 million on 13 Kmart stores in the Czech Republic and Slovakia. It soon converted these stores to the Tesco name. Initially, Tesco's central European operations suffered operating losses largely due to hefty development costs, but the company announced in early 1998 that it aimed to be a major food retailer in the region, that it would spend £350 million through the year 2000 to continue to expand its base, and that it expected to be making a profit there by the turn of the century. In 1997, Tesco acquired the Irish food retailing businesses of Associated British Food plc for £630 million ($1 billion), thereby gaining leading market share positions in both the Republic of Ireland (through 75 stores) and Northern Ireland (through 34 stores).

Tesco continued to experiment with additional new formats and introduce new and innovative services. One example of this occurred during 1994, when Tesco opened the first two Tesco Express gasoline stations, both located in London. The Express format was a combination filling station and convenience store. By late 1997, 15 Express gas stations had opened. In 1997, Tesco opened the first Tesco Extra unit in Pitsea, Essex. This store covered 102,000 square feet, and 25% of the sales area consisted of expanded nonfood departments. It soon became the company's number-one store in terms of sales.

Furthermore, to enhance the quality of its customer outreach programs, Tesco introduced the Tesco Clubcard in February 1995, becoming the first British retailer with a loyalty card. In 1997, the company created a new unit called Tesco Personal Finance in order to provide its customers with a vast array of financial services including a Tesco Visa Card, a Tesco savings account, in-store bank branches, Tesco Travel Money and Insurance, and Clubcard Plus, a combination loyalty card and savings account.

The year 1997 was also marked by management changes at the top; Mr. MacLaurin retired and was succeeded by John Gardiner. Mr. Gardiner had been appointed deputy chairman of Tesco in 1993 and also served as chairman of Larid Group plc. During that same year, Terry Leahy was appointed Tesco's CEO. Mr. Leahy had joined Tesco in 1979 as the company's first marketing director and played a key role in Tesco's rise to the top of U.K. food retailing. Now energized by a new management team, Tesco aimed to build upon its multi-format empire in the United Kingdom, continue to develop innovative products and services (particularly financial services), turn its central European operations into profitable ones, and seek other overseas expansion opportunities, such as those in the emerging markets of Asia.

Mr. Leahy's emergence as a prominent figure guiding Tesco at the turn of the century soon became apparent to observers. One of the things that he is credited with is the development of a four-pronged growth strategy. During the early part of the 21st century, Tesco directed its expansion efforts towards four areas: its core U.K. business, its retailing services, its international operations, and its nonfood business. The nonfood component of the company's growth strategy presented the greatest challenge for Mr. Leahy because the company was essentially starting from scratch. As Mr. Leahy's plans unfolded, Tesco aimed to make its nonfood business as strong as its food business, a goal that called for tremendous growth, especially considering the massive might of its food business. During his first years in charge, Leahy did not disappoint, and Tesco achieved remarkable success in all four of its expansion fronts.

During the year 2000, Tesco introduced its e-commerce business Tesco.com, one of several new business developments that accelerated the company's financial growth during the opening years of the 21st century. Tesco's grocery home shopping service rapidly developed into the largest of its type in the world. While its retailing services segment gathered momentum, Tesco concentrated on growing its non-food business. The company began to add electronic products, toys, sports equipment, cookware, and home furnishings to its stores' inventories. In September 2002, the company added the Cherokee clothing brand to its U.K. stores, giving a substantial boost to the company's nonfood business. On the international front, Tesco entered Thailand in 1998, South Korea in 1999, Taiwan in 2000, Malaysia in 2002, and China in 2004. The company's existing operations abroad were strengthened by several acquisitions, including the 2002 purchase of HIT, a 13-store chain located in Poland; the 2003 purchase of Kipa, a four-store chain in Turkey; and the 2003 acquisition of the C Two-Network, a chain of 78 food stores in Japan.

Significant progress was being achieved in Tesco's retailing services, international operations, and non-food business; but its key executives did not forget the heart of the company, the United Kingdom business. Tesco's market share in Britain increased steadily and impressively during the nascent years of the 21st century. Tesco outperformed its major rivals and increased its share of the market from 15.4% in 1998 to 28% in 2004. Highlights of Tesco's progress in its core business area included its rise to become the leading organics retailer in the U.K. in 2001 and the impressive strength of its brands Value, Finest, and Tesco. Perhaps the most notable achievement in the company's core business area was Tesco's January 2003 acquisition of the 870-unit convenience store chain T&S Stores plc. Tesco plans to convert 450 of the units into Tesco Express stores by 2007.

As Tesco continues to grow in its four target areas, the company's brand remains solid in Britain and abroad. Many industry observers who have struggled to discover any weakness throughout the company's sprawling operations recognize Tesco's achievements in high quality for its products and services. Tesco stands today as a Value Zone retail giant whose stature only promises to grow and become more intimidating to competitors as the 21st century progresses. In 2004, one of out every eight pounds spent in Britain went to Tesco's revenues, and the company's expansion program represented more than half of all the new supermarket space planned for the United Kingdom.

In this chapter, we have discussed the challenge for businesses to sustain high levels of quality in products or services. We have explored several Value Zone Hall of Fame companies in different regions of the world and in several different industries. In each case, we have presented evidence of ways that Cintas, Johnson Controls, and Tesco plc have sustained quality for periods of 25 years or more with remarkable success. In each case, our research involving the Value Zone Hall of Fame companies has provided strong evidence that each of these companies is known for products and services of exceptional quality and has typically institutionalized quality as core to its culture. In essence, quality is pervasive throughout these organizations and is practiced diligently by employees, managers, executives, suppliers, and business alliance partners. Let's now look at how the Value Zone Hall of Fame companies have sustained compelling competitiveness and dominance in the industries that they compete in.

Chapter Twelve
Gain and Sustain Competitive Advantage

One of the most critical elements of the Value Zone is the eighth element, competitive advantage. Companies that are in the Value Zone have clearly identifiable strategic "best practices" that help them to gain and sustain competitive advantage. The companies discussed in this book that have achieved Value Zone Hall of Fame status have each been able to maintain a competitive edge for at least 25 years or longer. It is quite remarkable that these companies have been able to sustain a competitive advantage in the industries that they compete in for so long. I think that it is quite appropriate to borrow a phrase from Rutgers University head football coach Greg Schiano that helped catapult Rutgers into national rankings in the NCAA football championship race for the first time in the school's history. He urged his team in practice and during games to "keep chopping wood." In other words, if you keep doing the basic things to sustain your competitive posture, you will attain the desired results. This is something that the companies in the Value Zone Hall of Fame have done; that is, they "keep chopping wood," which leads to sustained revenue growth and profitability. We have already discussed in Chapter Three all of the economic, political, and miscellaneous challenges that could impede a business in sustaining a competitive advantage. In this chapter, we will examine several companies that have been able to remain competitive despite a number of obstacles.

SYSCO Corporation

SYSCO Corporation (an acronym for Systems and Services Company) is the largest marketer and distributor of foodservice products in North America, commanding a current market share of approximately 14%. With more than 160 distribution facilities located throughout the United States and Canada, SYSCO provides food and food-related products and services to approximately 390,000 restaurants, schools, hospitals, nursing homes, hotels, businesses, and other foodservice customers. Restaurant customers account for almost 67% of total revenues. The company's line of products includes about 275,000 items. These items include seafood, poultry, fresh and frozen meats, fully prepared entrees, produce, canned and dry foods, desserts, imported specialties, paper and disposable items, china and silverware, restaurant and kitchen equipment and supplies, and cleaning supplies. SYSCO was founded in 1969 and has grown consistently since its beginning. SYSCO has achieved its consistent success by acquiring dozens of smaller distributors, a practice which has resulted in double-digit increases in sales and earnings nearly every year.

SYSCO was founded through the combination of nine foodservices distributors. John Baugh was the guiding force; he convinced the owners of eight other small food distributors to combine their companies to form what he envisioned becoming a national foodservice distribution organization. This organization would be able to distribute any food regardless of regional availability. The other eight original companies were: Frost-Pack Distributing Company (Grand Rapids, Michigan); Global Frozen Foods, Inc. (New York, New York); Houston's Food Service Company (Houston, Texas); Louisville Grocery Company (Louisville, Kentucky); Plantation Foods (Miami, Florida); Texas Wholesale Grocery Corporation (Dallas, Texas); Thomas Foods, Inc. and its Justrite Food Service, Inc. subsidiary (Cincinnati, Ohio); and Wicker, Inc. (Dallas, Texas). The combined 1969 total revenues for the nine founding companies were $115 million.

SYSCO became a publicly owned company during 1970 and in that same year bought Arrow Food Distributor, its first acquisition. In its nascent years, the company grew by acquiring small foodservice distribution companies. These companies were carefully chosen; a major factor in each choice was geographic region. These acquisitions helped Baugh achieve an early goal of providing consistent service to customers throughout the U.S. To deal with growth during the 1970s, SYSCO built warehouses to support its rapid expansion, later incorporating freezers into its warehouses and adding multi-temperature refrigerated trucks to transport produce and frozen foods. These strategic moves enabled SYSCO to gain and sustain competitive advantage.

During the 1970s, SYSCO grew steadily with the exception of a brief earnings drop in 1976 caused by a canned food glut and excessive start-up costs due to increasing capacity. One reason for such rapid recovery and regular growth was SYSCO's continued strategy of consistently diversifying into new products, such as fish, meat, and fresh produce. In 1976, SYSCO acquired Mid-Central Fish and Frozen Foods Inc., thus expanding the company's distribution capabilities around the nation. In 1979, SYSCO's sales passed the $1 billion mark for the first time, and in 1981, the company was rated as the largest U.S. foodservice distribution company. That year, SYSCO set up Compton Foods in Kansas City to purchase meat and subsequently began to supply supermarkets and other institutions with meat and frozen entrees.

In 1983, SYSCO's chief financial officer John E. Woodhouse became CEO of the company, while Mr. Baugh remained chairman. The following year, SYSCO continued its acquisition strategy by purchasing three operations of PYA Monarch, then a division of Sara Lee Corporation. One of SYSCO's largest acquisitions occurred in 1988 when the company paid $750 million for CFS Continental, which at the time was the third-largest food distributor in the country. This acquisition enabled SYSCO to serve an increased number of markets and provide services to 148 out of the top 150 markets. Although much of the United States and especially Texas experienced hard financial times during the 1980s, SYSCO Corporation remained a top competitor because it was a national company in a fairly recession-proof industry.

SYSCO continued to be a formidable competitor by acquiring more foodservice distributors in the late 1980s, including Olewine's Inc. in Harrisburg, Pennsylvania; Lipsey Fish Company, Inc. of Memphis, Tennessee; Hall One Chinese Imports, Inc. from Cleveland, Ohio; and Fulton Prime Foods, Inc. out of Albany, New York. By the end of the 1980s, sales had reached $6.85 billion, making SYSCO twice as large as its closest competitor in foodservice distribution and second only to McDonald's in the overall foodservice industry. Despite its size and growth (it boasted 43 acquisitions since its founding), SYSCO still only accounted for less than 8% of overall foodservice distributor volume. This clearly showed the fragmented nature of the foodservice distribution industry and provided evidence that SYSCO had plenty of room for future growth.

During the early 1990s, SYSCO continued to fiercely compete for more market share by making several additional acquisitions, thus increasing its geographic reach. One significant purchase was the 1990 acquisition of the Oklahoma City-based foodservice distribution business of Scrivner, Inc. In 1991, SYSCO acquired four of Scrivner's northeastern U.S. distribution businesses, including Jamestown, New York; the 1992 acquisition of Philadelphia-based Perloff Brothers, Inc.; and the 1993 acquisitions of the St. Louis Division of Clark Foodservice, Inc. and the Ritter Food Corporation of Elizabeth, New Jersey.

In 1991, SYSCO created a subsidiary called the SYGMA Network, Inc. The purpose of this strategic initiative was to gain competitive advantage by consolidating SYSCO's chain restaurant distribution systems to improve servicing for the chain restaurants. By 1997, the SYGMA Network included 11 distribution centers serving customers in 37 states and reporting revenues of $1.3 billion. By 1995, Mr. Baugh had assumed the title of senior chairman. He retired in late 1997. Mr. Woodhouse was then named chairman, and Bill M. Lindig, who had been with the firm since 1970, became CEO. Despite the fact that SYSCO's revenues had grown to $12.12 billion, its competitive positioning in the foodservice distribution market was less than 10%. Commenting on this, Mr. Lindig was quoted in the *Houston Business Journal* stating: "We could grow at 20 percent a year for the next five years and we'd still have only 20 percent of the market." By stretching itself as a company, SYSCO actually achieved a compound growth rate of 16.4% from 1978 to 1997.

During the mid-1990s, SYSCO's senior leadership recognized that the company's growth coupled with a decentralized management structure created control problems. These problems were compounded by the fact that SYSCO was expecting to grow from 58 operating companies to 75. To remedy this problem, corporate management decided to add four senior vice presidents of operations, each of whom would have full responsibility for about ten SYSCO operating companies. Nineteen companies would still report directly to corporate headquarters.

In the late 1990s, SYSCO decided to slow down the pace of acquisitions and opt to gain competitive advantage by selectively targeting new high-growth markets. These selected new market targets included Alaska and Canada. To implement this new strategic and competitive direction, the company bought Strano Foodservice of Peterborough, Ontario in 1996 (thereby establishing a SYSCO presence in the Toronto market) and Alaska Fish and Farm, Inc. in early 1997.

To gain and sustain competitive during the mid-1990s, SYSCO launched a "fold-out" expansion strategy as a catalyst for faster growth. Leveraging this strategy, SYSCO developed a sales base in new markets that were distant from an existing operation, built a new distribution center, and staffed it with experienced staff, creating a stand-alone operating company that served a new market. In 1995, SYSCO opened its first distribution center in Connecticut using this program. Over the next four years, "fold-out" operating companies were added in Florida, Wisconsin, North Carolina, Alabama, and California.

SYSCO's revenues were an impressive $14.45 billion during 1997, and it had record profits of $302.5 million. Despite the company's slower growth rate, the "fold-out" expansion strategy was still keeping SYSCO growing much faster than the foodservice industry as a whole, giving it a significant competitive advantage. SYSCO's profits reached $362.3 million on revenues of $17.42 billion. Meanwhile, new fold-outs were being created about every six months, and several significant acquisitions were completed in 1999. One of SYSCO's key competitive strategies in 1999 was to take advantage of the resurgence of beef by buying two leading purveyors of beef: Irvine, California-based Newport Meat Company and Atlanta-based Buckhead Beef Company. SYSCO also acquired the Portsmouth, Virginia company Doughtie's Foods that year.

In an effort to continue succession planning by promoting from within, Mr. Lindig was chosen as chairman in 1999. He retired the following year when Charles Cotros became SYSCO's fourth CEO and chairman. Mr. Cotros, who had been the firm's president, had joined SYSCO in 1974. One of Cotros' first strategic initiatives was overseeing one of the company's largest deals, the 2000 purchase of FreshPoint Holdings, one of the biggest distributors of wholesale produce in the United States. Based in Dallas, FreshPoint reaped annual sales of approximately $750 million and sold to more than 20,000 customers, including restaurants, hotels, cruise ships, and wholesale grocers.

Another strategic and very competitive initiative during the beginning of 2001 that SYSCO launched was the acquisition of a pair of specialty meat supply operations in Texas: Freedman Food Service and Texas Meat Purveyors. These newly acquired companies specialized in supplying fresh meat to upscale restaurants and generated annual revenues in excess of $200 million. SYSCO then diversified itself by buying Guest Supply Inc., a New Jersey firm, for $200 million. This firm supplied guest care and housekeeping items to hotels. Guest Supply's reported revenues for 2000 totaled approximately $366 million. SYSCO significantly improved its competitive positioning by bolstering its presence in Canada and buying SERCA Foodservice from Sobey's, Inc. for about $280 million in early 2002. SERCA was based in Toronto and reported annual revenues of $1.4 billion. It provided 100,000 food products, as well as foodservice supplies and equipment, to 80,000 customers. SYSCO's competitive position in its Canadian distribution operations now covered all of Canada. SYSCO added to these acquisitions in May 2002 when it opened its first niche fold-out: a Buckhead Beef branch that began providing fresh-cut meat to the New York metropolitan area. Broad-line fold-out operations were opened in

Sacramento, California; Las Vegas, Nevada; and Columbia, South Carolina. Meanwhile, SYSCO was working to expand the FreshPoint produce brand across North America. Late in the year, SYSCO moved into the ethnic food market with the acquisition of St. Paul, Minnesota-based Asian Foods, Inc., the largest Asian food distributor in the United States, with annual revenues of more than $100 million.

At the beginning of 2003, Mr. Cotros retired and was succeeded as chairman and CEO by Richard J. Schnieders, who had moved up to president and COO since joining SYSCO in 1982. Clearly, succession planning was key to SYSCO's ability to sustain substantial competitive advantage. With its fifth CEO, SYSCO continued its strategic initiatives to fill in gaps in its geographic reach across the broad-line distribution sector in North America by acquiring other companies. In July 2004, SYSCO reached even more territory by going global and purchasing International Food Group Inc., of Plant City, Florida, a distributor of supplies to quick-service chain restaurants in Central and South America, the Caribbean, Europe, Asia, and the Middle East. International Food reported 2003 revenues of $77.8 million. By the latter part of 2004, SYSCO had successfully completed 121 acquisitions over the course of its 35-year history.

To gain even more of a competitive advantage, SYSCO began to seek ways to improve its efficiency, such as launching a national reengineering of its supply chain that included the construction of approximately nine regional redistribution centers over a ten-year period. These regional centers were designed to supply a number of SYSCO operating companies within a certain region. The first, which opened in February 2005 in Front Royal, Virginia, was slated to serve 14 broad-line SYSCO companies in the firm's northeastern region (which encompassed Virginia, Maryland, Delaware, Pennsylvania, New Jersey, and western New York state). Schnieders called this "the largest strategic project in SYSCO's history." In August 2005, SYSCO announced that it had selected Alachua, Florida as the site for its second redistribution center, which would serve the Southeast. SYSCO planned to open the center in the fall of 2006.

By the end of 2004, SYSCO's consistent revenue growth had reached $29.34 billion, a 12.2% increase over 2003, while earnings rose 16.6% to $907.2 million. Fourth-quarter profits during 2004, however, did not meet Wall Street expectations, in part because of a high rate of inflation on the food SYSCO bought from suppliers. To remain competitive and to control expenses during the next fiscal year, SYSCO eliminated 1,500 jobs from its payroll. However, SYSCO managed to achieve gains in both sales and earnings for the 29th straight year in fiscal 2005. Despite the fact that the gains were not very large (6% for earnings totaling $961.5 million and just 3.2% for revenues), earnings did surpass the $30 billion mark for the first time. SYSCO continues to sustain its large competitive advantage by managing its costs, emphasizing superior customer service, and maintaining a strong management team that has been strengthened over the years by a company policy of retaining the managers of acquired firms to keep the firm moving forward. As a Value Zone Hall of Fame company, SYSCO is well positioned to maintain its record of steady increases in its share of the foodservice distribution sector, which had reached 14% by 2005.

Omnicom Group Inc.

Omnicom Group Inc., one of the largest advertising groups in the world, operates as the parent company for three separate, independent advertising networks: the BBDO Worldwide Network, the DDB Needham Worldwide Network, and the TBWA International Network. During the latter part of the 1990s, Omnicom also operated two independent agencies—Cline, Davis & Mann and Goodby, Silverstein & Partners—along with a variety of marketing service and specialty advertising companies through Omnicom's Diversified Agency services division. Omnicom was created in 1986 as a holding company, but its history stretches much further back. Each of its three subsidiary agencies significantly influenced the growth and development of the U.S. advertising industry. Let's learn how Omnicom has been able to achieve and sustain substantial competitive advantage in this fiercely competitive industry by briefly examining the recent histories of each of its three subsidiaries.

Batten, Barton, Durstine & Osborn (BBDO)

BBDO has a history of competitive and aggressive expansions. One example of this expansion policy was the company's decision to sign with the Republican National Committee's presidential candidate Dwight D. Eisenhower in 1952. Another example was BBDO's decision to sign institutional customers outside the political realm such as CBS Broadcasting (1959) and the SCM Corporation (1961). BBDO also won product-oriented accounts such as Tupperware (1959), Autolite (1961), McGregor Sporting Goods (1964), and Pepperidge Farm (1964). During this time, BBDO also expanded globally by opening up offices in London, Paris, Milan, Frankfurt, and Vienna. In 1964, BBDO acquired the Atlanta-based firm Burke Dowling Adams and with it the accounts of Delta Air Lines and the various governmental agencies of the state of Georgia. Clyne Maxon firm of New York, with its $60 million in billings, was also merged with BBDO in 1966. The worldwide recession during the 1970s led to losses in domestic billings. However, during these years of economic stagnation, BBDO's international expansion served to offset losses incurred in the domestic market.

During the mid-1990s, Bruce Crawford, who had a background heading up the agency's foreign operations, was named president of BBDO. During his eight-year tenure, billings at BBDO tripled to $2.3 billion, and his cost containment controls kept the company profitable. One analyst said of BBDO in 1981, "I've never seen a company so conscious of cost controls." To remain competitive, BBDO continued its succession planning by promoting from within when Crawford retired on March 31, 1985. A very competent executive, Allen Rosenshine, succeeded him. To remain competitive during the 1980s, Rosenshine began to dismantle what had been a decentralized and entrepreneurial management culture within the BBDO network in order to create more centralized leadership.

That same year, BBDO and its various sub-agencies won hundreds of awards for creativity. The most notable of these was the Grand Prix Gold Lion at the Cannes Film Festival, which BBDO won for producing the year's best television commercial. In this case, the ad that won this highly regarded award was the "Archeology" commercial made for Pepsi Cola.

To remain competitive and sustain growth and profitability, BBDO needed to expand globally. It would do this through mergers and acquisitions. The merger with Needham and Doyle Dane Bernbach would provide BBDO with greater global presence, particularly in France, Canada, and Great Britain. BBDO's leadership team felt strongly back then that this improvement of the agency's foreign business was necessary for BBDO to maintain its position as a formidable global player in the advertising industry.

Doyle Dane Bernbach (DDB)

Doyle Dane Bernbach has been praised by the advertising industry as the agency that exemplified innovation and creativity. In the world of advertising, imitation is the rule. The exception to this rule has frequently been the Doyle Dane Bernbach agency. In fact, advertising guru David Ogilvy stated about them that, "They just sort of created an original school out of air."

The 1949 union of Ned Doyle, William Bernbach, and Maxwell Dane turned out to be a perfect blend of talents that benefited DDB in remarkable ways. Doyle was the sales executive in charge of winning and retaining clients; Dane took care of administration and financial matters; and Bernbach was the innovative and creative advertising genius. Each of these leaders understood his role, and thus it became quite apparent in the advertising world that this nascent company would be a major force in the industry. One significantly strategic and competitive approach that they employed was to hire and retain the most creative people they could find, no matter where they came from.

The inspiration that led to DDB's industry-wide reputation of being creative and innovative came from Bernbach and especially from his preoccupation with the "road not taken." Bernbach was an "outside of the box" thinker with refreshing ideas. He was sympathetic towards the consumer base that found that most advertisements were boring. His vision was that ad campaigns should be exciting and fun while still focusing on a product's features and value. He reportedly felt that research and statistics were not as important as ideas and emotions. He believed that advertising was an art, and as an artist, his chief concerns were imagery, impression, and perspective.

Bernbach was also a great teacher and mentor. He was patient and precise but gentle in his criticism of others and had the ability to nurture the natural ability of his subordinates. His "students" formed the firm's Creative Team: a small group of copy writers, artists, art directors, and photographers that produced the agency's campaigns. Bernbach led the group not as a dictator but as one who worked with his subordinates in what he called a "horizontal hierarchy." In Bernbach's view, his group members were peers and had equal input.

During the 1950s, Doyle Dane Bernbach surged into the advertising mainstream by elevating the brand names of some of its clients who were struggling for recognition. The company achieved this through very aggressive and competitive advertising in four notable campaigns for four near-unknown companies: Polaroid Cameras, Levy Bakery Goods, Ohrbach's Department Store, and El Al Israel Air Lines. Like Doyle Dane Bernbach, these companies were striving to establish themselves in their respective markets. Polaroid was overshadowed by Kodak, Ohrbach's was overshadowed by Macy's, and few people during that time had ever heard of Levy's Bread or El Al Air. To overcome this lack of public recognition, the agency developed and launched strikingly different ads featuring everything from a cat dressed in a woman's hat to a Native American claiming that "you don't have to be Jewish to enjoy Levy's real Jewish rye." These ads succeeded in selling large quantities of cameras, clothes, bread, and airline tickets and also helped establish Doyle Dane Bernbach as a major player in the advertising industry. In fact, the agency's billings soared from $8 million in 1954 to $27.5 million by 1959.

During the early 1960s, Doyle Dane Bernbach landed two new accounts that improved the company's reputation: Avis Car Rentals and Volkswagen. In the rent-a-car business, Hertz was the dominant player, while Avis was far behind in second place. Avis wanted more market share. Typically, most advertising portrays clients in as favorable and strong a position as possible. However, Doyle Dane Bernbach took a different and radical tactic with an ad campaign that stressed Avis' weak position vis-à-vis Hertz and announced that Avis was "number two" in the car rental market. The ads said, "We try harder. We have to." This strategy was a success. In just two years, Avis increased its market share by over 25%.

Let's now consider a similar story involving Volkswagen. These small German cars were not popular in the American marketplace, or so it appeared. Once again, Doyle Dane Bernbach transformed a liability into a strength. Discerning through market research that the American consumer had tired of the large and overly embellished American-made cars of the 1950s, Doyle Dane Bernbach's ad campaign message was simply: "Think small." The art of the ads was minimalist, usually portraying a tiny picture of the Volkswagen against a blank white backdrop. The text was also odd. The short, simple copy was blocked in paragraphs. Not only did Americans purchase these "ugly" Volkswagens by the thousands, but the car also became an icon for an entire "nonconformist" generation. Continuing to sustain competitive advantage, Doyle Dane Bernbach won a number of big accounts, including American Airlines, Seagram, International Silver, Heinz Ketchup, Sony, Uniroyal, Gillette, Bristol-Myers, and Mobil Oil. Yes, the 1960s ushered in a new era for advertising, a sort of "creative revolution," and Doyle Dane Bernbach was leading the way.

New challenges emerged during the 1970s as the industry began once again to use conventional advertising techniques. Combined with an economic recession in the early 1970s, this trend presented problems for Doyle Dane Bernbach. For example, Doyle Dane Bernbach lost the $20 million Alka-Seltzer account in

1970, despite the successful "that's a spicy meat-ball" commercial. Equally troublesome was the loss of other accounts, including Lever Brothers, Whirlpool, Sara Lee, Quaker Oats, Cracker Jack, Uniroyal, and Life Cereal. However, the agency's growth during the 1960s provided it with enough revenue to absorb these losses. In 1974, Neil A. Austrian joined the company as executive vice president, and with his expertise in the business aspects of advertising (expertise that had been missing at the agency), he gradually transformed the company into a more organized advertising network. Subsidiaries were acquired to strengthen Doyle Dane Bernbach's global presence and to offer more comprehensive client services. Once again, the agency's billings rose as reported in 1975. In fact, this was the first time that billings had risen in the new decade, a trend that continued for the next seven years.

On October 2, 1982, William Bernbach passed away, leaving a void of creativity at the agency. This circumstance posed the question: could Doyle Dane Bernbach survive without Bill Bernbach? The question was very troubling for the firm. Because of this dilemma, 1982 earnings fell 30%, a situation which was compounded in the next two years by the loss of key accounts, including American Airlines in 1983 and Polaroid in 1984. The Polaroid loss was especially shocking to the agency because its commercials had helped make Polaroid the world's best-selling camera.

At the beginning of 1986, Doyle Dane Bernbach laid off 24 staff members and reported a $113 million loss in net earnings. The future merger with BBDO and Needham Harper Worldwide represented a key strategic business decision. It appeared doubtful that Doyle Dane Bernbach would be able to continue if its fiscal situation did not improve. The security afforded by the Omnicom umbrella would bring financial relief to the agency and allow the firm to concentrate on what it did best: namely, innovative and creative advertising.

Needham Harper

Chicago-based agency Needham Harper traditionally avoided advertising in East Coast markets like New York, preferring clients in the Midwest. The agency was founded in 1924 by Maurice Needham in Illinois, and it went through a series of mergers until 1984, when it was finally named Needham Harper. This agency was not ranked among the largest worldwide agencies. Its business came mainly from smaller firms that felt neglected and disrespected by large advertising agencies and therefore would use the services of Needham Harper. These types of clients were the foundation of this agency's business.

In addition to Maurice Needham, the other person associated with the agency was Paul Harper. Paul Harper came to work at the agency in 1945 when it was Needham, Louis & Brorby. Maurice Needham gave Harper, who had a Yale degree and military background in the Marine Corps during World War II, an opportunity to work in the advertising business. He started out as a copy writer and soon did exceptionally well in broadcast advertising. Some notable examples of his talent were his commercials for Johnson's Wax on the "Fibber McGee and Molly" radio show. Harper's successes led to a position in management, and then in 1964, he became president of the company and led the acquisition by Needham of Doherty, Clifford, Steers and Shenfield in 1965. During this period, the name of the agency was changed to Needham, Harper & Steers. In 1967, he became chairman and chief executive officer of the agency, and he retained this position until his retirement in 1984.

During the 1950s and 1960s, the advertising industry grew as more companies invested in advertising. Needham, Harper & Steers grew with the industry, despite the fact that it was a mid-size firm. The agency focused on smaller accounts while also retaining several large midwestern clients such as the Household Finance Corporation and the Oklahoma Oil Company. One of the ways that the agency sustained competitive advantage was by creating catchy slogans like the "Never borrow money needlessly" slogan for Household Finance and "Put a tiger in your tank" for Oklahoma Oil.

In 1972, the firm went public. It followed the industry trend and began to publicly trade its shares. However, this move did not prove fruitful. Investors frowned upon investments in advertising agencies simply because they viewed them as unstable investments that were impacted by the fluctuations of the economy. Smaller advertising firms were especially vulnerable and therefore posed more risk to potential investors. Therefore, unlike the larger agencies such as Ogilvy & Mather and Interpublic, Needham, Harper & Steers did not do well in attracting a strong investment interest. Therefore, Needham, Harper & Steers "went private" again in 1976, a move which helped it to regain and sustain its competitive edge.

Despite the fact that it serviced many small and mid-size accounts, Needham, Harper & Steers began to gain a reputation for attracting "blue chip" clients. For example, the agency landed big accounts with Xerox in 1968, McDonald's in 1970, Honda in 1977, and Sears in 1982. The agency created the famous "Brother Dominic" commercials for Xerox and the "you deserve a break today" slogan for McDonald's. Surprisingly, McDonald's took its domestic business away from Needham, Harper & Steers in 1984 and turned it over to a competitor, Leo Burnett. More bad news occurred in 1986 when the agency lost the $40 million Xerox account. It was at about this time that the formation of Omnicom occurred.

1986 Formation of Omnicom

The merger of Needham, Harper & Steers with BBDO and Doyle Dane Bernbach would greatly influence each firm's business culture and persona. For example, the merger reshaped the "personality" of Needham, Harper & Steers. Despite the fact that the three agencies intended to operate as autonomous and separate divisions of Omnicom, the merger had many more complications than just a simple name change. One example of such a complication occurred when a number of clients expressed displeasure about the prospect of sharing the agency with competitors. The conflict-of-interest problem became especially pronounced when Campbell's Soup, a Needham, Harper & Steers client, would not stay with Omnicom if Heinz, a Doyle Dane Bernbach client, remained a customer. Stroh's and Busch beer and Honda and Volkswagen automobiles experienced similar conflicts.

Customers wanted to receive the same advertising attention to which they had been accustomed. Some of Needham, Harper & Steers' clients were glad that Keith Reinhard, who had joined the firm in 1964, would continue with the newly merged Omnicom. Mr. Reinhard became president of Needham, Harper & Steers/Chicago in 1980, achieved the rank of chairman and CEO in 1982, and became chairman and CEO of Needham Harper Worldwide in 1984. His employees, managers, colleagues, and customers were impressed with his integrity and hard work. He consistently delivered the message to his staff that the merger with Omnicom would help Needham, Harper &Steers to attract and retain large clients while enabling the agency to remain loyal to its smaller customers as well. He also believed that the added New York presence would attract clients in that market.

Once the merger was complete, there were some real challenges ahead. The overall responsibility of making sense and profits out of this three-company merger belonged to BBDO's key leader, Allen Rosenshine. It was clear from the beginning of this amalgamation that achieving profits and harmony was not going to be easy, and as predicted, the process of combining three competing agencies under one umbrella corporation was cumbersome, tiresome, and a real challenge. There was even some speculation that this merger would not work. Omnicom invested over $40 million in the merger and in costs related to restructuring, leaving the company without profit and with a slow and lethargic start for its first year. A number of clients were opposed to the merger and stopped doing business with the company. For example, RJR Nabisco was displeased and exited abruptly. In fact, RJR Nabisco's chairman remarked, "As a client, I see disruption, but little value. With very few exceptions, the wave of mergers has benefited the shareholders and managers of the agencies." By the time the dust settled after the merger, the three Omnicom agencies had lost $184 million in billings, a consequence that was directly attributable to the act of the merger itself. Obviously, this strategic merger did not promise to bring sustained competitive advantage for the three agencies.

The merger had not made any real progress by the end of 1986, when Omnicom's 1987 financial totals report showed that the numbers were low. The report highlighted the fact that the company earned only $32 million from commissions and fees of $785 million, or 4.1%, in what traditionally was a double-digit margin business. However, the year did have its shining moments, including the acquisition of several large accounts. During that year, Omnicom agencies landed a U.S. Navy account; a large portion of new Pepsi business, including Slice soft drinks and Pizza Hut; and the account for NEC Home Electronics. In total, Omnicom registered $280 million in new business during 1987; however, this was not enough to offset other difficulties. The merger was not delivering the desired and expected results. This was discouraging Omnicom's leaders. In fact, Rosenshine reported this dissatisfaction to the media in 1988.

Bruce Crawford, a former BBDO executive, returned as Omnicom's chief executive officer. He was given the responsibility of directing and expediting the restructuring of Omnicom in early 1989 and immediately began paring away superfluous managerial layers and divesting poorly performing businesses. His goal was not to gain economies of scale but to build businesses by leveraging a simple management structure and minimizing overhead.

Crawford divested a number of Omnicom businesses and shut down others that were performing poorly. At the same time, he expanded the merged agency's presence in Britain and Europe, where Omnicom trailed behind other U.S.-based international advertising agencies. As the 1990s began, the strategy was beginning to work and Omnicom was now beginning to demonstrate some life. This was the kind of vitality that the merger's creators had envisioned. Despite the effects of a suffocating economic recession during the early 1990s, Omnicom reported healthy financial gains. In fact, 1991 revenues increased to $1.2 billion with consistent profit growth. This growth trend continued after the recession when the company recorded an 18% increase in revenues to $2.3 billion in 1995 and a 26% gain in net income to $140 million. Now that's gaining and sustaining competitive advantage.

By the end of the mid-1990s, there were no more lingering doubts about the decision to merge in 1986. Omnicom now was a powerful, dominant, and creative force in the advertising industry. Its three agency networks were earning numerous prestigious awards and gaining prestigious new clientele. BBDO, selected by Advertising Age International as "The Most Creative Agency Network" in the world in 1996, was awarded multinational accounts for Sara Lee, Mars, Visa, Pepsi, and Bayer. At the Cannes International Advertising Festival in 1996, DDB Needham won more awards than any other agency in the world, the fifth year out of the previous six years that the agency was number one. New clients added to DDB Needham's portfolio during the year included L'eggs, CompuServe, Wells Fargo Bank, Clorox, Wilson Sporting Goods, Hamilton Beach, and Lockheed Martin. TBWA International's progress during 1996 bolstered Omnicom's global reach. To support the agency's global expansion, new offices were opened in Latin America (Brazil, Chile, and Argentina), Asia (Singapore, Hong Kong, China), Europe (Warsaw, Munich, Berlin, and Cyprus), and in Durban, South Africa (the agency's third South African office). TBWA also followed the pattern of success established by its sister agencies by winning an impressive list of new clients while earning recognition for its innovativeness. The agency's Nissan commercial was named the "Best of 1996" by *Time, USA Today, Entertainment Weekly,* and *Rolling Stone*; new clients included Novartis and Canon in Europe as well as Gramercy Picture and Sara Lee's Champion Sportswear in the United States.

On top of this vibrant trio of agencies stood Omnicom, selected in 1997 as *Fortune* magazine's most respected advertising group and ranked by the *Wall Street Journal* as number one in the advertising industry in terms of total return to shareholders. Amid the accolades and applause directed at its three subsidiary agency companies, Omnicom posted strong financial totals, registering a 26%

gain in net income in 1996 to $176.3 million and an increase in revenues from $2.26 billion to $2.64 billion. Much of the credit for Omnicom's robust growth went to Crawford. He believed in the concept of Omnicom and made it work as a viable corporate entity. When he stepped down as chief executive officer in January 1997, he passed the leadership baton to John D. Wren. Mr. Wren continued to build on Crawford's legacy of success by nurturing growth and creativity. This enabled Omnicom to sustain its competitive advantage in the 21st century. Throughout this book, we have repeatedly emphasized the point that being in the Value Zone is all about sustaining high performance. In our concluding chapter, we will sum up what we have learned in our research of these 38 companies that have clearly qualified to be included in the Value Zone Hall of Fame.

Chapter Thirteen
Conclusion

In this book, we have learned about some remarkable companies that were able to sustain exceptional organizational performance for 25 years and even longer in some cases. Despite intense competition, these companies achieved great results on a consistent basis. In this book, we also identified eight critical Value Zone elements that provided the basis for tracking the business results of each of the 38 companies that were studied. All of these companies used strategic "best practices" throughout the 25-year period of this study to help them *create meaningful and sustainable value for their stakeholders. Based on our findings, we assert that it is the creation of meaningful and sustainable value that can position a business in the High Value area of the Value Zone.*

Each company that was examined in this book has consistently demonstrated exceptional leadership, an enduring and resilient culture, a well-managed financial portfolio with consistent and sustained growth in revenues and profits, a history of sustained market expansion, an innovative mindset, consistent improvement of the efficiency and effectiveness of its business operations, the ability to create high-quality products and services, and fierce and tenacious competitiveness.

It is quite remarkable that according to our research, only 38 out of 74,293 publicly owned companies in a variety of industries were able to sustain consistent business performance for a continuous period of 25 years or longer. (Our benchmark time period began in 1981 and ended in 2005.) To distinguish these solidly performing companies from the rest of the companies that were examined, we created the 1981 through 2005 Value Zone Hall of Fame. While some of the companies included in our research were not necessarily well-known, we hope that you found their stories refreshing and interesting (see the list of companies on the next page). Even more importantly, we told their stories so that readers can learn how these companies, which competed in a number of industries across the globe, were able to sustain their positive business results for such long periods of time.

In Chapter Three of this book, we highlighted some interesting events that occurred during our benchmark period. We hope that you enjoyed reading that chapter as it took you on a journey back in time to see what challenges the leaders of the 38 Value Zone Hall of Fame companies (Figure 13.1 below) were faced with and how they navigated their enterprises through tumultuous environments of change and uncertainty. Perhaps as you read about the history of these companies, you sensed a common thread throughout each enterprise. There was clearly an exceptional succession plan in these firms; the preceding leaders carefully mentored each succeeding generation of leaders about the culture and the key strategic initiatives that would sustain company performance. It also seemed quite clear from our research that of all the elements in the Value

Zone, leadership and culture provided the underpinnings of all of the rest of the elements.

```
┌─────────────────────────────────────────────────────────────────────┐
│                                                                       │
│        >═══  ┌──────────────────────────────────┐  ═══<              │
│              │   Value Zone Hall of Fame         │                    │
│              └──────────────────────────────────┘                    │
│                                                                       │
│       Abertis SA                        Home Depot Inc                │
│       ABM Industries Inc                Johnson & Johnson             │
│       Aeon Company Limited              Johnson Controls Inc          │
│       Alliance Unichem PLC              Land Securities PLC           │
│       Arthur J Gallagher & Company      Longs Drug Stores            │
│       Automatic Data Processing         Lowe's Companies Inc          │
│       Becton Dickinson & Company        McDonalds Corp.              │
│       Biomet Inc                        Morrison (WM) Supermarkets PLC│
│       Cbrl Group Inc                    Nbty Inc                      │
│       Cintas Corp.                      Nordstrom Inc                 │
│       Comcast Corp.                     Omnicom Group Inc             │
│       Diagnostic Products Corp.         Pall Corp.                   │
│       Family Dollar Stores Inc          Pick N Pay Stores Limited    │
│       Federal Realty Investment Trust   Stryker Corp.               │
│       Fraport AG                        Sysco Corp.                  │
│       G & K Services Inc                Teleflex Inc                  │
│       Greene King PLC                   Tesco PLC                     │
│       Grupo Bimbo SA De CV              Wal Mart Stores Inc           │
│       Grupo Continental SA              Walgreen Company              │
│                                                                       │
└─────────────────────────────────────────────────────────────────────┘
```

Figure 13.1

Our time capsule in Chapter Three revealed startling events occurring between 1981 and 2005 that would in some way affect the 38 companies researched in this book. Along with tens of thousands of others, these firms were faced with incredible challenges that were brought on by internal and external forces of change. In reviewing those years, we learned that all public and private sector organizations faced turbulent times, unpredictable economies, unprecedented occurrences of natural disasters, political unrest, a growing world population, regional warfare, threats of terrorism, a growth in the number of countries boasting weapons of mass destruction, disruptive technologies, an alarming decline in ethical values, a growing energy crisis, and healthcare problems at levels never faced by mankind before. It is amazing that despite these unprecedented obstacles, these companies were able to achieve sustained revenue growth and profitability.

Outstanding leadership is at the heart of the Value Zone. We learned about company leaders like Biomet's Dane Miller, who made his company a premiere developer and marketer of orthopedic products. Former Home Depot CEO Bob Nardelli helped his company's founders to centralize their operations in order to provide a more structured organization. This was greatly needed because the company achieved rapid growth by driving a more consistent approach in its corporate policies. In Asia, AEON's leaders stressed the importance of remaining constantly focused on enhancing global management standards, determining local customer requirements, and maximizing teamwork and group synergy. AEON's leaders were guided by three core principles: respect for humanity, contribution to local communities, and the pursuit of peace centered on customers.

ADP former CEO Josh Weston created ADP's culture of associates and clients. Weston's concept of teams is what drove him to view everyone who worked in ADP as an associate. He also introduced the term "client" to replace the term "customer" in ADP culture. His rationale was that a customer represented a one-time transaction, but a client represented repeated business and an enduring professional relationship. Roberto Servitje described two key areas of central importance to Grupo Bimbo's leadership culture: productivity and being "people-oriented." This firm's culture is also manifested in projects like "Reforestamos México," an initiative that established this organization as an advocate of green management and a significant contributor to environmental protection and preservation in Mexico.

During succession planning, future leaders of Johnson & Johnson were groomed to adhere to their company's Corporate Credo like breathing air. We learned about an example of this incredible adherence to the J&J corporate culture during the tenure of former CEO and chairman of Johnson & Johnson James Burke. Burke faced a significant test of the Credo and the J&J culture during September 1982 when tragedy struck J&J after seven people died from ingesting Tylenol capsules that had been laced with cyanide. Burke and his leadership team were decisive in their adherence to the Credo; they cancelled all advertising and recalled all Tylenol products from store shelves. Despite the great financial loss suffered by J&J, this decision was a "no-brainer" for Burke and the J&J leaders. The Credo and the corporate culture compelled Burke and J&J leaders to "do the right thing."

As the 21st century was ushered in, the dynamics of the global marketplace changed drastically, and sustaining exceptional financial performance became a challenge for business leaders worldwide. During this time, Wal-Mart exemplified exceptional leadership in sustained revenue growth and profitability. Its founder Sam Walton envisioned Wal-Mart becoming the number-one retailer in the U.S. If he were still alive today, Mr. Walton would be astounded to see that his Arkansas-based retail chain has grown to become one of the largest companies in the world. Only the combined revenues of the Exxon-Mobil Corporation now exceed Wal-Mart's revenues worldwide.

Family Dollar's successful business strategy for market expansion was paying huge dividends by fiscal 2003 when Family Dollar reported achieving 30 consecutive quarters of record sales and earnings. Howard Levine, who was named CEO in 1998, continued to drive this growth streak and oversaw Family Dollar's expansion to its 5,000th store on August 28, 2003 in Jacksonville, Florida. During 2004, Family Dollar continued its aggressive expansion efforts by opening more than 500 new stores including eight new distribution centers.

Walgreen is currently the largest drugstore chain in the United States in terms of revenues. More than 60% of those revenues are from retail prescriptions. In 2003, Walgreen reported that it filled 400 million prescriptions, a figure representing about 13% of all retail prescriptions in the U.S. One of Walgreen's many innovations was the development of drive-through pharmacies. Other creative innovations by Walgreen included its Health Initiatives Manager, a prescription benefit application that services small and medium-sized employers and managed care organizations, and one-hour photo-finishing offered by 50% of its stores.

Pall Corporation is the largest manufacturer of filtration, separation, and purification products in the world, and it demonstrates exceptional efficiency in its manufacturing operations. One area in which Pall demonstrates remarkable efficiency and effectiveness is its worldwide pricing. In order to ensure that supplies and prices remain consistent globally, manufacturing for each of Pall's product lines takes place in at least two Pall facilities, and the size of each facility is limited to no more than 450 employees. This environment promotes a team spirit of collaboration.

Tesco's grocery home-shopping service rapidly developed into the largest of its type in the world, an advancement that helped the company to sustain its competitiveness during the year 2000. One of several strategic initiatives that accelerated the company's financial growth during the opening years of the 21st century was Tesco's e-commerce business on Tesco.com. Tesco also concentrated on growing its non-food business by adding electronic products, toys, sports equipment, cookware, and home furnishings to its stores' inventories. In September 2002, Tesco added the Cherokee clothing brand to its U.K. stores, giving a substantial boost to the company's non-food business. The company's existing operations abroad were strengthened by several acquisitions, including the 2002 purchase of HIT, a 13-store chain located in Poland; the 2003 purchase of Kipa, a four-store chain in Turkey; and the 2003 acquisition of the C Two-Network, a chain of 78 food stores in Japan. Despite this competitive expansion, Tesco's key executives did not forget that the heart of the company was the United Kingdom business, and they made sure that they maintained Tesco's market share lead in Britain.

The founder of Johnson Controls, affectionately known as the "The Professor," had an eye for high quality and insisted that only trained Johnson mechanics install his company's devices. His successors reinforced this policy. The Professor insisted that the Johnson Service Company was to serve not just as a producer of regulation equipment but also as a single source for design, installation, and service, a policy which in his mind guaranteed the highest quality. Johnson's temperature-control business grew and fit in well with the country's building boom, and it continued with the help of other expansion projects to produce highly innovative products with consistent quality. To this day, Johnson Controls is known for the high quality of its products.

The Value Zone: Gaining And Sustaining Remarkable Results
In this book, we have learned about companies that have been able to gain and then sustain positive business results. The 38 companies that were able to achieve this distinction are very diverse. Because our study was limited to publicly owned companies, we concede that it is quite possible that there are private companies that have also achieved similar results. Any firm that can provide internal financial annual reports displaying sustained revenue growth and profitability for 25 years or longer will be included in the Value Zone Hall of Fame. Moreover, if you are willing to share some of the strategic initiatives that you have used to sustain your company's performance, we will be glad to include your company on our list of Value Zone Hall of Fame companies at our website. We plan to provide newsletters featuring case studies about privately owned firms who would like to share their success stories.

Because our research in this book was based on companies in the public domain that were in business and reported results from 1981 through 2005, it is very possible that there are other companies that were able to achieve business results that qualify them for inclusion in the Value Zone Hall of Fame. If your company has earned this distinction, please share with us the time frame of your achievement and the financial records that support your claim. We will be happy to include your firm's achievement in our list of Value Zone Hall of Fame companies at our website.

There is one other distinction that we would like to share with you. In our research, we have discovered that there are companies that have been able to achieve sustained revenue growth with profitability for periods longer than 25 years. Therefore, we have added the Value Zone Hall of Fame Ring of Honor for companies that have achieved this sustained profitable growth for a period of 50 years or longer. Based on our research, we have identified one company that has distinguished itself in this special category: Johnson & Johnson. As shown by its historical financial records, this company has been able to sustain revenue growth and profitability for 73 consecutive years (please see the Johnson & Johnson Historical Financial Performance Table in the Appendix). How was this company able to achieve these remarkable results? How can an enterprise that owns 237 companies with operations in over 57 countries produce sustained value for its clients all over the world? How was it able to do this decade after decade? We will briefly highlight some of the reasons why Johnson & Johnson was able to achieve this distinction.

First, we looked at the eight Value Zone elements and clearly found examples of exceptional business practices embedded in each of the elements. Based on the company's consistent history of developing great leaders, a pattern emerged suggesting that an institutionalized culture of producing great leaders made the difference. Throughout their company's history, Johnson & Johnson's leaders demonstrated remarkable abilities to develop strategic initiatives that enabled them to achieve their financial objectives, expand their markets, and create innovative products and services. Furthermore, the company is now able to efficiently manage its assets, provide high-quality products and services, and sustain a powerful competitive posture in all the industries in which it competes. We have provided some examples in this book of Johnson & Johnson's exceptional business practices and remarkable results. We have concluded that Johnson & Johnson's Corporate Credo and its leadership team's strict adherence to the key tenets of the Credo are the keys to the company's sustained success. The Credo is timeless and universal, transcending all cultures among mankind. It enables Johnson & Johnson leaders to make decisions that consistently result in sustained value for clients all over the world. If your company has achieved this remarkable distinction of sustaining revenue growth and profitability for 25 years or more, we invite you to share it with us and will include your story on our website and add your company's name to the Value Zone Hall of Fame. If your company was able to sustain revenue growth and consistent profitability for 50 years or longer, your firm will earn the distinction of being in the Value Zone Hall of Fame Ring of Honor.

The Value Zone represents sustained value. To achieve this sustained value, we believe that public and private enterprises must design and build strategic initiatives that are driven by great leadership, have a clearly defined culture, result in consistent growth in revenues and profits, constantly seek to expand, are highly innovative, are remarkably efficient and effective, provide products and services that are of the highest quality, and are fiercely competitive.

Appendix
Thomson Financial 25 Yr. Income Statement

Scaling Factor: 1000000 USD

Abertis

	1981	1982	1983	1984	1985	1986	1987	1988	1989	1990	1991	1992	1993	1994
Net Sales	42.13	50.98	57.35	79.02	95.30	113.33	135.85	160.19	185.77	215.40	745.72	760.10	256.43	277.0
Net Income	7.80	4.41	7.55	10.02	10.05	19.31	38.67	48.33	67.67	67.67	79.42	97.08	97.48	117.52

	1995	1996	1997	1998	1999	2000	2001	2002	2003	2004	2005
Net Sales	321.78	340.17	372.30	404.34	457.54	531.14	681.49	761.58	1226.30	1489.14	1824.24
Net Income	135.00	142.33	149.03	141.66	149.24	162.76	171.95	195.33	355.21	467.29	511.23

ABM

	1981	1982	1983	1984	1985	1986	1987	1988	1989	1990	1991	1992	1993	1994
Net Sales	272.85	303.68	329.12	374.12	424.17	484.31	528.44	638.36	679.13	679.13	745.72	760.10	256.43	277.08
Net Income	6.13	6.91	7.76	7.49	5.00	5.65	4.92	8.73	11.23	11.23	11.99	12.65		15.17

	1995	1996	1997	1998	1999	2000	2001	2002	2003	2004	2005
Net Sales	965.38	1086.93	1252.47	1501.83	1629.72	1807.56	1950.04	2180.93	2262.48	2416.22	2587.76
Net Income	18.22	21.72	27.24	33.93	39.67	44.34	32.83	46.73	38.96	30.47	43.72

Alliance

	1981	1982	1983	1984	1985	1986	1987	1988	1989	1990	1991	1992	1993	1994
Net Sales	216.80	284.91	336.15	370.93	441.15	492.64	544.64	711.11	783.0	873.35	920.1	1048.7	1177.6	1324.66
Net Income	216.80	3.57	3.01	2.74	4.04	3.85	4.85	7.19	8.94	10.62	13.0	21.0	24.83	29.64

	1995	1996	1997	1998	1999	2000	2001	2002	2003	2004	2005
Net Sales	1402.73	1478.50	1712.30	5353.40	6094.00	6191.20	7314.10	8023.50	8799.30	8898.40	9171.20
Net Income	33.38	24.20	40.30	71.70	78.70	76.70	96.00	108.80	128.50	167.10	210.70

AJ Gallagher

	1981	1982	1983	1984	1985	1986	1987	1988	1989	1990	1991	1992	1993	1994
Net Sales	42.5	48.0	53.36	64.18	81.57	118.85	118.85	156.04	173.21	198.18	231.68	272.73	317.66	356.38
Net Income	N/A	3.0	4.27	6.30	9.88	15.41	16.21	16.90	17.25	17.69	18.79	23.47	32.27	4.54

	1995	1996	1997	1998	1999	2000	2001	2002	2003	2004	2005
Net Sales	412.00	456.68	488.03	540.66	577.55	740.60	910.04	1101.22	1202.40	1477.60	1488.30
Net Income	41.4	45.80	53.32	56.5	67.75	87.78	125.2	129.74	146.20	188.50	28.60

ADP

	1981	1982	1983	1984	1985	1986	1987	1988	1989	1990	1991	1992	1993	1994
Net Sales	558.44	669.26	752.83	888.0	1030.0	1204.0	1384.0	1549.16	1677.69	1714.04	1771.0	1940.57	2223.37	2468.0
Net Income	47.36	57.79	64.52	75.13	87.0	105.96	132.0	170.30	187.57	211.7	227.0	256.18	294.20	334.12

	1995	1996	1997	1998	1999	2000	2001	2002	2003	2004	2005
Net Sales	2893.74	3566.60	4112.19	4798.06	5540.14	6287.51	6853.57	7004.26	7147.02	7754.94	8499.10
Net Income	394.83	454.70	513.50	605.30	700.45	843.71	927.06	1102.38	1018.15	935.57	1056.40

Becton Dickinson

	1981	1982	1983	1984	1985	1986	1987	1988	1989	1990	1991	1992	1993	1994
Sales/or Revenue	1066.09	1113.92	1119.52	1126.85	1143.79	1311.57	1581.96	1709.37	1811.46	2012.65	2172.17	2365.32	2465.41	2559
Net Income	77.10	77.77	36.88	63.40	88.92	111.91	141.85	161.94	168.94	180.47	187.22	198.21	210.09	224

	1995	1996	1997	1998	1999	2000	2001	2002	2003	2004	2005
Net Sales/or Revenue	2712.53	2769.76	2810.52	3116.87	3418	3618.3	3754.3	4033.07	4527.94	4934.8	5414.7
Net Income	249.00	280.77	297.43	235.57	274.9	392.21	437.76	479.37	546.55	467.35	722.17

Biomet Inc

	1981	1982	1983	1984	1985	1986	1987	1988	1989	1990	1991	1992	1993	1994
Net Sales/or Revenue	2.02	3.52	7.10	10.56	33.08	44.10	55.86	97.56	135.76	162.38	209.69	274.80	335.37	373.30
Net Income	N/A	0.26	0.72	1.5	3.47	5.22	8.08	13.18	21.48	29.93	39.47	51.81	63.96	69.82

	1995	1996	1997	1998	1999	2000	2001	2002	2003	2004	2005
Net Sales/or Revenue	452.27	535.16	580.35	651.41	757.41	920.58	1030.66	1191.90	1390.30	1615.25	1879.95
Net Income	79.20	63.52	86.60	104.14	70.19	59.00	49.18	91.79	106.53	113.26	130.97

Cbrl Group Inc

	1981	1982	1983	1984	1985	1986	1987	1988	1989	1990	1991	1992	1993	1994
Net Sales/or Revenue	28.46	35.42	45.66	56.86	67.50	80.86	99.03	125.81	170.05	225.52	300.21	400.58	517.62	640.90
Net Income	0.90	1.31	2.05	2.73	2.42	3.61	4.69	7.24	10.92	15.27	22.87	33.94	45.65	56.96

	1995	1996	1997	1998	1999	2000	2001	2002	2003	2004	2005
Net Sales/or Revenue	783.09	943.29	1123.85	1317.10	1531.63	1772.71	1963.69	2066.89	2198.18	2380.95	2567.55
Net Income	66.04	63.52	86.60	104.14	70.19	59.00	49.18	91.79	106.53	113.26	130.97

Cintas Corp.

	1981	1982	1983	1984	1985	1986	1987	1988	1989	1990	1991	1992	1993	1994
Net Sales/or Revenue	54.63	61.75	62.85	83.24	107.82	123.73	163.38	204.51	243.62	284.54	322.48	401.56	452.72	523.22
Net Income	3.72	4.62	5.5	7.36	9.24	11.26	13.94	17.15	22.06	26.61	31.43	36.49	44.87	52.17

	1995	1996	1997	1998	1999	2000	2001	2002	2003	2004	2005
Net Sales/or Revenue	615.10	730.13	839.95	1198.31	1751.57	1901.99	2160.70	2271.05	2686.59	2814.06	3067.28
Net Income	62.74	75.18	90.84	122.86	138.94	193.39	222.45	234.25	249.25	272.21	300.52

Comcast Corp.

	1981	1982	1983	1984	1985	1986	1987	1988	1989	1990	1991	1992	1993	1994
Net Sales/or Revenue	39.46	62.84	84.44	103.01	117.31	130.85	309.25	449.91	562.28	657.04	721.00	900.35	1338.23	1375.30
Net Income	4.90	6.53	9.03	12.17	14.57	1.00	-9.38	-47.56	-148.75	-178.41	-155.57	-217.94	-98.87	-75.33

	1995	1996	1997	1998	1999	2000	2001	2002	2003	2004	2005
Net Sales/or Revenue	3,362.95	4038.40	4912.60	5145.30	6209.20	8218.60	9674.20	12460	18348	20307	22255
Net Income	-37.85	-52.5	-223.30	973.10	1116.70	2045.10	225.6	-274	-50	970	928

Diagnostic Products Corp.

	1981	1982	1983	1984	1985	1986	1987	1988	1989	1990	1991	1992	1993	1994
Net Sales/or Revenue	9.00	12.00	14.81	17.68	22.68	29.03	36.92	47.01	60.35	60.35	90.0	103.49	106.79	126.45
Net Income	N/A	N/A	2.77	2.88	3.91	6.30	9.27	12.43	15.20	17.27	19.32	17.29	14.17	16.70

	1995	1996	1997	1998	1999	2000	2001	2002	2003	2004	2005
Net Sales/or Revenue	159.65	176.83	186.26	196.64	216.19	247.87	283.43	324.09	381.39	443.17	481.10
Net Income	24.17	22.95	18.25	20.21	20.49	28.25	39.03	47.31	61.80	61.7	67.15

Family Dollar Stores Inc

	1981	1982	1983	1984	1985	1986	1987	1988	1989	1990	1991	1992	1993	1994
Net Sales/or Revenue	181.71	207.42	264.44	340.92	410.09	487.73	560.34	669.49	756.89	874.40	89.35	1158.70	1297.43	1428.44
Net Income	9.12	10.70	15.73	23.56	28.01	30.51	24.80	27.33	21.52	28.73	40.24	55.67	64.43	61.96

	1995	1996	1997	1998	1999	2000	2001	2002	2003	2004	2005
Net Sales/or Revenue	1546.89	1714.63	1994.97	2361.93	2751.18	3132.64	3665.36	4162.65	4750.17	5281.89	5824.81
Net Income	58.11	60.59	74.68	103.29	140.08	172.02	189.51	216.93	247.48	262.69	217.51

Fed. Realty Investment Trust

	1981	1982	1983	1984	1985	1986	1987	1988	1989	1990	1991	1992	1993	1994
Net Sales/or Revenue	14.02	14.80	21.15	27.27	34.25	44.80	60.42	68.11	82.85	90.95	97.65	100.20	115.34	137.76
Net Income	2.67	3.35	8.04	10.31	9.86	14.92	6.05	5.36	4.78	4.89	4.80	6.99	16.11	20.47

	1995	1996	1997	1998	1999	2000	2001	2002	2003	2004	2005
Net Sales/or Revenue	154.39	179.06	204.27	238.48	264.71	279.28	300.50	318.03	357.88	394.27	410.33
Net Income	23.11	28.74	44.63	37.59	48.37	50.20	51.92	27.15	77.31	57.50	72.39

Fraport AG

	1981	1982	1983	1984	1985	1986	1987	1988	1989	1990	1991	1992	1993	1994
Net Sales/or Revenue	386.45	412.24	435.06	462.28	511.62	549.72	604.71	673.40	744.08	826.63	885.78	980.80	1051.59	1126.23
Net Income	10.23	10.24	16.93	20.71	32.76	35.63	37.57	110.66	1.33	-15.05	-14.32	13.59	17.95	

	1995	1996	1997	1998	1999	2000	2001	2002	2003	2004	2005
Net Sales/or Revenue	1184.49	1208.24	1215.19	1258.47	1340.18	1536.18	1580.60	1803.60	1834.30	1998.10	2089.80
Net Income	22.60	43.06	45.75	53.17	70.56	129.00	101.10	-120.80	115.20	136.40	161.20

G & K Services Inc

	1981	1982	1983	1984	1985	1986	1987	1988	1989	1990	1991	1992	1993	1994
Net Sales/or Revenue	38.31	42.12	47.17	56.06	63.83	71.59	80.76	94.01	108.82	118.66	176.23	194.72	207.90	225.23
Net Income	2.16	2.43	0.58	2.15	3.21	3.90	4.74	7.36	8.31	10.21	7.07	8.58	11.12	14.79

	1995	1996	1997	1998	1999	2000	2001	2002	2003	2004	2005
Net Sales/or Revenue	262.48	305.41	350.91	502.59	519.97	577.39	603.58	625.91	705.59	733.45	788.78
Net Income	18.29	22.72	29.00	32.06	37.03	37.81	33.78	38.27	33.69	35.38	39.93

Greene King PLC

	1981	1982	1983	1984	1985	1986	1987	1988	1989	1990	1991	1992	1993	1994
Net Sales/or Revenue	55.75	62.77	68.20	74.20	80.23	90.16	93.85	100.52	103.59	109.16	126.26	128.58	133.59	146.10
Net Income	4.99	5.00	5.23	5.22	5.93	7.37	8.26	9.46	13.74	14.33	16.08	16.89	14.95	15.23

	1995	1996	1997	1998	1999	2000	2001	2002	2003	2004	2005
Net Sales/or Revenue	154.43	164.97	253.60	282.90	292.60	414.10	431.70	494.50	535.60	552.70	732.60
Net Income	16.63	18.05	14.80	34.90	36.20	33.00	45.50	43.30	47.20	52.00	54.10

Grupo Bimbo SA De CV

	1981	1982	1983	1984	1985	1986	1987	1988	1989	1990	1991	1992	1993	1994
Net Sales/or Revenue	13.88	23.70	43.20	73.64	131.48	277.25	663.61	1457.10	1457.10	3021.24	3781.23	4499.13	5089.68	6186.24
Net Income	0.82	0.35	2.20	5.91	12.60	19.22	47.52	135.55	150.34	204.82	201.46	261.02	331.71	161.08

	1995	1996	1997	1998	1999	2000	2001	2002	2003	2004	2005
Net Sales/or Revenue	10159.64	15074.30	18563.01	25091.67	28788.29	28788.29	33855.33	41373.27	46663.00	51545.00	56102.00
Net Income	249.96	847.10	994.33	1233.27	1969.63	1844.66	1503.18	972.83	1192.00	2027.00	2820.00

Grupo Continental SA

	1981	1982	1983	1984	1985	1986	1987	1988	1989	1990	1991	1992	1993	1994
Net Sales/or Revenue	4.86	7.79	13.26	19.67	33.98	65.88	152.67	359.12	677.26	1001.25	1315.70	1505.32	1882.51	2059.07
Net Income	0.08	-0.12	-1.54	3.04	2.12	6.69	14.54	7.84	-11.26	27.45	98.13	70.76	120.24	89.25

	1995	1996	1997	1998	1999	2000	2001	2002	2003	2004	2005
Net Sales/or Revenue	3081.90	3766.03	4700.42	6316.71	7561.91	9025.67	9298.36	9760.97	9952.26	9978.35	10623.77
Net Income	216.11	332.49	470.75	737.02	809.07	1014.41	1100.50	1267.07	1137.57	1079.87	1205.04

Home Depot Inc

	1981	1982	1983	1984	1985	1986	1987	1988	1989	1990	1991	1992	1993	1994
Net Sales/or Revenue	22.32	51.54	117.65	256.18	432.78	700.73	1011.46	1453.66	1999.51	2758.54	3815.36	5136.67	7148.44	9238.76
Net Income	0.86	1.21	5.32	10.26	14.12	8.33	23.87	54.09	76.75	111.95	163.43	249.15	362.86	457.40

	1995	1996	1997	1998	1999	2000	2001	2002	2003	2004	2005
Net Sales/or Revenue	12476.70	15470.36	19535.50	24156.00	30219.00	38434.00	45738.00	53553.00	58247.00	64816.00	73094.00
Net Income	604.50	731.52	937.74	1183.00	1637.00	2337.00	2581.00	3044.00	3664.00	4304.00	5001.00

Johnson & Johnson

	1981	1982	1983	1984	1985	1986	1987	1988	1989	1990	1991	1992	1993	1994
Net Sales/or Revenue	5399.00	5760.90	5972.90	6124.50	6421.30	7002.90	8012.00	9000.00	9757.00	11232.00	12447.00	13753.00	14138.00	15734.00
Net Income	467.60	523.40	489.00	514.50	613.70	329.50	833.00	974.00	1082.00	1143.00	1461.00	1625.00	1787.00	2006.00

	1995	1996	1997	1998	1999	2000	2001	2002	2003	2004	2005
Net Sales/or Revenue	15734.00	21620.00	2629.00	23657.00	27471.00	29139.00	33004.00	36298.00	41862.00	47348.00	50514.00
Net Income	2403.00	2887.00	3303.00	3059.00	4167.00	4800.00	5693.00	6597.00	7197.00	9298.00	10411.00

Johnson Controls

	1981	1982	1983	1984	1985	1986	1987	1988	1989	1990	1991	1992	1993	1994
Net Sales	1128.39	1251.52	1323.42	1425.27	1787.05	2639.38	2676.82	3099.60	3683.60	4504.00	4559.00	5156.50	6181.70	6870.50
Net Income	48.13	53.84	59.0	23.78	77.92	89.55	83.20	103.50	94.60	84.10	86.80	114.90	128.80	155.90

	1995	1996	1997	1998	1999	2000	2001	2002	2003	2004	2005
Net Sales/or Revenue	8330	10009	11145	12586	16139	17154	18427	20103	22646	26553	27479
Net Income	186.40	5.20	214.00	332.50	412.70	468.00	474.9	600.50	682.90	817.40	757.20

Land Securities PLC

	1981	1982	1983	1984	1985	1986	1987	1988	1989	1990	1991	1992	1993	1994
Net Sales/or Revenue	103.89	118.16	130.63	137.70	148.40	171.50	204.10	213.20	249.00	296.30	359.70	406.70	436.90	448.90
Net Income	32.50	40.69	45.61	50.70	59.00	79.50	89.50	96.00	105.50	124.20	155.50	164.60	170.00	180.60

	1995	1996	1997	1998	1999	2000	2001	2002	2003	2004	2005
Net Sales/or Revenue	460.40	462.20	471.00	484.00	500.20	528.20	647.20	936.70	1067.60	1285.80	1641.40
Net Income	179.70	171.90	178.40	196.70	216.4	252.00	233.10	263.60	229.40	288.00	-35.90

Longs Drug Stores

	1981	1982	1983	1984	1985	1986	1987	1988	1989	1990	1991	1992	1993	1994
Net Sales/or Revenue	893.20	1005.37	1123.23	1214.44	1375.77	1480.83	1635.44	1772.46	1925.45	2110.57	2333.77	2365.92	2475.48	2499.22
Net Income	25.86	30.27	30.89	36.39	40.09	37.72	38.59	49.22	55.86	61.29	59.62	55.38	52.99	49.75

	1995	1996	1997	1998	1999	2000	2001	2002	2003	2004	2005
Net Sales/or Revenue	2558.27	2644.38	2828.34	2952.92	3266.90	3672.41	4027.13	4304.73	4426.27	4526.52	4607.87
Net Income	48.73	46.23	58.61	57.73	63.36	68.97	44.88	47.10	31.33	29.76	36.56

Lowe's Companies Inc

	1981	1982	1983	1984	1985	1986	1987	1988	1989	1990	1991	1992	1993	1994
Net Sales/or Revenue	883.61	888.04	1034.03	1430.58	1688.74	2072.57	2283.48	2442.18	2516.80	2650.55	2833.11	3056.25	3846.42	4538.00
Net Income	18.89	17.86	25.13	50.62	61.44	59.71	55.10	55.95	69.20	74.91	71.09	76.49	84.72	131.79

	1995	1996	1997	1998	1999	2000	2001	2002	2003	2004	2005
Net Sales/or Revenue	6110.52	7075.44	8600.24	10136.89	12244.88	15905.60	18778.56	22111.11	26491.00	30838.00	36464.00
Net Income	223.56	226.03	292.15	357.48	482.42	672.80	809.87	1032.58	1482.00	1872.00	2176.00

McDonalds Corp

	1981	1982	1983	1984	1985	1986	1987	1988	1989	1990	1991	1992	1993	1994
Net Sales	2515.84	2769.54	3062.92	3414.80	3760.86	4240.17	4893.54	5566.26	6142.00	6639.60	6695.00	7133.30	7408.10	8320.80
Net Income	264.83	300.60	342.64	385.95	428.53	476.23	549.06	645.86	723.00	788.30	840.40	943.90	1035.60	1177.20

	1995	1996	1997	1998	1999	2000	2001	2002	2003	2004	2005
Net Sales/or Revenue	9794.50	10686.50	11408.80	12421.40	13259.30	14243.00	14870.00	15405.70	17140.50	19064.70	20460.20
Net Income	1386.80	1545.00	1617.20	1550.10	1947.90	1977.30	1636.60	992.10	1508.20	2278.50	2602.20

Morrison Supermarkets

	1981	1982	1983	1984	1985	1986	1987	1988	1989	1990	1991	1992	1993	1994
Net Sales/or Revenue	171.21	198.52	223.99	270.43	336.24	367.99	423.31	482.11	603.66	778.48	909.90	1117.97	1316.70	1538.41
Net Income	5.28	4.6	4.16	5.88	6.39	9.19	13.35	16.01	19.65	22.42	30.94	39.70	54.20	60.97

	1995	1996	1997	1998	1999	2000	2001	2002	2003	2004	2005
Net Sales/or Revenue	1779.37	2099.38	2176.02	2297.00	2533.78	2970.10	3500.37	3918.32	4288.50	4944.08	12116.10
Net Income	70.78	$77.66	81.42	93.64	106.53	118.43	142.13	154.12	179.22	197.54	205.70

Nbty Inc

	1981	1982	1983	1984	1985	1986	1987	1988	1989	1990	1991	1992	1993	1994
Net Sales/or Revenue	24.71	30.00	35.66	36.35	40.03	43.56	48.32	50.99	62.66	70.77	73.59	100.91	138.43	156.06
Net Income	-0.31	1.02	1.10	-0.55	-1.38	N/A	0.68	0.22	0.24	0.72	1.02	3.81	9.77	7.78

	1995	1996	1997	1998	1999	2000	2001	2002	2003	2004	2005
Net Sales/or Revenue	178.76	194.40	281.41	572.12	630.89	720.86	806.90	964.08	1192.55	1652.03	1737.19
Net Income	5.14	13.35	17.23	38.84	27.28	51.51	41.93	95.79	81.59	111.85	78.14

Nordstrom Inc

	1981	1982	1983	1984	1985	1986	1987	1988	1989	1990	1991	1992	1993	1994
Net Sales/or Revenue	407.81	522.05	612.94	787.89	982.67	1301.86	1629.92	1920.23	2327.95	2671.11	2893.90	3179.82	3421.98	3589.94
Net Income	19.66	24.78	27.01	40.24	40.71	50.08	72.94	92.73	123.33	114.91	115.82	135.82	136.62	140.42

	1995	1996	1997	1998	1999	2000	2001	2002	2003	2004	2005
Net Sales/or Revenue	3894.48	4113.52	4453.06	4851.62	5027.89	5124.22	5528.54	5634.13	5975.08	6491.67	7131.39
Net Income	202.96	165.11	147.51	186.21	206.72	202.56	101.92	124.69	103.58	242.84	393.45

Omnicom Group Inc

	1981	1982	1983	1984	1985	1986	1987	1988	1989	1990	1991	1992	1993	1994
Net Sales/or Revenue	410.86	465.97	555.56	631.37	673.40	753.53	811.37	881.29	1007.17	1178.23	1236.16	1385.16	1516.48	1756.21
Net Income	27.77	24.62	28.66	36.66	30.14	-4.08	34.77	39.19	46.79	52.01	57.05	65.50	85.35	108.13

	1995	1996	1997	1998	1999	2000	2001	2002	2003	2004	2005
Net Sales/or Revenue	2257.54	2641.60	3124.81	4092.04	5130.55	6154.23	6889.41	7536.30	8621.40	9747.20	10481.10
Net Income	139.96	176.33	232.05	294.70	380.85	516.73	503.14	643.46	675.88	723.50	790.70

Pall Corp.

	1981	1982	1983	1984	1985	1986	1987	1988	1989	1990	1991	1992	1993	1994
Net Sales/or Revenue	169.08	195.52	214.74	242.14	275.92	332.04	385.14	429.23	497.00	564.50	656.98	685.07	687.22	700.85
Net Income	24.80	24.99	27.82	30.73	34.25	40.94	48.09	57.40	57.68	66.24	79.92	90.23	78.31	98.92

	1995	1996	1997	1998	1999	2000	2001	2002	2003	2004	2005
Net Sales/or Revenue	822.82	960.38	1062.01	1087.29	1147.07	1224.10	1235.42	1290.82	1613.64	1770.75	1902.28
Net Income	119.22	138.50	67.32	93.63	51.51	146.64	118.01	73.23	103.20	151.57	140.82

Pick N Pay Stores Limited

	1981	1982	1983	1984	1985	1986	1987	1988	1989	1990	1991	1992	1993	1994
Net Sales/or Revenue	745.00	974.00	1235.00	1501.00	1825.00	2145.00	2468.00	3038.00	3869.00	4381.00	5189.00	5911.00	6424.00	6686.00
Net Income	17.00	24.00	28.00	31.00	34.00	35.00	43.00	53.00	68.00	83.00	87.00	84.00	93.00	106.00

	1995	1996	1997	1998	1999	2000	2001	2002	2003	2004	2005
Net Sales/or Revenue	7920.00	9169.00	9794.00	10971.00	12503.00	13791.00	15126.00	18818.00	26194.00	29276.00	31885.00
Net Income	79.00	106.00	135.00	111.00	159.00	267.00	319.00	400.00	454.00	516.00	650.00

Stryker Corp.

	1981	1982	1983	1984	1985	1986	1987	1988	1989	1990	1991	1992	1993	1994
Net Sales/or Revenue	42.87	55.08	70.19	84.29	101.55	121.05	148.10	178.64	225.86	280.63	364.83	477.05	557.34	681.92
Net Income	3.87	4.71	5.75	6.94	8.40	10.08	12.73	15.86	19.23	23.63	33.08	47.70	60.21	72.40

	1995	1996	1997	1998	1999	2000	2001	2002	2003	2004	2005
Net Sales/or Revenue	871.95	910.06	980.14	1103.21	1103.21	2289.40	2602.30	3011.60	3625.30	4262.30	4871.50
Net Income	87.01	104.46	125.32	$39.57	19.40	221.00	271.80	345.60	453.50	465.70	675.20

Sysco Corp.

	1981	1982	1983	1984	1985	1986	1987	1988	1989	1990	1991	1992	1993	1994
Net Sales/or Revenue	1386	21713	1963	2311	2627	3172	3655	4384.70	6851	7590	8149	8892	10021	10942
Net Income	26.81	34.21	40.10	4 5.15	50.33	58.33	61.83	80.18	107.89	132.46	153.83	172.23	201.81	216.75

	1995	1996	1997	1998	1999	2000	2001	2002	2003	2004	2005
Net Sales/or Revenue	12118.05	13395.13	14454.59	15327.54	17422.82	19303.27	21785.00	23351.00	26140.00	29335.40	30281.91
Net Income	251.82	276.91	302.53	324.82	362.27	453.63	597.00	680.00	778.00	907.21	961.46

Teleflex Inc

	1981	1982	1983	1984	1985	1986	1987	1988	1989	1990	1991	1992	1993	1994
Net Sales/or Revenue	103.22	111.69	129.34	153.31	171.82	218.15	271.77	328.22	360.07	441.13	479.54	570.34	666.80	812.67
Net Income	7.11	10.95	9.50	11.31	13.31	16.43	19.67	24.01	26.80	28.57	29.81	32.01	33.69	41.20

	1995	1996	1997	1998	1999	2000	2001	2002	2003	2004	2005
Net Sales/or Revenue	10101.0	12094.0	13887	15915	17158.0	18796.00	20988.00	23653.0	26337.00	30814.00	33974.00
Net Income	48.87	57.16	70.07	82.55	95.22	109.22	112.31	125.27	109.10	119.52	139.00

Wal Mart

	1981	1982	1983	1984	1985	1986	1987	1988	1989	1990	1991	1992	1993	1994
Net Sales/or Revenue	1643.20	2445.0	3376.25	4666.91	6400.86	8451.49	11909.0	15959.2	20649.0	25810.6	32601.5	43886.90	55483.7	67344.5
Net Income	55.68	82.66	123.55	195.72	270.29	327.08	450.09	627.64	837.22	1075.90	1291.02	1608.48	1994.79	2333.2

	1995	1996	1997	1998	1999	2000	2001	2002	2003	2004	2005
Net Sales	82494.0	93627.0	104859	117958.0	137634.0	165013.00	191329.0	217799.0	244524.0	256329.0	285222.0
Net Income	2681.00	2740.00	3056.00	3526.00	4430.00	5575.00	6295.00	6671.00	8039.00	8861.00	10267.00

Walgreen Company

	1981	1982	1983	1984	1985	1986	1987	1988	1989	1990	1991	1992	1993	1994
Net Sales	1743.47	2039.50	2360.61	2744.63	161.94	3660.55	4281.61	4883.52	5380.13	6047.49	6733.04	7474.9	8294.84	9234.98
Net Income	42.13	56.06	69.79	85.4	94.17	103.14	103.54	129.06	154.24	174.58	194.97	220.63	245.29	281.93

	1995	1996	1997	1998	1999	2000	2001	2002	2003	2004	2005
Net Sales	10395.10	11778.41	13363.00	15307.0	17838.80	21206.90	24623.00	28681.1	32505.4	37508.2	42201.60
Net Income	320.79	371.75	436.00	537.00	624.10	776.90	885.60	1019.20	1175.7	1360.20	1559.50

(Scaling Factor : 1000000 JPY)

Aeon Co

	1981	1982	1983	1984	1985	1986	1987	1988	1989	1990	1991	1992	1993	1994
Net Sales	592372	652037	706067	763653	821952	867750	919440	992790	1181583	1350949	1436647	1532331	1609298	1713226
Net Income	10551	6501	6054	6369	7487	9820	7815	12154	11732	12691	14563	13854	8287	25901

	1995	1996	1997	1998	1999	2000	2001	2002	2003	2004	2005
Net Sales	1881934	2094933	2238276	2340141	2465827	2522209	2738638	2934591	3086504	3546215	4195843
Net Income	23154	31141	35297	11279	18128	15151	22515	-16139	51257	55316	62066

Bibliography

Abertis Infraestructuras, S.A.

"Abertis Infraestructuras, S.A." *International Directory of Company Histories.* Vol. 65. St. James Press, 2004. Reproduced in Business and Company Resource Center. Farmington Hills, Mich.: Gale Group, 2006.

"Abertis se fija en Europe del este." *Epoca*, April 30, 2004, 83.

Blitz, James. "Autostrade, Acesa Strengthen Ties." *Financial Times*, March 27, 2001, 30.

Gonzalez, Emilio. "Abertis, en busca de la consolidaci?" *Epoca*, July 11, 2003, 78.

Levitt, Joshua. "Acesa Move Opens up Battle for Iberpistas." *Financial Times*, March 21, 2002, 22.

Schafer, Thilo. "Spanish Roads Operator Attracts Four Bids." *Financial Times*, May 28, 2003, 28.

"Spanish Acesa Group Acquires 5% of Portuguese Operator Brisa." *European Report*, April 6, 2002, 600.

Thomson One Banker. Analytics 1981-2006 10k Reports.

Wise, Peter. "Brisa Road Deal Points to Merger." *Financial Times*, September 17, 2002, 16.

ABM Industries Incorporated

75 Years of American Building Maintenance Industries. San Francisco: American Building Maintenance Industries, 1985.

"ABM Industries Acquires 'Big Apple' from Ogden Corp." *Business Wire*, August 1, 1997.

"ABM Industries Acquires Polaris of Indianapolis," *Business Wire*, May 1, 1997.

"ABM Industries Incorporated." *International Directory of Company Histories.* Vol. 25. St. James Press, 1999. Reproduced in Business and Company Resource Center. Farmington Hills, Mich.: Gale Group, 2006.

Thomson One Banker. Analytics 1981-2006 10k Reports.

Troxell, Thomas N., Jr. "Cleaning Up." *Barron's*, March 2, 1981.

Aeon Company Limited

Thomson One Banker. Analytics 1981-2006 10k Reports.

Alliance Unichem PLC

Thomson One Banker. Analytics 1981-2006 10k Reports.

Arthur J. Gallagher

Thomson One Banker. Analytics 1981-2006 10k Reports.

Automatic Data Processing Inc.

ADP 1995 Annual Report.

ADP 1996 Annual Report.

ADP 1997 Annual Report.

"ADP Acquires Bank of America Units." *Datamonitor NewsWire*, November 2, 2004.

"ADP Acquires the Vincam Group." *Business Wire*, March 11, 1999.

"ADP Blunder Places 7,000 in ID Danger." *Contra Costa Times*, April 9, 2005.

"ADP's Josh S. Weston Retires as Chairman; CEO Arthur F. Weinbach Becomes Chairman." *ADP Press Release*, April 16, 1998.

"Automatic Data Processing Inc." *HRMagazine*, September 2001, 190.

"Automatic Data Processing, Inc." *International Directory of Company Histories*. Detroit: St. James Press, 1994.

"Automatic Data Processing, Inc." *International Directory of Company Histories*. Vol. 47. St. James Press, 2002. Reproduced in Business and Company Resource Center. Farmington Hills, Mich.: Gale Group, 2006.

"Automatic Data Processing Hews to Winning Formula," *Wall Street Journal*, December 24, 1992.

Automatic Data Processing Inc. *Notable Corporate Chronologies*. Online Edition. Thomson Gale, 2005. Reproduced in Business and Company Resource Center. Farmington Hills, Mich.:Gale Group, 2006.

Crone, Richard K. "Notes on the Infobahn: ADP Positioned to Control Funds at Point of Payroll." *American Banker*, January 9, 1995, 6A.

"Cunningham Graphics to be Acquired by ADP." *Business Wire*, May 3, 2000.

Marjanovic, Steven. "Checkfree, ADP to Start PC Payment System Aimed at Small Business." *American Banker*, July 20, 1995, 8.

"Payroll Specialist." *Investor's Reader*, July 26, 1972.

"ProBusiness to Be Acquired by Automatic Data Processing for $17.00 Per Common Share in Cash." *Business Wire*, January 6, 2003.

"They Make Money Paying Us." *Forbes*, January 4, 1993.

Weston, Josh. "Soft Stuff Matters." *Financial Executive*, July/August 1992.

Becton, Dickinson and Co.

"BD Blasted as 'Unscrupulous Competitor' by RTI." *Health Industry Today*, January 2000.

"BD Enters Glucose Monitoring." *The BBI Newsletter*, February 2003.

"BD Files Patent Infringement Complaint Against Tyco Healthcare." *Business Wire*, December 23, 2002.

"Becton, Dickinson & Co." *CDA-Investnet Insiders' Chronicle*, June 7, 1993: 11.

Becton Dickinson and Co. *Notable Corporate Chronologies*. Online Edition. Thomson Gale, 2005. Reproduced in Business and Company Resource Center. Farmington Hills, Mich.: Gale Group, 2006.

"Becton, Dickinson & Co." *Nursing Home and Elder Business Week*, July 3, 2005.

"Becton Dickinson Facelift Unveils New Direction, New Logo for 'BD'." *Health Industry Today,* October 1999.

"Becton Dickinson Repurchase." *Wall Street Journal,* September 28 1994, C18.

"Fast-track AS/RS Cuts Costs." *Modern Materials Handling,* Februbary 1993: 62.

"Glucose Testing Strips Recalled." *Drug Topics,* February 9, 2004.

Healey, Thomas S. *Qualities.* Becton Dickinson and Co., 1993, 193.

International Directory of Company Histories. Detroit: St. James Press.

"Shareholders Applaud Double-Digit Profit Growth." Record (Hackensack, NJ), February 14, 1996, B1.

Siekman, Philip. "Becton Dickinson Takes a Plunge with Safer Needles." *Fortune,* October 1, 2001, 157.

"Switch to VNA cuts product damage." *Modern Materials Handling,* January 1993: 46.

Wall Street Journal: 11-25-92.; 01-13-93.; 04-09-93.; 04-21-93.

"Whistle-Blower to Share in $3.3 Million Settlement." *Baltimore Sun,* June 20, 1995, C12.

Thomson One Banker. Analytics 1981-2006 10k Reports.

Biomet, Inc

Andrews, Greg. "Cha-Ching! CEO's Salaries Outpace Earnings at Hoosier Firms*." Indianapolis Business Journal,* May 4, 1992, Sec. 1, 1.

"Biomet: Wall Street Likes What It Sees," *Indiana Business,* April 1985, Sec. 1, 55.

Howey, Brian. "Biomet: Bringing R&D to Market," *Indiana Business,* May 1988, Sec. 1, 72.

Kaelble, Steve. "International Business Person of the Year," *Indiana Business,* October 1992, Sec. 1, 1.

Kurowski, Jeff, 'Indiana Business's Industrialist of the Year: Dane Miller, CEO, Biomet,' Indiana Business, December 1989, Sec. 1, 1.

Miller, Jim. "Biomet Founder Recalls Years Filled With 'Sheer Excitement'." *Elkhart Truth,* October 29, 1992, Business section.

Panzica, Lisa. "Getting a Knee Up on the Competition." *Tribune Business Weekly,* September 22, 1993, Sec. 1, 14.

Sasso, Greg. "Biomet Announces Record Second Quarter and First Half Results," *Business Wire,* December 10, 1992.

Shankle, Greta. "FDA proposes Stiffening Regulation of the Medical Device Industry." *Indianapolis Business Journal,* January 10, 1994, Sec. 1, 11A.

Welles, Ed, ed. "Stock Pick; Biomet, Inc." *Common Stocks, Common Sense,* December 1993, 3-4.

Thomson One Banker. Analytics 1981-2006 10k Reports.

CBRL Group, Inc.

Carlino, Bill. "Magruder Exits Darden to Join Cracker Barrel." *Nation's Restaurant News,* July 17, 1995, 1.

"Cracker Barrel Protesters Don't Shake Loyal Patrons." *Nation's Restaurant News*, August 26, 1991, 3.

"Cracker Barrel Set the Survey's Standard for Family Dining for the Fourth Straight Year." *Restaurant & Institution*, February 1, 1994.

Farkas, David. "Kings of the Road." *Restaurant Hospitality*, August, 1991, 118.

Ganem, Beth Carlson. "My Country, Right or Wrong." *Restaurant Hospitality*, February 1993, 73.

Gutner, Todd. "Nostalgia Sells." *Forbes*, April 27, 1992, 102.

Harper, Roseanne. "Cracker Barrel Plunges Back into HMR with Carmine's Purchase." *Supermarket News*, April 20, 1998, 49.

Hayes, Jack. "After Free Fall Cracker Barrel Rolls As a Top Contender in Family Segment." *Nation's Restaurant News*, November 17, 1997, 1.

Kramer, Louise. "Cracker Barrel Expands Test of Corner Market." *Nation's Restaurant News*, June 5, 1995, 7.

Oleck, Joan. "Bad Politics." *Restaurant Business*, June 10, 1992, 80.

Papiernik, Richard L. "Cracker Barrel Springs a Leak, Bottom-Line Fix Under Way." *Nation's Restaurant News*, November 25, 1996, 11.

Rhein, Liz. "Along the Interstate with Cracker Barrel." *Restaurant Business*, June 10, 1987, 113.

Tarquinio, J. Alex. "Restaurants: King of Grits Alters Menu to Reflect Northern Tastes." *Wall Street Journal*, September 22, 1997, B1.

Thomson One Banker. Analytics 1981-2006 10k Reports.

Walkup, Carolyn. "Family Chains Beat Recession Blues with Value, Service." *Nation's Restaurant News*, August 5, 1991, 100.

"With New Prexy in Place, CBRL Group Readies Expansion." *Nation's Restaurant News*, October 5, 1998.

Yanez, Luisa. "Food Fight on the Interstate." *Restaurant Business*, September 20, 1992, 50.

Cintas Corp.
Boulton, Guy. "Cintas Caps Strong Year with 2-1 Stock Split." *Cincinnati Enquirer*, October 23, 1997, C14.

———. "Cintas' Fiscal-Year Profit Climbs 21% to $90.8M." *Cincinnati Enquirer*, July 11, 1997, C10.

"Cintas Corp. Announces Completion of Acquisition of Unitog Co." *PR Newswire*, March 24, 1999.

"Cintas Corp." *International Directory of Company Histories*. Detroit: St. James Press, 1998.

Cintas Corp. *Notable Corporate Chronologies*. Gale Group, 2003. Reproduced in Business and Company Resource Center. Farmington Hills, Mich.: Gale Group, 2006.

"Cintas Keeps NASCAR as Partner." *Business Courier Serving Cincinnati-Northern Kentucky*, February 18, 2000, 11.

Sekhri, Rajiv. "Cintas Acquires First-Aid Company for $7.2 Million." *Business Courier Serving Cincinnati-Northern Kentucky*, November 21, 1997, 9.

Taylor, John. "Labor Union Organizers Target Cintas." *Omaha World Herald*, February 20, 2003, 1D.
Thomson One Banker. Analytics 1981-2006 10k Reports.

Comcast Corp.
"About Us: Key Events." *Comcast*. http://www.comcast.com/about_us.
"Adelphia Creditors Would Take Offer If It Is All Cash." *Wall Street Journal*, February 25, 2005, A5.
"AT&T Broadband Merging." *Denver Business Journal*, December 21, 2001.
"Bumpy Road Led to Alliance of AOL, Google." *Wall Street Journal*, December 21, 2005: B1.
"Comcast Completes Acquisition of Majority Interest in The Golf Channel." *PR Newswire*, April 7, 2000, 6116.
"Comcast in Fiber-Network Push." *Wall Street Journal*, December 8, 2004, B8.
"Comcast Gives Up on Disney." *MEDIAWEEK*, May 3, 2004, 25.
"Comcast Reports Strong 1999 Results." *PR Newswire*, April 7, 2000, 6691.
"Comcast's Newly Acquired TechTV Will Be Merged with Its Videogame/Lifestyle Channel G4 to Create G4TechTV." *Broadcasting & Cable*, May 17, 2004, 6.
"DirecTV to File Complaint Over Fees." *Wall Street Journal*, June 29, 2005, A3.
"EU Approves Acquisition of MGM by Sony-Led Group." *Wall Street Journal*, March 31, 2005.
Higgins, John M. "Comcast Sure on Rebuilding AT&T Ops." *Broadcasting & Cable*, March 3, 2003, 8.
International Directory of Company Histories. Farmington Hills: St. James Press.
"Please Hold, Mr. Roberts will Connect You." *Business Week*, October 26, 1992.
Thomson One Banker. Analytics 1981-2006 10k Reports.

Diagnostic Products Corp.
Thomson One Banker. Analytics 1981-2006 10k Reports.

Family Dollar Stores, Inc.
Clune, Ray. "Family Dollar Sticks to Its Niche." *Daily News Record*, December 6, 1993, 4-5.
D'Innocenzio, Anne. "Building the Family Image." *Women's Wear Daily*, January 26, 1994, 18.
"Family Dollar to Open Ariz. Units in Slow, Steady March West." *Discount Store News*, March 8, 1999, 3.
"Family Dollar Posts Record Earnings, Celebrates 40th Anniversary." *Discount Store News*, February 7, 2000, 5.
"Family Dollar Quietly Invades Northeast." *Discount Store News*, December 7, 1992, 4-5.

"Family Dollar Stores, Inc." *International Directory of Company Histories.* Vol.
    62. St. James Press, 2004. Reproduced in Business and Company Resource
    Center. Farmington Hills, Mich.: Gale Group, 2006.
"Family Dollar Succession." *Home Textiles Today,* January 20, 2003, 27.
Foust, Dean. "The Family Feud at Family Dollar Stores." *Business Week,* Sep-
    tember 21, 1987, 32-33.
Greene, Richard. "The Leon and Al Show." *Forbes,* September 29, 1980, 52-54.
Grover, Mary Beth. "Tornado Watch." *Forbes,* June 22, 1992, 66-69.
Halverson, Richard. "Leadership at Family Dollar Moves to the Next Genera-
    tion." *Discount Store News,* May 19, 1997, 3.
Howell, Debbie. "Family Dollar Continues Record Pace, Will Surpass 5,000
    Stores." *DSN Retailing Today,* July 21, 2003, 1.
Johnson, Jay L. "Face to Face with Howard Levine." *Discount Merchandiser,*
    December 1999, 11.
Keefe, Lisa. "Guess Who Lost." *Forbes,* September 7, 1987, 60-61.
Lillo, Andrea. "Family Dollar Grows Sales, Stores." *Home Textiles Today,* Oc-
    tober 16, 2000, 21.
Palmer, Jay. "Back to Basics." *Barron's,* August 29, 1988, 20-21.
Tronell, Thomas. "Bucking a Slump." *Barron's,* January 21, 1980, 39, 41.
Thomson One Banker. Analytics 1981-2006 10k Reports.

Federal Realty Investment Trust

Thomson One Banker. Analytics 1981-2006 10k Reports.

Fraport AG

Thomson One Banker. Analytics 1981-2006 10k Reports.

G&K Services, Inc.
Byrne, Harlan S. "G&K Services Inc. Acquisition To Boost Firm's Results."
    Barron's, October 22, 1990.
———. "G&K Services: Its Canadian Venture Is Beginning To Turn a Profit."
    Barron's, August 30, 1993, 43.
"G&K Services, Inc." *International Directory of Company Histories.* Vol. 16.
    St. James Press, 1997. Reproduced in Business and Company Resource
    Center. Farmington Hills, Mich.: Gale Group, 2006.
"G&K Services, Inc." *The Wall Street Transcript,* December 12, 1994.
Jones, John A. "G&K Services Growing Fast in Booming Uniform Business."
    Investor's Business Daily, May 22, 1995.
Thomson One Banker. Analytics 1981-2006 10k Reports.
Youngblood, Dick. "Fink's G&K Services Enjoys a Clean Rate of Growth."
    Minneapolis Star Tribune, October 2, 1995.

Golden State Foods Corporation (McDonalds Corp.)

Britton, Charles. "Golden State Foods ... Under the Arches." *Southern California Business,* July 1, 1987, 8.

Desloge, Rick. "Wetterau Says McDonald's." *St. Louis Business Journal,* March 2, 1998, 1A.

"Golden State Foods Corporation" *International Directory of Company Histories.* Vol. 32. St. James Press, 2000. Reproduced in Business and Company Resource Center. Farmington Hills, Mich.: Gale Group, 2006.

Hernandez, Greg. "Golden State's Chief Executive Retires." *Los Angeles Times, Orange County Edition,* May 28, 1999, C6.

Segal, Robert. "McDonald's Primary Distributors Are Sold." *The Voice of Foodservice Distribution,* July 1998, 33.

Stanton, Russ. "Duo Purchases Golden State Foods." Los *Angeles Times, Orange County Edition,* February 24, 1998, D21.

Thomson One Banker. Analytics 1981-2006 10k Reports.

Greene King plc

"£182m Morland Deal Fuels Greene King Marketing Rejig." *Marketing Week,* August 12, 1999, 9.

"Abbot Ale Gets Bottled Up." *Super Marketing,* June 4, 1993, 40.

Blackwell, David. "Beard Growth for Greene King." *Financial Times,* July 1, 1998, 26.

"Brewer Limits the Damage from Beer." *Financial Times,* December 13, 1993, 23.

"Brewery and Leased Pubs Help Greene King Lift Profit by 10%." *Caterer & Hotelkeeper,* July 8, 2004, 8.

Burt, Tim. "Greene King Static at 20.4m Pound Sterling." *Financial Times,* July 8, 1994, 20.

Dennis, Mike. "Greene King Renews Attack on Take-Home." *Super Marketing,* February 18, 2000, 16.

"Financial Results." *Greene King plc.* http://www.greeneking.co.uk. June 2003.

Fry, Andy. "Greene King Widens Realm." *Marketing,* May 10, 1990, 5.

Gourvish, T.R., and R.G. Wilson. *The British Brewing Industry 1830-1980.* Cambridge, England: Cambridge University Press, 1994.

"Greene King." *Investors Chronicle,* December 17, 1993, 54.

"Greene King Ahead to 22m Pounds Sterling." *Financial Times,* July 14, 1995, 19.

"Greene King Appoints CKT to Launch Irish 'Hybrid' Ale." *Marketing Week,* May 17, 1996, 13.

"Greene King Back to Basics After Failure of Morland Takeover." *Guardian,* July 29, 1992, 10.

"Greene King Below Expectations at 9.6m Pounds Sterling." *Financial Times,* December 14, 1993, 20.

"Greene King Benefits from Magic Spell." *Financial Times,* December 12, 1996, 25.

"Greene King Buys Neighborhood Estate from Laurel." *Caterer & Hotelkeeper*, July 15, 2004, 8.

"Greene King plc." *International Directory of Company Histories*. Vol. 31. St. James Press, 2000. Reproduced in Business and Company Resource Center. Farmington Hills, Mich.: Gale Group, 2006.

"Greene King plc." *International Directory of Company Histories*. Farmington Hills: St. James Press, 2000.

Greene King plc. *Notable Corporate Chronologies*. Online Edition. Thomson Gale, 2005. Reproduced in Business and Company Resource Center. Farmington Hills, Mich.: Gale Group, 2006.

"Greene King plc Offer to Buy Magic Pub Would Give It 1,139 Pubs." *Wall Street Journal*, June 19, 1996.

"Greene King Sells Morland Stake." *Financial Times*, September 7, 1994, 24.

"Greene King Takes Over Magic Pub." *Financial Times*, June 19, 1996, 25.

"Greene King to Close Maltings." *Financial Times*, October 15, 1998, 29.

"History." *Greene King plc*. http://www.greeneking.co.uk. June 2003.

"Improved Beer Sales Volumes Help Greene King to 10.7m Pounds Sterling." *Financial Times*, December 16, 1994, 24.

Jackson, Tony, and Christopher Price. "Whitbread Sells Holdings in Regional Brewers." *Financial Times*, March 11, 1994, 19.

"Magic Casts Its Spell on Greene King." *Financial Times*, December 6, 1997, 16.

Mazur, Laura. "Brewing a Storm." *Management Today*, June 1989, 48.

"McCann Nets L2.5m Greene King Rands in Centralisation." *Marketing Week*, March 5, 1998, 13.

McKenzie, Sophie. "Pump Action." *Marketing Week*, September 8, 1995, 60-63.

Oram, Roderick. "Greene King 13% Ahead at 11m Pounds Sterling." *Financial Times*, December 12, 1995, 26.

Rawstorne, Philip. "A Fight to the Bitter End." *Financial Times*, July 24, 1992, 23.

"Retail Side Helps Greene King to 16% Advance." *Financial Times*, June 19, 1996, 28.

Thomson One Banker. Analytics 1981-2006 10k Reports.

Tieman, Ross. "Greene King Aided by Magic's Spell." *Financial Times*, June 26, 1997, 36.

"UK: Morland to Sell to Greene King." *Daily Telegraph*, June 5, 1998, 29.

"UK: Offer for Marston Pubs from Greene King." *Daily Telegraph*, December 24, 1998, 21.

"UK: Wolves Finally Captures Marston." *Daily Telegraph*, February 5, 1999, 29.

Grupo Bimbo SA DeCV

"American Capital and Employees of Four-S Sell Bakery for $34 Million." *PR Newswire*, March 30, 1999.

"Bimbo Acquires Pacific Pride in California." *Milling and Baking News*, April 2, 1996, 1.

"Bimbo's Big Buy." *LatinFinance*, March, 2002, 10.

"Bimbo Modifies Company Name, Increases Stock Buy-Back Fund." *InfoLatina S.A. de C.V.*, December 1999.

"Bimbo Turnover Exceeds 400M-Euro Mark." *The Financial Times*, September 2, 2004.

"Grupo Industrial Bimbo." *International Directory of Company Histories*. Detroit: St. James Press, 1998.

"Servitje Urges Redefining of Companies." *Milling and Baking News*, June 27, 1995, 1.

Thomson One Banker. Analytics 1981-2006 10k Reports.

Grupo Continental SA
Thomson One Banker. Analytics 1981-2006 10k Reports.

The Home Depot
Document Number: I2501150877

Frederick, Jim. "Home Depot Vs. Lowe's: Both Giants Have Growing Room, But One's a Better Value." *Money*, March 1, 1999, 60.

"The Home Depot." *Management Horizons*, July 1990.

"The Home Depot, Inc." *International Directory of Company Histories*. Vol. 18. St. James Press, 1997. Reproduced in Business and Company Resource Center. Farmington Hills, Mich.: Gale Group, 2006.

"Home Depot Finds the World a Small Place." *Wall Street Journal*, December 2, 2004.

"Home Depot and the Home Center Industry." *Mid-Atlantic Journal of Business*, December 1994.

Home Depot Inc. *Notable Corporate Chronologies*. Online Edition. Thomson Gale, 2005. Reproduced in Business and Company Resource Center. Farmington Hills, Mich.: Gale Group, 2006.

"Home Depot, Lowe's Settlement Could Mean Rebates for Millions." *Wall Street Journal*, December 2, 2004.

"Home Depot Renovates." *Fortune*, November 23, 1998, 200.

"The 'How' in Home Improvement." *New York Times*, June 14, 1992.

Howell, Debbie. "Home Depot to Focus on Modernization, New Ventures in '04."

International Directory of Company Histories. Farmington Hills: St. James Press.

O'Connor, Marjie. "Home Depot buys wholesaler." *Contractor*, January 2000, 1.

"Shelter from the Recession." *Time*, June 10, 1991.

Thomson One Banker. Analytics 1981-2006 10k Reports.

Wall Street Journal: 04-28-93.; 08-25-93.; 12-23-93.; 12-21-94.; 01-20-95.; 07-06-95.; 08-18-95.; 12-22-95.; 01-29-96.; 02-21-96.

"Will Home Depot be 'The Wal-Mart of the '90s?'" *Business Week*, March 19, 1990.

"Will Home Depot Be 'The Wal-Mart of the '9Os?'" *Business Week*, March 19, 1990.

Zemke, Ron. *The Service Edge*. New York: NAL Books, 1986.

Johnson & Johnson

Abelson, Reed. "Johnson Takes Ally to Try to Keep Lead in Stents." *New York Times*, February 25, 2004, C1.

"Abbott Laboratories, Five Rivals Offer Drug Discount Card for Uninsured." *Chicago Tribune*, January 12, 2005.

Alpert, Bill. "Bitter Pills: Once Invincible, J&J Faces Fresh Competition Across Its Product Spectrum." *Barron's*, June 9, 2003, 17-18.

———. "Breach of Discipline?: Possible J&J Buy of Guidant Draws Skeptics." *Barron's*, December 13, 2004, 14.

Alsop, Ronald. "Johnson & Johnson (Think Babies!) Turns Up Tops." *Wall Street Journal*, September 23, 1999, B1.

Barker, Robert. "Picture of Health: Johnson & Johnson Seems to Have Cured What Ailed It." *Barron's*, March 30, 1987, 15+.

Barrett, Amy. "J&J Stops Babying Itself." *Business Week*, September 13, 1999, 95-97.

———. "Johnson & Johnson: A Shopping Spree Waiting to Happen." *Business Week*, June 17, 2002, 58, 60.

———. "Staying on Top." *Business Week*, May 5, 2003, 60-63, 68.

Brief History of Johnson & Johnson. New Brunswick: Johnson & Johnson, 1989.

A Brief History of Johnson & Johnson. http://www.jnj.com/company/comphist. htm, 09-96.

Burton, Thomas M. "Behind the J&J Guidant Talks: Heart Implants." *Wall Street Journal*, December 8, 2004, B1.

"Changing a Corporate Culture." *Business Week*, May 14, 1984, 130+.

"Drug Makers Win Big Patent Victory." *Wall Street Journal*, June 14, 2005.

Dumaine, Brian. "Is Big Still Good?" *Fortune*, April 20, 1992, 50-60.

Easton, Thomas and Stephan Herrera. "J&J's Dirty Little Secret." *Forbes*, January 12, 1998, 42-44.

Fannin, Rebecca. "The Pain Game." *Marketing and Media Decisions*, February 1989, 34-39.

Foster, Lawrence G. *A Company That Cares: One Hundred Year Illustrated History of Johnson & Johnson*. New Brunswick, NJ: Johnson & Johnson, 1986.

Guzzardi, Walter. "The National Business Hall of Fame." *Fortune*, March 12, 1990, 118-26.

Harris, Roy J., Jr., and Elyse Tanouye. "Johnson & Johnson to Buy Neutrogena in Bid to Boost Consumer-Products Unit." *Wall Street Journal*, August 23, 1994, A3.

Hensley, Scott. "J&J Say New-Drug Pipeline Is Filling After Four-Year Push." *Wall Street Journal*, May 27, 2005, B3.

———. "Johnson & Johnson Agrees to Buy Alza in $12 Billion Stock Deal." *Wall Street Journal*, March 28, 2001, B15.

Hensley, Scott, Thomas M. Burton, and Dennis K. Berman. "Johnson & Johnson to Buy Guidant." *Wall Street Journal*, December 16, 2004, A3.

Hwang, Suein L. "J&J to Acquire Unit of Kodak for $1.01 Billion." *Wall Street Journal*, September 7, 1994, A3.

International Directory of Company Histories. Farmington Hills: St. James Press.

"J&J Completes Scios Deal." *Chemical Market Reporter*, May 5, 2003, 4.

"J&J Sets Up New Company Veridex." *Pharma Marketletter*, June 21, 2004.

"J&J's Acquisition of Breast Biopsy Equipment Maker Termed 'a Perfect Fit'." *Health Industry Today*, July 1997, 7.

Jacobs, Richard M. "Products Liability: A Technical and Ethical Challenge." *Quality Progress*, December 1988, 27-29.

Johnson & Johnson: Global Expansion in the Face of Intense Competition. Mountain View, Calif.: Frost & Sullivan, 1993.

"Johnson & Johnson." International Directory of Company Histories, Vol.75. St. James Press, 2006. Reproduced in Business and Company Resource Center. Farmington Hills, Mich.: Gale Group, 2006.

Johnson & Johnson Notable Corporate Chronologies. Online Edition. Thomson Gale, 2005. Reproduced in Business and Company Resource Center. Farmington Hills, Mich.: Gale Group, 2006.

"Johnson & Johnson Recalls Some Cypher Drug-Eluting Stents." *Wall Street Journal*, January 14, 2005.

"J&J Buys Merck Interest in European Joint Venture." *Chemist & Druggist*, March 6, 2004.

Kador, John. *Great Engagements: The Once and Future Johnson & Johnson.* New Brunswick, N.J.: Johnson & Johnson, 2004.

Kardon, Brian E. "Consumer Schizophrenia: Extremism in the Marketplace." *Planning Review*, July/August 1992, 18-22.

Keaton, Paul N. and Michael J. Semb. "Shaping up That Bottom Line." *HRMagazine*, September 1990, 81-86.

Kulpa, Jennifer. "J&J Pulls Confide Home HIV Test." *Drug Store News*, August 4, 1997, 21.

Langreth, Robert, and Ron Winslow. "At J&J, a Venerable Strategy Faces Questions." *Wall Street Journal*, March 5, 1999, B1.

———. "J&J Plans Job Cuts, $800 Million Charge." *Wall Street Journal*, December 4, 1998, A3.

Leon, Mitchell. "Tylenol Fights Back." *Public Relations Journal*, March 1983, 10+.

Matthes, Karen. "Companies Can Make It Their Business to Care." *HR Focus*, February 1992, 4-5.

McGinley, Laurie. "Johnson & Johnson Ordered to Give Up HIV Test Business." *Wall Street Journal.* http://interactive5.wsj.com/inap-bin/bb?sym@eqlJNJ&page@eql1, July 29, 1996.

McLeod, Douglas, and Stacy Adler. "Tylenol Death Payout May Top $35 Million." *Business Insurance,* May 20, 1991, 1, 29.

McNulty, Mike. "Ansell Acquires Condom Business." *Rubber & Plastics News,* 01 May 2000, 1.

Moore, Thomas. "The Fight to Save Tylenol." *Fortune,* November 29, 1982, 44+.

Moukheiber, Zina, and Robert Langreth. "J&J: An Unfinished Symphony." *Forbes,* December 10, 2001, 62.

Murray, Eileen, and Saundra Shohen. "Lessons from the Tylenol Tragedy on Surviving a Corporate Crisis." *Medical Marketing and Media,* February 1992, 14-19.

"News Releases." *Johnson & Johnson.* http://www.jnj.com/news_finance/cn_index.html.

O'Reilly, Brian. "J&J Is on a Roll." *Fortune,* December 26, 1994, 178-80+.

PR Newswire: 05-22-92.

"Shareholders Overwhelmingly Approve Acquisition Agreement with Johnson & Johnson." *Business Wire,* April 27, 2005.

Rublin, Lauren R. "More Than a Band-Aid: Johnson & Johnson's Has a Strong Prescription for Growth." *Barron's,* April 17, 2000, 37-38, 40, 42.

Taylor, Alex, III. "Can J&J Keep the Magic Going?" *Fortune,* May 27, 2002, 117-18+.

Thomson One Banker. Analytics 1981-2006 10k Reports.

Tully, Shawn. "Blood Feud." *Fortune,* May 31, 2004, 100.

Silverman, Edward R. "J&J Will Slash 4,100 Positions." *Newark Star-Ledger,* December 4, 1998.

———. "More Than Medicine: Johnson & Johnson's CEO Defends the Company's Slow-Growing Divisions." *Newark Star-Ledger,* June 18, 2000.

Smith, Lee. "J&J Comes a Long Way from Baby." *Fortune,* June 1, 1981, 58+.

Waldholz, Michael. "Johnson & Johnson Defends Emphasis on Long-Term Growth As Profit Surges." *Wall Street Journal,* August 8, 1985.

Warner, Susan. "From Band-Aids to Biotech." *New York Times,* April 10, 2005, section 14NJ, p. 1.

Weber, Joseph. "A Big Company That Works." *Business Week,* May 4, 1992, 124-32.

———. "No Band-Aids for Ralph Larsen," *Business Week,* May 28, 1990, 86-87.

Winslow, Ron. "Head Start: Johnson & Johnson Finds an Elusive Gene and Races to Exploit It." *Wall Street Journal,* May 26, 2000, A1+.

———. "J&J Agrees to Buy DePuy for $3.5 Billion." *Wall Street Journal,* July 22, 1998, A3.

Winters, Patricia. "J&J Sets Nighttime Tylenol." *Advertising Age,* February 18, 1991, 1, 46.

———. "Tylenol Expands with Cold Remedies." *Advertising Age*, August 27, 1990, 3, 36.

Johnson Controls

Berss, Marcia. "Watizzit? Johnson Controls is a Strange Mixture—Car Seats, Thermostats, Plastic Bottles and Auto Batteries." *Forbes*, August 28, 1995, 100.

Byrne, Harlan S. "Johnson Controls: Back in Gear." *Barron's*, June 5, 2000, 21-22.

———. "Johnson Controls: Strong Market Positions Help It Ride Out the Recession." *Barron's*, February 24, 1992, 51-52.

"C&D Buys Battery Unit of Johnson Controls." *Electronic News*, March 8, 1999, 34.

Connole, Joe. "Johnson Controls to Storm into Europe." *Business Journal-Milwaukee*, May 16, 1988, 1+.

Content, Tom. "Johnson Controls Buys French Unit: Deal Opens Door to Europe." *Milwaukee Journal Sentinel*, July 26, 2001, 1D.

———. "Johnson Controls Elevates Barth: Keyes to Remain Chairman As Part of Succession Plan." *Milwaukee Journal Sentinel*, July 25, 2002, 1D.

———. "Johnson Controls Plans to Boost Battery Power: Acquisition of German Firm to Bring Access to New Technology for Cars and Light Trucks." *Milwaukee Journal Sentinel*, August 24, 2001, 1D.

———. "Johnson Controls to Buy Varta Unit: Acquisition Would Boost Glendale Firm's Hold on Car Batteries in Europe." *Milwaukee Journal Sentinel*, August 7, 2002, 1D.

Dubashi, Jagannath. "Slump Control: Johnson Controls Thought One Good Deal Would Eliminate Two Pet Peeves." *Financial World*, May 29, 1990, 49.

Gallagher, Kathleen. "Johnson Controls in Driver's Seat with Diverse Sales." *Milwaukee Journal Sentinel*, August 19, 2001, 4D.

Gardner, Greg. "JCI Buys Itself a Prince." *Ward's Auto World*, August 1996, 35.

Gordon, Joanne. "Interior Motives: Johnson Controls Puts Spy Cameras in Cars—to Find Out What Features You Really Want." *Forbes*, September 2, 2002, 74-75.

International Directory of Company Histories. Detroit: St. James Press.

"Johnson Controls, Saft Launch EV, HEV Battery Supply JV." *Electric and Hybrid Vehicles Today*, January 13, 2006.

"Johnson Controls Acquires Varta Automotive Battery." *Automotive Industries*, October 2002, 62.

"Johnson Controls to Buy Imsa Battery Stake." *American Metal Market*, July 21, 2004, 4.

"Johnson Controls Makes a Deal." *Health Data Management*, March 2006.

"Johnson Controls Says $3.2 Billion York Acquisition Done." *Associated Press*, December 9, 2005.

"Johnson Opens PET Facility." *American Metal Market*, July 11, 1995, 7.

Kerfoot, Kevin. Crain's Detroit Business, October, 1992.

Kisiel, Ralph and David Sedgwick. "Large Firms: Over $500 Million in Sales." *Automotive News*, January 29, 1996, 24.

Lappen, Alyssa A. "Damn the Analysts, Full Speed Ahead." *Forbes*, March 20, 1989, 171+.

Lazo, Shirley A. "Sitting Pretty: Johnson Controls' Record Earnings Drive 2 Cent Payout Hike." *Barron's*, November 20, 1995, 37.

Marsh, Peter. "A Sitting Target for Two Rivals." *Financial Times*, April 15, 1996, 10.

———. "Standing Up to Seating Challenge." *Financial Times*, February 23, 1998, FTS7.

Miller, James P. "Johnson Controls' Container Business Will Be Sold to Unit of Germany's Viag." *Wall Street Journal*, December 10, 1996, A3.

Pryweller, Joseph. "Former CEO Plans Buyback of Part of Becker Group." *Crain's Detroit Business*, January 25, 1999, 57.

Right for the Times: Johnson Controls 100th Anniversary. Milwaukee, Wis.: Johnson Controls, Inc., 1985.

Rose, Robert L. "Johnson Controls Agrees to Purchase of Becker Group." *Wall Street Journal*, April 28, 1998, B22.

———. "Johnson Controls Gets a Big Boost from the Bottom." *Wall Street Journal*, February 3, 1997, B4.

———. "Johnson Controls Plans to Expand into Asia, Pacific." *Wall Street Journal*, September 26, 1996, B2.

———. "Johnson Controls to Buy Prince Unit As Car-Interior Industry Consolidates." *Wall Street Journal*, July 19, 1996, A3.

Rose, Robert L., and Robert L. Simison. "Johnson Controls and UAW Reach Pact." *Wall Street Journal*, February 21, 1997, A3, A4.

Schmid, John. "Johnson Controls Closing 16 Plants: Milwaukee Area Spared in Company's Plan to Trim 5,000 Jobs Worldwide." *Milwaukee Journal Sentinel*, August 10, 2006.

"TechnoTrim, Inc. Opening Facility in Glasgow." *Kentucky Manufacturer*, October 1992, 14.

Tetzell, Rick. "Mining Money in Mature Markets." *Fortune*, March 22, 1993, 77.

Thomson One Banker. Analytics 1981-2006 10k Reports.

Treece, James B. "Johnson Controls Gains Japan Auto Base." *Automotive News*, July 17, 2000, 6.

Wermiel, Stephen. "Justices Bar "Fetal Protection' Policies." *Wall Street Journal*, March 21, 1991, B1, B5.

Wiegner, Kathleen K. "Bright Spot." *Forbes*, July 5, 1982, 175+.

Wielgat, Andrea. "Sagem Expands JCI's Reach in Europe." *Automotive Industries*, March 2002, 8.

Land Securities PLC

Thomson One Banker. Analytics 1981-2006 10k Reports.

Longs Drug Stores Corp.

Alaimo, Dan. "Video Role Expanding at Longs Drug Stores." *Supermarket News*, August 28, 1995, 33.

Brookman, Faye. "Drug Chains Shift to Central Control." *Stores*, August 1996, 58-59.

Campanella, Frank W. "Longs' Way Up." *Barron's*, February 11, 1980.

Carlsen, Clifford. "Longs Drug Still Addicted to Its Expansion Plan." *San Francisco Business Times*, November 27, 1992, 1+.

"A Company Overview of Longs Drug Store Corporation." *Business Wire*, November 4, 2005.

"Era Comes to an End at Long Stores." *Chain Drug Review*, April 26, 2004, 96.

Ginsberg, Steve. "Longs Drug's Rx: $85M Expansion." *San Francisco Business Times*, December 5, 1997, 1+.

Hemmila, Donna. "Longs Writes a Prescription for Its Ailing Profits: New Stores." *San Francisco Business Times*, September 19, 1997, 3+.

International Directory of Company Histories. Detroit: St. James Press.

Levenson, Maurice, George I.H. Rho, and Robert M. Greene. "The Value Line Investment Survey, Part 3: Ratings & Reports." *Drug Store Industry*, April 12, 1996, 799.

Liedtke, Michael. "Longs Drug Stores Revitalizes its Bottom Line." *Contra Costa Times*, November 29, 1995.

Longs Drug Stores Corp. *Notable Corporate Chronologies*. Online Edition. Thomson Gale, 2006. Reproduced in Business and Company Resource Center. Farmington Hills, Mich.: Gale Group, 2006.

"Longs Drug Stores Corporation." International Directory of Company Histories, Vol. 25. St. James Press, 1999. Reproduced in Business and Company Resource Center. Farmington Hills, Mich.:Gale Group. 2006.

"Longs Experiences a Watershed Year." *Chain Drug Review*, August 5, 2002.

"Longs Unveils Senior Advantage." *Drug Store News*, 18 November 18, 2002, 22.

Paris, Ellen. "Managers As Entrepreneurs." *Forbes*, October 31, 1988, 62+.

Rosendahl, Iris. "Longs Drugs Stores—Pharmacy Chain of the Year." *Drug Topics*, April 25, 1994, 16.

Symons, Allene. "Managing Expansion Through Acquisition." *Drugstore News*, April 24, 2000, 130.

Thomson One Banker. Analytics 1981-2006 10k Reports.

Westover, Kyle J. *Longs Drugs: A Tradition of Caring, 1938-1988*. Walnut Creek, Calif.: Longs Drug Stores, 1988.

Winkler, Connie. "How Longs Got Centralized." *American Druggist*, February 1995, 37+.

Lowe's Companies Inc.

"Analyst Predicts Two to Dominate Industry." *Chilton's Hardware Age*, May 1995, 12.

Auchmutey, Jim. "Handyman's Special." *Barron's*, June 18, 1980.

————. "Warehouses Stack the Deck." *Hardware Age*, March 1981.

"Big-Store Bonanza." *Forbes*, December 20, 1993, 14-15.

Cochran, Thomas. "Handyman's Special." *Barron's*, June 18, 1980.

————. "Lowe's Gets Ready to Raise the Roof." *Sales Management*, July 7, 1975.

Curtis, Carol E. "How Much Sheetrock, Ma'am?" *Forbes*, August 30, 1982, 70.

————. "Playing Do-It-Yourself." *Forbes*, May 10, 1982, 314.

————. "Warehouses Stack the Deck." *Hardware Age*, March 1981.

David, Gregory E. "Stomping Elephant." *Financial World*, September 28, 1993, 40-41.

"Eagle Is Sold to Home-Store Giant Lowe's." *The Seattle Times*, November 23, 1998.

Feder, Barnaby J. "In Hardware War, Cooperation May Mean Survival." *New York Times*, June 11, 1997, D1, D7.

"Hardware Chain Nails Down Northwest Deal." *The Seattle Times*, November 24, 1998.

Hartnett, Michael. "Lowe's Plan: Think Big." *Stores*, November 1993, 58-60.

"Home Depot, Lowe's Settlement Could Mean Rebates for Millions." *Wall Street Journal*, December 2, 2004.

International Directory of Company Histories. Detroit: St. James Press.

Korn, Don. "Lowe's Gets Ready to Raise the Roof." *Sales Management*, July 7, 1975.

"Lowe's Co. Increases Sales." *Do-It-Yourself Retailing*, January 1992, 84.

"Lowe's Companies, Inc." *International Directory of Company Histories*. Vol. 21. St. James Press, 1998. Reproduced in Business and Company Resource Center. Farmington Hills, Mich.: Gale Group, 2006.

Lowe's Companies Inc. *Notable Corporate Chronologies*. Online Edition. Thomson Gale, 2006. Reproduced in Business and Company Resource Center. Farmington Hills, Mich.: Gale Group, 2006.

"Lowe's to Expand into Canada with Toronto Stores in 2007." *Associated Press*, June 6, 2005.

"Lowe's Has Added First Home Office Products." *Television Digest*, September 26, 1994, 14.

"Lowe's Looks to Smaller Markets to Help Drive Growth." *Do-It-Yourself Retailing*, November 2003, 14.

"Lowe's Names COO, President of Contractor Yards Division." *Chilton's Hardware Age*, January 1995, 9.

"Lowe's and NationsRent Form Strategic Partnership; NationsRent Stores to Operate Inside Lowe's." *PR Newswire*, April 6, 2000.

"Lowe's Plans to Borrow $250 Million." *Do-It-Yourself Retailing*, June 1992, 27.

"Lowe's Publishes Home Page." *Do-It-Yourself Retailing*, December 1995, 19.

"Lowe's Steps It Up." *Do-It-Yourself Retailing*, August 1995, 259.

"Lowe's Vision—The Wal-Mart of Home Centers." *Chain Store Age Executive*, May 1989.

"Lowe's Zeroes in on Customers." *Chain Store Age Executive*, August 1979.

Lubove, Seth. "A Chain's Weak Links." *Forbes*, January 21, 1991, 76.

Mallory, Maria. "This Do-It-Yourself Store Is Really Doing It." *Business Week*, May 2, 1994, 108.

McCormack, Karyn. "Casualties of War." *Financial World*, May 20, 1997, 45-46, 48, 53.

McIntyre, Deni. *No Place Like Lowe's: 50 Years of Retailing for the American Home*. North Wilkesboro, N.C.: Lowe's, 1996.

"Robert L. Tillman Assumes President and CEO Position at Lowe's." *PR Newswire*, August 1, 1996.

Serwer, Andy. "Lowe's Hits the Nail on the Head." *Fortune*, June 24, 2001.

"Strickland Positions Lowe's for Conquest." *Building Supply Home Centers*, March 1993, 48-50.

Sutton, Rodney K. "Lowe's Conversion Ends in Its Rebirth." *Building Supply Home Centers*, June 1994, 36-38, 40, 42.

Thomson One Banker. Analytics 1981-2006 10k Reports.

Upbin, Bruce. "Merchant Prices." *Forbes*, January 20, 2003.

Morrison (WM) Supermarkets PLC

Thomson One Banker. Analytics 1981-2006 10k Reports.

Nbty Inc.

Thomson One Banker. Analytics 1981-2006 10k Reports.

Nordstrom Inc.

Bergmann, Joan. "Nordstrom Gets the Gold." *Stores*, January 1990.

———. "Nordstrom Prepares for Dallas Debut." *WWD*, February 12, 1996, 29.

Blumenthal, Robin Goldwyn. "Fashion Victim: A Hipper Nordstrom Is Trying to Tailor a Comeback, and It Just Might Succeed." *Barron's*, April 3, 2000, 20, 22.

Browder, Seanna. "Great Service Wasn't Enough." *Business Week*, April 19, 1999, 126-27.

Byron, Ellen. "Nordstrom Regains Its Luster: Challenge Awaits As Rivals Encroach on Image of Affordable Luxury." *Wall Street Journal*, August 19, 2004, B2.

Coffee, Peter. "Nordstrom Names Starbucks Supplier." *Nation's Restaurant News*, September 28, 1992, 50.

Daily News Record: 08-06-92.; 08-11-92.; 08-12-92.

De Voss, David. *New York Times Magazine*, August 27, 1989.

———. "The Rise and Rise of Nordstrom." *Lear's*, October 1989.

"Down the Tube: Nordstrom." *The Economist*, June 5, 1993, 80.

Falum, Susan C. "At Nordstrom Stores, Service Comes First—But at a Big Price." *Wall Street Journal*, February 20, 1990.

Greenwald, John. "Losing Its Luster: Despite Exquisite Service, Nordstrom Has Suffered a Profit Slump." *Time*, March 24, 1997, 64+.

Haber, Holly. "Co-president of Nordstrom Retiring." *Puget Sound Business Journal*, February 4, 2000, 13.

Hamilton, Joan O'C. and Amy Dunkin. "Why Rivals Are Quaking As Nordstrom Heads East." *Business Week*, June 15, 1987, 99.

HFD-The Weekly Home Furnishings Newspaper: 09-28-92.

Holmes, Stanley. "Can the Nordstroms Find the Right Style?" *Business Week*, July 30, 2001, 59, 62.

Hoover's Company Profile Database: 1996.

International Directory of Company Histories. Detroit: St. James Press.

Kossen, Bill. "A Good Fit? Northwest Retail Giant Attempts to Stay Nimble As It Tries to Bounce Back." *Seattle Times*, May 29, 2001, C1.

———. "Success Came a Step at a Time." *Seattle Times*, May 29, 2001, A1.

Lee, Louise. "Nordstrom Cleans Out Its Closets." *Business Week*, May 22, 2000, 105-106, 108.

Los Angeles Times: 08-12-92.

Lubove, Seth. "Don't Listen to the Boss, Listen to the Customer." *Forbes*, December 4, 1995, 45.

McAllister, Robert. "Nordstrom Tightens Its Belt for the Long Haul." *Footwear News*, September 6, 1993, 1.

Merrick, Amy. "Nordstrom Accelerates Plans to Straighten Out Business." *Wall Street Journal*, October 19, 2001, B4.

Moin, David. "A Big Job Ahead: Top Nordstrom Execs Map Rebuilding Plan." *WWD*, December 7, 2000, 1.

———. "Shakeup in Seattle: CEO Out, Family Back at Nordstrom Helm." *WWD*, September 1, 2000, 1.

Mulady, Kathy. "Back in the Family: Fourth Generation Takes Control After a Brief Change in Company Leadership." *Seattle Post-Intelligencer*, June 27, 2001, D1.

———. "Still in Style: From Small Shoe Store to Upscale Retailer, Company Has Kept Founder's Values." *Seattle Post-Intelligencer*, June 25, 2001, E1.

———. "A Time of Change: Company Makes Huge Leaps with Expansion, Public Stock Offering." *Seattle Post-Intelligencer*, June 26, 2001, D1.

New York Times: 08-06-92.; 11-11-92.; 11-12-92.; 01-12-93.

"Nightmare at Nordstrom." *Personnel Journal*, September 1990.

"Nordstrom, Inc." *International Directory of Company Histories*. Vol. 67. St. James Press, 2005. Reproduced in Business and Company Resource Center. Farmington Hills, Mich.: Gale Group, 2006.

Nordstrom, John W. *The Immigrant in 1887*. Seattle: Dogwood Press, 1950.

"Nordstrom Announces Partnership with Streamline." *PR Newswire*, October 8, 1998, 7775.

"Nordstrom Announces Partnership with Two Japanese Retailers to License Exclusive-Branded Product in Japan." *PR Newswire*, June 23, 1999.

"Nordstrom Employees Ring New York Stock Exchange's Opening Bell as Company Moves to Trade on Big Board." *PR Newswire*, June 10, 1999, 6357.

"Nordstrom Gets the Gold." *Stores*, January 1990.

Nordstrom History. Nordstrom, 1990.

Nordstrom Inc. *Notable Corporate Chronologies*. Online Edition. Thomson Gale, 2006. Reproduced in Business and Company Resource Center. Farmington Hills, Mich.: Gale Group, 2006.

"Nordstrom Launches Online Store at www.Nordstrom.com." *PR Newswire*, October 21, 1998, 6363.

"Nordstrom Opens at Dadeland Mall." *PR Newswire*, November 12, 2004.

"Nordstrom Opens First Store in Irvine, California at Irvine Spectrum Center." *PR Newswire*, September 30, 2005.

"Nordstrom Is Adding Home to Its Wardrobe." *HFN —The Weekly Newspaper for the Home Furnishing Network*, March 1, 2004, 1.

Palmeri, Christopher. "Filling Big Shoes." *Forbes*, November 15, 1999, 170, 172.

"Press Releases." *Nordstrom Inc.* http://www.nordstrom.com. March 2003.

"The Rise and Rise of Nordstrom." *Lear's*, October 1989.

Schwadel, Francine. "Nordstrom's Push East Will Test Its Renown for the Best in Service." *Wall Street Journal*, August 1, 1989.

"Search for Software to Distribute Apps Proves Challenging." *PC Week*, August 31, 1992, 73.

Sinisi, John. *Wall Street Journal*, November 11, 1992.

Solomon, Charlene Marmer. "Nightmare at Nordstrom." *Personnel Journal*, September 1990.

———. *Wall Street Journal*, February 20, 1990.

"Starbucks, Nordstrom au lait-up." *Brandweek*, September 28, 1992, 7.

Spector, Robert, and Patrick D. McCarthy. *The Nordstrom Way: The Inside Story of America's #1 Customer Service Company*. 2nd ed. New York: Wiley, 2000.

Spurgeon, Devon. "In Return to Power, the Nordstrom Family Finds a Pile of Problems." *Wall Street Journal*, September 8, 2000, B1.

Stevenson, Richard W. "Watch Out Macy's, Here Comes Nordstrom." *New York Times Magazine*, August 27, 1989.

Thomson One Banker. Analytics 1981-2006 10k Reports.

The Value Line Investment Survey (Part 3 - Ratings & Reports): 08-28-92; 11-27-92.

Wall Street Journal: 08-01-89; 08-12-92; 12-14-92; 01-12-93.

Yang, Dori Jones. "Nordstrom's Gang of Four." *Business Week*, June 15, 1992, 122-23.

Yang, Dori Jones, and Laura Zinn. "Will 'the Nordstrom Way' Travel Well?" *Business Week*, September 3, 1990, 82.

Omnicom Group Inc.

"Advertising's 'Big Bang' is Making Noise at Last." *Business Week*, April 4, 1991.

"Agency Nets Merge, Trim, Consolidate." *Advertising Age*, October 19, 1987, 2.

"A Bad Night at the Opera May Be Transposed into a Brighter Day for Omnicom Ad Agency." *Wall Street Journal, Eastern Edition*, November 14, 1988, C2.

Beatty, Sally Goll. "Credit Saison/Omnicom Team for Direct Marketing." *Comline-Tokyo Financial Wire*, November 6, 1997.

"Chilko Widow Files $20M Suit Against DDB." *Advertising Age*, August 8, 1988, 1.

Chura, Hillary. "Omnicom Outpaces Market with 14% Increase in 2003." *Advertising Age*, February 23, 2004, 8.

"D'Arcy Acquires Controlling Stake in Omnicom Unit." *Wall Street Journal, Eastern Edition*, February 5, 1988, 28.

"First National Ad Campaign by Newspaper Association." *New York Times*, September 12, 1997, C6.

"GGT Group to Merge with TBWA International." *ADWEEK Eastern Edition*, May 18, 1998, 12.

"Press Releases." *Omnicom Group Inc.* http://www.omnicomgroup.com. June 2003.

Thomson One Banker. Analytics 1981-2006 10k Reports.

Pall Corp.

"Filtration, Separations and Purification Company Acquires Division of Ciphergen." *Biotech Business Week*, December 27, 2004.

"Filtration, Separations and Purification Company Acquires Euroflow." *Drug Week*, February 25, 2005.

"Germany Mandates Blood Filtration." *Membrane & Separation Technology News*, October 1, 2000.

Hardy, Maurice. "Going Global: One Company's Road to International Markets." *Journal of Business Strategy*, November-December, 24-27.

"His Business Knows No Borders." *U.S. News & World Report*, March 7, 1988, 52.

Hord, Christopher. "Pall's Krasnoff Heads Quiet Diversification." *Long Island Business News*, May 30, 1994, 15.

Kanner, Bernice. "Blood Simple." *Chief Executive*, April 1999, 30.

"Pall Names Krasnoff Chairman and Chief." *Wall Street Journal*, July 12, 1994, B10.

"Purely by Chance." *Long Island Business News*, June 30, 2000, 5A.

Slutsker, Gary. "To Catch a Particle." *Forbes*, January 23, 1989, 88-89.

Teitelman, Robert. "Focused Functions." *Financial World*, July 11, 1989, 54-55.

Thomson One Banker. Analytics 1981-2006 10k Reports.

Pick N Pay Stores Limited

Thomson One Banker. Analytics 1981-2006 10k Reports.

Stryker Corp.

"Bigger Niche at Stryker." *New York Times*, December 16, 1980.

Brewer, Geoffrey. "20 Percent—or Else." *Sales & Marketing Management*, November 1994, 66.

Gowrie, David. "Giving Back the Ability to Walk." *Hackensack (New Jersey) Record*, October 28, 1998.

Jones, John A. "Stryker Keeps Moving with Strong Research Commitment." *Investor's Business Daily*, January 20, 1992.

Kramer, Farrell. "Stryker Becomes a Synonym for Consistency." *Investor's Daily*, July 6, 1990.

Rogers, Doug. "Stryker Skillfully Handles a Steady Run of New Products." *Investor's Daily*, March 21, 1991.

Sawaya, Zina. "Focus Through Decentralization." *Forbes*, November 11, 1999, 242.

Seebacher, Noreen. "Stryker Products: Just What the Doctor Ordered." *Detroit News*, May 6, 1991.

Stavro, Barry. "The Hipbone's Connected to the Bottom Line." *Forbes*, December 3, 1984.

Stroud, Michael. "Stryker: Another Play on Endoscopy Boom." *Investor's Business Daily*, October 25, 1991.

Thomson One Banker. Analytics 1981-2006 10k Reports.

Sysco Corp.

Anders, K.T. "SYSCO's Strategy." *Supermarket Business*, September 1998, 182.

Bagamery, Anne. "Don't Sell Food, Sell Peace of Mind." *Forbes*, October 11, 1982, 58.

Civin, Robert. "Sysco: Distribution's $7-Billion Entrepreneur." *Institutional Distribution*, April 1990.

"Distribution's Multi-Branch Giants." *Institutional Distribution*, October 1985, 169.

Fisher, Daniel. "Little Things Mean a Lot for Giant Sysco." *Houston Business Journal*, August 18, 1995, 24.

Geelhoed, E. Bruce. *The Thrill of Success: The Story of SYSCO/Frost-Pack Food Services, Incorporated*. Muncie, Ind.: Bureau of Business Research, College of Business and Department of History, Ball State University, 1983.

"Great Distributor Organization Study: SYSCO Corporation." *Institutional Distribution*, June 1980.

Greer, Jim. "First in the Food Chain." *Houston Business Journal*, April 28, 2000, 16A.

———. "Sysco Stock Hits Record High, Emerges from Cisco's Shadow." *Houston Business Journal*, March 5, 2004.

Harrison, Dan. "Sysco Eyes $10 Billion." *Institutional Distribution*, April 1989, 52.

Hassell, Greg. "The Sage of Sysco: Retired Founder Still at Work." *Houston Chronicle*, July 10, 1998.

——. "Sysco's President Will Be Its Next Chief Executive." *Houston Chronicle*, November 6, 1999.

——. "Sysco Will Purchase FreshPoint." *Houston Chronicle*, January 8, 2000.

Jones, Jeanne Lang. "Keeping Sysco on Course." *Houston Post*, January 8, 1995.

Kreimer, Susan. "Sysco to Expand Presence in Canada." *Houston Chronicle*, December 6, 2001.

Lawn, John. "Sysco's Strategy: 'Divide and Multiply.'" *Foodservice Distributor*, January 1995, 32.

Loeffelholz, Suzanne. "Voracious Appetite: Sysco's Ability to Digest Its Acquisitions Can Only Mean More Deals Ahead." *Financial World*, April 18, 1989, 72.

Mack, Toni. "V.P.s of Planning Need Not Apply." *Forbes*, October 25, 1993, 84.

Reiter, Jeff. "Sysco and Dairy." *Dairy Foods*, October 1995, 113.

Ruggless, Ron. "John F. Woodhouse." *Nation's Restaurant News*, January 1995.

Salkin, Stephanie. "Sysco's Schnieders Previews Growth Agenda." *ID*, May 2002, 17-18.

"Sysco: Swallowing Up Its Competitors to Grow in Food Distribution." *Business Week*, August 17, 1981, 116+.

"SYSCO Corporation: Serving Up Steady Growth." *Better Investing*, December 2004, 36-38.

"Sysco Corporation: Since 1980." *Institutional Distribution*, September 15, 1986, 60.

Thomson One Banker. Analytics 1981-2006 10k Reports.

Telefex Inc.

Thomson One Banker. Analytics 1981-2006 10k Reports.

Tesco PLC

"1995 Annual Report—Chairman's Statement." *Tesco PLC*. http://www.tesco.co.uk/report95/Cstat.html.

"Careers: Company CV - Tesco." *Marketing*, June 6, 2002, 42.

Bird, Michael. "At Your Convenience." *In-Store Marketing*, December 2002, 9.

Board, Laura. "Tesco Offers to Acquire T&S." *Daily Deal*, October 31, 2002, 54.

"Brain Food: Speaking Out—Sire Terry Leahy, CEO, Tesco." *Management Today*, September 1, 2004, 19.

Church, Chris. "How Tesco Took the Low Road to Scotland." *Grocer*, September 30, 1995, 14.

Corina, Maurice. *Pile It High, Sell It Cheap: The Authorized Biography of Sir John Cohen*. London: Weidenfeld & Nicolson, 1971.

Fallon, James. "Tesco Grows Restless." *Supermarket News*, August 10, 1992, 1ff.

"The Grocer Focus on Tesco Supplement." *Grocer*, September 20, 1997.

Harrington, Sian. "On Top of the World." *Grocer*, June 19, 2004, 44.

Hollinger, Peggy. "The Skier Keeping Tesco away from Slippery Slopes." *Financial Times*, February 28, 1997, 25.

———. "Tesco Considers Expanding into South-East Asia." *Financial Times*, August 4, 1997, 1.

———. "A French Blot on Tesco's Copybook." *Financial Times*, December 10, 1997, 30.

International Directory of Company Histories. Farmington Hills: St. James Press.

Mills, Lauren. "Terry's All Gold at Tesco." *In-Store*, October 2004, 17.

Mitchell, Alan. "There Is More in Store for Tesco with T&S Buy." *Marketing Week*, November 14, 2002, 34.

Mowbray, Simon. "Spot the Difference Tesco Once Told Suppliers That Its Days of Copying Their Brands Were Over." *Grocer*, September 4, 2004, 36.

O'Connor, Robert. "Tesco, Safeway, Sainsbury Target Ireland." *Chain Store Age Executive*, December 1997, 134ff.

Powell, David. *Counter Revolution: The Tesco Story.* London: Grafton, 1991.

Price, Chris. "Tesco Checks Out As Leader." *Financial Times*, September 21, 1996, WFT5.

Reier, Sharon. "Branding the Company." *Financial World*, November 26, 1991, 32+.

Tesco Abbreviated History and Facts Sheet. Cheshunt: Tesco Plc, 1991.

"Tesco Considering Telecoms Market." *EuropeMedia*, July 3, 2002.

"Tesco Enters Into Joint Venture in China." *European Cosmetics Market*, August 2004.

"Tesco First 14 Weeks 1997 Like-for-Like Sales Up 5.1%." *Dow Jones Newswires.* http://interactive3.wsj.com/inapbin/bb?sym@eqlU.TSC&page@eql1. June 6, 1997.

"Tesco Makes Forey into China Market." *Asia Africa Intelligence Wire*, August 6, 2004, 34.

Tesco Plc Annual Report and Accounts 1992.

"Tesco to Unite e-Com Service." *Supermarket News*, April 17, 2000, 4.

Thomson One Banker. Analytics 1981-2006 10k Reports.

Wal Mart Stores Inc.

"At Wal-Mart, Emergency Plan Has Big Payoff." *Wall Street Journal*, September 12, 2005, B1.

Clark, Evan. "Wal-Mart in Japanese Venture." *WWD*, March 15, 2002, 2.

Facts about Wal-Mart Stores Inc. Bentonville: Wal-Mart Stores, 1992.

International Directory of Company Histories. Detroit: St. James Press.

"Meet Your New Neighborhood Grocer." *Fortune*, May 13, 2002.

"Mexican Market Mover: Wal-Mart Takes Top Spot South of the Border." *Dallas Morning News*, May 2, 2000, 1D.

"New Prototype for Wal-Mart Supercenter." *Discount Store News*, March 18, 1996, F4.

"Plaintiffs in Suit Claim Wal-Mart Fudged on Study." *Los Angeles Times*, December 30, 2004, C2.

"Sainsbury Gains on Rivals." *Daily Telegraph*, June 3, 2005.

Thomson One Banker. Analytics 1981-2006 10k Reports.

"Wal-Mart CEO Glass Takes a Break; Chief Resigns after Leading Chain to Explosive Growth." *The Washington Post*, January 15, 2000, E1.

"Wal-Mart's Coughlin to Plead Guilty to Wire-Fraud, Tax-Evasion Charges." *Wall Street Journal*, January 6, 2006. "Wal-Mart's Labor Agreement Is Criticized by Former Official." *Wall Street Journal*, February 15, 2005, A14.

"Wal-Mart Makes Euro 10.3 Billion Offer for the U.K.'s Asda; U.S. Retailing Giant Cuts in on Kingfisher, Signaling Big Changes in Europe." *Wall Street Journal Europe*, June 15, 1999, 3.

"Wal-Mart to Open Store on Net." *Discount Store News*, March 4, 1996, 1.

Wal-Mart Stores Inc. Fact Sheet. http://www.hoovers.com. August 2004.

"Wal-Mart World." *Newsweek International*, May 20, 2002, 50.

Wilson, Melinda. "The Detroit News." *The Meijer Challenge*, September 21, 1992.

Zwiebach, Elliott. "Wal-Mart Sets Record Supercenter Openings." *Supermarket News*, October 5, 1998.

Walgreen Company
Bacon, John U. *America's Corner Store: Walgreens' Prescription for Success.* Hoboken, N.J.: Wiley, 2004.

Baeb, Eddie. "Headaches Awaiting Walgreen's New CEO: Grow Store Base, Guard Margins." *Crain's Chicago Business*, July 23, 2001, 3.

Block, Toddi Gutner. "We Need You, You Need Us: Drug Benefit Managers Have Grabbed Power in the Retail Pharmacy Industry. Walgreen Co. Is Grabbing It Back." *Forbes*, May 8, 1995, 66-67, 70.

Brookman, Faye. "Innovative Chain Ranks No. 1." *Stores*, April 1993, 21-23.

Byrne, Harlan S. "Good Prescription: Walgreen's Long Skein of Profit Gains Continues." *Barron's*, October 12, 1998, 15.

———. "Prescription for Profits." *Barron's*, January 12, 2004, 23.

———. "Rx for Growth." *Barron's*, January 7, 2002, 14.

———. "A Winning Prescription." *Barron's*, March 7, 1994, 21.

"A Century of Growth Comes Full Circle." *Chain Store Age*, December 2000, 250, 252.

Clepper, Irene. "Walgreens: One of the Oldest and Still Growing." *Drug Topics*, April 8, 1996, 116, 118.

Dubashi, Jagannath. "Walgreen: Just What the Doctor Ordered." *Financial World*, May 1, 1990, 20.

"Flourishing Walgreen: It Has Found the Right Prescription for a Retail Drug Chain." *Barron's*, April 14, 1958, 9.

Garbato, Debby. "A Model of Efficiency." *Retail Merchandiser*, June 2004, 16, 18, 20.

Heller, Laura. "Steering Chain Along a Profitable Course." *Drug Store News*, March 25, 2002, 20, 22.

Henkoff, Ronald. "A High-Tech Rx for Profits." *Fortune*, March 23, 1992, 106-07.

Jones, Sandra. "Walgreen Doctoring Stores." *Crain's Chicago Business*, September 8, 2003, 3.

Kogan, Herman, and Rick Kogan. *Pharmacist to the Nation: A History of Walgreen Co., America's Leading Drug Store Chain.* Deerfield, Ill.: Walgreen Co., 1989.

Kramer, Louise. "Walgreen to Take on New York City." *Crain's New York Business*, July 5, 2004, 3.

Kruger, Renée Marisa. "Walgreens: America's Corner Drugstore." *Retail Merchandiser*, December 2000, 25-27.

Lambert, Emily. "In the Pill Box." *Forbes*, April 26, 2004, 54-56.

Simon, Ruth. "Pills and Profits." *Forbes*, June 30, 1986, 33.

Spurgeon, Devon. "Walgreen Takes Aim at Discount Chains, Supermarkets." *Wall Street Journal*, June 29, 2000, B4.

Thomson One Banker. Analytics 1981-2006 10k Reports. "Walgreen Company: The Accomplishments and Prospects of the Second Largest American Drug-Store Chain." *Barron's*, October 15, 1934, 16.

"The Walgreen Formula: Digging in for New Growth in Drug Retailing." *Business Week*, March 1, 1982, 84+.

"Walgreen Likely to Score Its Best Showing Ever." *Barron's*, July 25, 1966, 24.

Other References

2003 Hoovers Financial Reports.

Alexander, Keith L. Washington Post Staff Writer. April 21, 2002, H01.

America West 2002 Annual Report.

AMR 2002 Annual Report.

Atlanta & The World. The Atlanta Journal—Constitution. Atlanta, Ga. January 23, 2002.

Aviation Week & Space Technology 156, no. 25 (2002): 36.

Business Week (industrial/technology edition), New York: January 14, 2002, Iss. 3765: 124).

Continental Airlines 2002 Annual Report.

Corporate Finance, London: June 2002, Iss. 211: 5.

Dateline, Thursday January 23, 2003.

Delta Airlines 2002 Annual Report.

Financial Times, April 17, 2002.

Financial Times, January 18, 2002.

JetBlue Airlines 2002 Annual Report.

Marketing Science: Summer 2002; 21, 3; ABI/INFORM Global p. 294.
New York Times, March 26, 2003.
Northwest Airlines 2002 Annual Report.
Organization of the Petroleum Exporting Countries. http://www.opec.org/.
The Philadelphia Inquirer, April 22, 2002.
The Philadelphia Inquirer, December 13, 2001.
Reuters, January 10, 2002.
Reuters, July 10, 2003.
Southwest Airlines. http://www.southwest.com/.
Southwest Airlines 2002 Annual Report.
Southwest Airlines 2004 Annual Report.
Southwest Airlines 32nd Anniversary Special Report.
United Airlines 2002 Annual Report.
US Airways 2002 Annual Report.
USA Today, January 7, 2002
Wagner A. Kamakura; Vikas Mittal; Fernando de Rosa; Jose Afonso Mazzon.
    Assessing the Service-Profit Chain.
Wall Street Journal, July 11, 2003.